Romancing the Vote

LESLIE PETTY

Romancing the Vote

Feminist Activism in American Fiction, 1870–1920

THE UNIVERSITY OF GEORGIA PRESS
Athens and London

In memory of Cynthia Marshall (1953–2005)

© 2006 by the University of Georgia Press
Athens, Georgia 30602
www.ugapress.org
All rights reserved
Set in Minion by Bookcomp, Inc.

Most University of Georgia Press titles are
available from popular e-book vendors.

Printed digitally

Library of Congress Cataloging-in-Publication Data
Petty, Leslie, 1970–
Romancing the vote : feminist activism in American fiction,
1870–1920 / Leslie Petty.
viii, 231 p. ; 24 cm.
Includes bibliographical references (p. [211]–221) and index.
ISBN-13: 978-0-8203-5712-6

1. American fiction—19th century—History and criticism.
2. American fiction—20th century—History and criticism.
3. Feminist fiction, American—History and criticism.
4. Political fiction, American—History and criticism.
5. Feminism and literature—United States—History.
6. Politics and literature—United States—History.
7. Women—Suffrage—United States—History.
8. Women's rights in literature. 9. Suffrage in literature.
I. Title.
PS374.F45P48 2006
813'.6—dc22   200612101

British Library Cataloging-in-Publication Data available

*The illustration on the title page is reproduced by permission
of the National Museum of American History, Smithsonian Institution.*

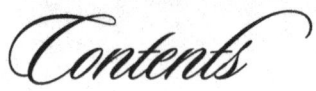

Contents

Acknowledgments, vii

Introduction, 1

CHAPTER ONE
"True Christian Philanthropy"; or, a Release from the "Prison-House" of Marriage: Fictional Representations of Feminist Activism in the 1870s, 17

CHAPTER TWO
Expanding the Vision of Feminist Activism: Frances E. W. Harper's *Iola Leroy* and Hamlin Garland's *A Spoil of Office*, 64

CHAPTER THREE
Making It New: Middlebrow Literary Culture and Twentieth-Century Suffrage Fiction, 103

CHAPTER FOUR
The Political Is Personal: What Henry James's *The Bostonians* Can Teach Feminist Activists, 168

Coda, 189

Notes, 199

Bibliography, 211

Index, 223

Acknowledgments

I have worked on this book quite a while, and it would be impossible to acknowledge everyone who has helped me along the way. I would, however, like especially to thank a few people and institutions indispensable to its completion. I began *Romancing the Vote* as a graduate student in English at the University of Georgia, and while there, I was blessed with an exceptional group of mentors and friends. Roxanne Eberle, Anne Mallory, and Barbara McCaskill were thoughtful readers of my work, and Bonnie Dow taught me a great deal about the historical and rhetorical context of first-wave feminism. I can never thank Kris Boudreau and Tricia Lootens enough for their patient and insightful guidance as dissertation directors; their influence has shaped every page of this book. Meg Amstutz, Olivia Edenfield, Elizabeth Edwards, Bob Fernandez, Ellen Lachney, Rachel Norwood, Caren Orum, Maddux Petty, Aarti Verma, Beth Ann Way, and Lance and Shannon Wilder formed the core of my support network in graduate school, and my relationships with them continue to sustain me.

In recent years, the English department at Rhodes College has become my professional home and my colleagues some of my closest friends. Working with them has made me a much better scholar and teacher and has directly contributed to the completion of this work. Special thanks to Dan Gates for his careful reading and commentary, to Bob Johnson for his encouragement, and to Jenny Brady, Gordon Bigelow, and Marshall Boswell for mentoring me through the revision process. Before she died, Cynthia Marshall was not only my chair but my chief advisor and role model. I deeply regret that she did not see the publication of this book, but it is dedicated to her memory and her peerless example.

I owe Nancy Grayson at the University of Georgia Press a debt of gratitude for her interest in this project. Also, Lisa Hogeland, Courtney Denney, and M. J. Devaney deserve kudos for their helpful suggestions, as do Amber Shaw and Frances Rabalais for their timely and thorough proofreading. Debbie Hashim and Dave Burgevin at the Smithsonian worked wonders securing for me a beautiful jacket image on very short notice, so I thank them as well.

Like most writers, I have benefited from institutional and financial support, so I gratefully acknowledge the Carrie Chapman Catt Center at Iowa State University for the honorable mention in the 2001 competition for the Catt Prize for Research on Women and Politics. This monetary award, along with the Freeman Research Award from the University of Georgia and the generosity of Rhodes College, underwrote my research endeavors. Thanks also to the Huntington Library for access to the Elizabeth Boynton Harbert Collection and to the New York Public Library for permission to reprint letters from the Elizabeth Garver Jordan Papers. An earlier version of chapter four appeared in *Women's Studies: An Interdisciplinary Journal*, and I appreciate being given permission to reprint it.

Most importantly, I want to thank my parents, Monk and Ellen Petty, and my sisters, Lizette Smith and Lisa Garcia-Arrese, for their contributions to this book. They always tell me that I have gotten where I am on my own, but they are wrong. My most cherished wish has been to make them proud, and that wish—along with their unfailing love—has sustained me throughout the writing process.

Introduction

In 1839, Sarah Josepha Hale published *The Lecturess*, a novel about a woman's rights activist whose transgressive behavior—she gives public lectures on gender reform and even ventures to the South to speak about abolition—leads directly to the loss of her husband and child and, eventually, to her death.[1] In this cautionary tale, Hale warns her readers about the dangers of women taking a public role in politics; at the time this was a national phenomenon that had attracted a great deal of attention because of women like Maria W. Miller Stewart and the Grimké sisters and it was a phenomenon that many believed would lead directly to the dissolution of American society.[2] Hale was also, however, originating a character—the feminist activist heroine—that became increasingly common on the national literary scene as the nineteenth century progressed toward the twentieth. Novels about politically active females, written by men and women both for and against feminist reform, were published in almost every decade of the nineteenth century and in the early years of the twentieth. Most of these works have received little critical consideration individually, and they have never been studied properly as a distinct tradition in American literature. This book attempts to recover this tradition and to analyze its literary and cultural influence, especially on the people involved in the movements depicted.

That this tradition has remained submerged is perhaps surprising, given the increased scholarly attention that has been paid over the past decade to the ways in which women's unprecedented political participation in nineteenth- and early twentieth-century America is manifested in the nation's literature. However, this interest has not often been extended to fictional representations. This study fills in some of the gaps left by literary historians and critics who have explored the issues of women's political power in American literature. One of the most obvious of these gaps is the failure to explore the myriad of texts that explicitly depict feminist activism; critics often do not treat seriously fiction that was written to promote reform. Because of these omissions, Henry James's *The Bostonians* (1886) is often read as a unique text about feminist reform activity in the United States instead of as part of a larger tradition of such fiction. Furthermore, while many literary scholars are interested in how women's political activities affected the nation's culture at large, few have considered literature's importance to creating and sustaining the movements from which these political activities stemmed.³ My central concern, then, is how American fiction, primarily novels, written about the woman's rights and other related movements contributed to the creation and continued viability of these movements.

I mainly explore texts sympathetic to the movements they portray, although I am also interested in the role of more ambiguous texts like James's. Specifically, I examine these novels as paradigms of feminist activism and reform communities and elucidate how they, whether wittingly or not, model for their readers ways to create and become members of similar communities in the real world. These narratives voice the hopes and anxieties surrounding some of the most important political movements in American history as well as encapsulate the paradoxical blend of progressive and conservative ideologies that drove them.

In attending to both the progressive and conservative elements in these novels, I am answering Cathy N. Davidson and Jessamyn Hatcher's call for a "posthagiographic model" of American feminist literary scholarship. Davidson and Hatcher argue that much of this scholarship has assumed that "women [. . .] were virtuous simply because they lacked the status, power and position attained by middle-class white men," and they rightly point out that this notion is flawed because "the same nineteenth-century middle-class woman unfairly excluded from the world of public politics might well be a tyrant to the slave or indentured servant who cleans her home and tends her children" (12). Nevertheless, they warn that "the backlash against white feminist literary criticism [. . .] [has often been] even more sanctimonious in its diligent fault-finding than had been the earlier attempts to valorize [. . .] nineteenth-century women" (13). A posthagiographic model, however, will be "more curious and less condemnatory," both about those with the majority of social power, like white males, and those with a relative amount of power, like white women (13).

I strive here to maintain such judicious curiosity about my subject. Without question, these novels discredit many traditional notions about gender and inspire their readers to seek fairness and equality for many American women. At the same time, they often perpetuate discriminatory ideas about other marginalized groups not only by privileging the experiences of white women but also by relying on widespread anxieties about racial and ethnic minorities to demonstrate the need for gender reform. I try to approach this paradox fairly, neither idealizing the feminist messages in these books nor dismissing them wholesale because of their sometimes latent (and sometimes overt) racial and class bias. Rather, I tease out how these two strands are dependent on each other. Comparing some of the novels about feminist activism (specifically, those emerging from the woman's rights/woman suffrage movement) to works written by authors outside this movement affords perspective on this Gordian knot of feminism and racism. Also, considering background information about contemporary racial attitudes helps me speculate about the "absent present" of race in books that seem determined not to acknowledge its importance.

Davidson and Hatcher's call for posthagiographic scholarship is part of their larger effort to discourage critical dependence on the separate spheres paradigm that has governed our understanding of nineteenth- and early twentieth-century middle-class culture for a long time.[4] As they observe, "[s]cholars [. . .] argue that the separate spheres ideology took on renewed power and urgency in nineteenth-century America. They insist that not only was nineteenth-century American society organized around the model of the separate spheres but also that the female sphere of sentiment, home and hearth suddenly became a source of great national value, pride and inspiration" (7). Framing the study of nineteenth-century American culture in terms of such a rigid division between public and private and concomitantly between male and female has had several damaging effects. One is that it has obscured the reality that public and private life "are intimately intertwined and mutually constitutive" (8). Another is that "the congealed binary logic of the separate spheres" has often kept the study of gender arbitrarily distinct from "other variables the construct has been symptomatically unable to address—crucially race, sexuality, class, nation, empire, affect, region and occupation" (8). Uncritical acceptance of the idea of separate spheres has had the effect of privileging white middle-class men and women, often making them seem like the universal subjects of nineteenth-century America.

I attempt to further the critical movement away from the "congealed binary logic of separate spheres" by demonstrating the fluidity of the subject matter at hand. One might assume that only women writers were interested in depicting feminist activism, especially in a sympathetic way; however, my research unearthed several male authors who create successful politically active heroines. In fact, I make the case that a white male, Hamlin Garland, is responsible for the most radical delineation of a feminist activist heroine in American literature. Furthermore, in addition to scrutinizing the intricacies of power relations in these novels by attending to variables such as race, class, sexuality and region, I repeatedly acknowledge the tenacious influence of separate spheres *rhetoric* on the debate about women's political participation in the nineteenth and early twentieth centuries. Women and men were crossing the line between the public and private all the time—sometimes by choice, sometimes by necessity—but most essays, sermons, and stories at the time insisted that a strict adherence to separate spheres ideology was vital to the success of American culture. I would argue that this insistence was in part a reaction to first-wave feminism, which threatened to expose the falseness of this ideology, a falseness that men and women must have intuited in their daily lives even as they professed a belief in its tenets. Feminist activist fiction negotiates these proscriptive messages by either challenging their viability or by appropriating them and redefining them for its own political use.

Such fictional negotiations seem to have begun almost simultaneously with the woman's rights movement itself. There is ample evidence to suggest that from the movement's inception, many of its members considered literature to be a prime medium for challenging and rewriting gender norms. The Seneca Falls Convention, organized by Elizabeth Cady Stanton and Lucretia Mott in 1848, is considered by most historians to be the event that launched the first wave of American feminism, and the nation's first journal devoted to issues of woman's rights, the *Una*, was founded by Paulina Wright Davis in February 1853, just five years later. The very title of the journal, an allusion to the virginal character in Spenser's *The Faerie Queene*, underscores the ties between feminist reform and literature in the nineteenth century and seems an attempt at reconciling the often complicated relationship between feminine virtue and feminist reform. In its first issue, an essay entitled "The Truth of Fiction, and Its Charms" suggests some ways in which literature can be of value to the nascent movement: "Making no pretensions to, and limited by none of the laws of narrative, truth and historic fact, [fiction] brings the truth of nature—the probable, the possible and the ideal—in their broadest range and utmost capabilities into the service of a favorite principle, and demonstrates its force and beauty, and practicability, in circumstantial details, which like a panorama, presents an image so like an experience that we realize it for all the purposes of knowledge, hope and resolution" (5). According to the author, the imaginative nature of fiction, bound by "none of the laws of narrative" makes it the perfect vehicle through which writers can envision a different world—a world that not only reflects the "ideal" of a "favorite principle" but that also demonstrates its "practicability." For those concerned with feminist reform, the pages of stories and novels became a space in which to depict vividly the problems with the current state of society and in which to imagine a "possible" world in which those conditions were challenged and transformed.

The second part of the essay shows another benefit of this kind of imaginative discourse: "In its progress, while the favorite interest and the admired characters are in peril, the reader, in brave and generous sympathy, adds his strength to the heroic effort, and his enthusiasm to the noble impulse, and grows capable, while he flatters himself that in like circumstances he would behave as magnanimously" (5). Again, there are important implications for reform-minded writers and readers. A reader who identifies and sympathizes with the action of the characters and the situations in the story "grows capable" of emulating those actions and believes that she "would behave as magnanimously" as the protagonist in the story when faced with the same situations. In the case of the *Una*, this type of empowerment would be especially important for its readers, predominantly white middle-class women who were acculturated in the "Cult of True Womanhood," which insisted that acting publicly in support of reform ideas was anathema for "proper ladies." [5]

The inaugural issue of this woman's rights journal contains other clues that suggest that literature was indeed viewed as central to the movement by its founders and proponents. A rather critical review of Charles Dickens's *Bleak House*, entitled "Mrs. Jellaby [sic]," appears, in which the well-known author is chastised for "turning his satirical talent so determinedly against many of the needful and important reforms of his time" and for "satirizing all methods of female activity" (4). The reviewer, however, does not merely condemn the authorial perspective; she also makes an observation that seems like a prototypical response of Judith Fetterley's "resisting reader," one who reads against the grain of the dominant discourse of a text and looks for ways to recuperate suppressed possibilities for the characters: "Mrs. Jellaby [sic], the principal personage in this satire, although caricatured to an extent which greatly injures the force of the delineation, yet shows more ability than any other character in the book" (4). By pointing out an alternate way to view a character ostensibly maligned in the text, the essay suggests that models for empowerment and female independence can also be gleaned from texts that do not seem expressly intended to foster reform impulses or that even seem to discourage them.

In addition to commenting on and evaluating existing fiction, this issue of the *Una* (as well as subsequent ones) contains several original short stories and poems that seem conventional in style but radical in content. Mari Boor Tonn observes that Paulina Wright Davis, the editor, "often included short stories and poems that imitated the style of popular journals but were 'feminist' in nature" (51). Tonn argues that this inclusiveness was pragmatic because "a paper comprised entirely of argumentative essays might not pique the interest and garner the support of those women not already sympathetic to the movement." The *Una*'s desire to cull reformers out of its readership guided the choices it made as to what kind of fiction to publish, and its strategies anticipate the strategies of almost all the authors included in this study. For example, this issue provides insight into how fiction might improve the woman's rights movement by fostering sympathetic identification in the reader with many of the concerns of feminist activists, thus encouraging her to join their struggles. Often this fiction relies on conventions of popular narrative employed in the service of unconventional content; furthermore, one can also see the potential importance of literature written about but not specifically to promote the movement.

As the ranks of feminist activists grew in the following decades, those in charge of the movement continued to treat literature as a vital part of their efforts. In the early 1870s, Elizabeth Cady Stanton included a poetry column in her short-lived radical feminist journal, *The Revolution*, and she began to serialize a story by Alice Cary entitled "The Born Thrall, or Woman's Life and Experience" that Stanton claimed would serve a function for the woman's rights movement analogous to *Uncle Tom's Cabin*'s role in the abolitionist movement (Dow 75). Unfortunately, Cary died before the story was complete. Twenty years later, however, Stanton reiterated her belief in the transformative potential of fiction in the preface to *Pray You Sir, Whose Daughter?* a suffrage novel written in 1892 by Helen Gardener: "As the wrongs of society can be more deeply impressed on a large class of readers in the form of fiction than by essays, sermons or the facts of science, I hail with pleasure all such attempts [to write novels exposing the 'false philosophy on which woman's character is based'] by the young writers of our day" (1). It is difficult to say conclusively and specifically what impact fictional portrayals of feminist activists had on the proliferation of the woman's rights agenda, but one cannot dispute that suffragists and other reformers believed in their capacity to enrich and expand their movements.

Although feminist activist heroines were on the American literary scene as early as the 1830s and real-world feminist activists were relying on the persuasive power of literature in the 1850s and 1860s, I have chosen to take up feminist activist fiction published between 1870 and 1920, when the Nineteenth Amendment was ratified, giving women the vote. There are several reasons for these historical boundaries. For one, the woman's rights movement changed dramatically after the Civil War. As the historian Ellen Carol DuBois points out in her groundbreaking work *Feminism and Suffrage*, the years after the Civil War mark the beginning of "an independent feminist movement" distinct from the abolitionist and temperance movements and not affiliated with the Republican party (20). For the first time, women founded reform institutions of which they were the organizers and leaders as well as the members. This organizational independence, however, is only part of the story. During the Civil War, many American women—not just those who were already politically engaged—were called on to take on nontraditional jobs, such as nursing and running family farms and businesses, and these new activities made women more self-reliant and less patient with stifling gender expectations. Furthermore, women often had their independence thrust on them; with so many young men dead, many young women had no prospects for marriage and thus greater access to education and professions became a must, a situation that increased the urgency for feminist reform. All of these developments made conditions ripe for the woman's rights movement to enter a critical stage in its development in the 1870s.

The restructuring of race relations that followed on the heels of the Civil War is also pertinent to this study. How newly freed slaves, as well as newly arrived immigrants, would be integrated into American society was one of the toughest questions with which the nation grappled between the Civil War and the first World War, and this struggle became inextricably intertwined with that for woman's rights. By defining itself as an "all-woman movement" after the Civil War, the feminist activist community eschewed race reform as a central tenet of its platform, thereby erasing the concerns of African American women. As a result, the movement's relationship with African Americans of both sexes was often antagonistic. In fact, some went so far as to argue that white women's rights were the answer to the "Negro Question," because they would restore white supremacy in politics. The period between the two wars saw another kind of ethnic flux in America as well. As the historian Matthew Frye Jacobson points out, the second half of the nineteenth and the early twentieth century was an era of "variegated whiteness," a time when immigrants from Europe and elsewhere were streaming into the country because of rapid industrialization. The history of the xenophobia exhibited toward these immigrants, most of whom were denigrated as ethnically "other" even though they were "technically" white, is contiguous with the history of American feminism. As Louise Michele Newman reminds us, "woman suffrage was debated along with immigration restriction and eugenics regulations, and the northern states' ratification of the Woman Suffrage Amendment in 1920 was soon followed by the passage of national legislation restricting immigration in 1923" (59). While it is a gross oversimplification to say that the woman's rights movement was monolithically racist or xenophobic, the often troubling history of the interplay between gender and race concerns in the United States cannot be ignored. Examining this interplay in feminist activist fiction written between the two wars is particularly fruitful, because its complications are embodied in authorial choices about characterization, conflict, and resolution. These novels add to our understanding of how to situate first-wave feminism within a larger historical and cultural context.

Why do I call these heroines "feminist activists"? In some ways, I am using the historically anachronistic term "feminist" in the rather generic way that Karlyn Kohrs Campbell employs the word to refer to "all those who worked for the legal, economic, and political advancement of women" (3).[6] However, I am also using it because the terms "woman's rights activist," "woman suffrage activist," and even "suffragist" are too reductive to account for all the activist heroines I discuss, although it is true that they all support women's political enfranchisement and their social equality. Female reform activity in nineteenth- and early twentieth-century America and its literary counterpart comprised a vast network of organizational affiliations and coalitions, a point demonstrated by the regular column "Concerning Women" in the *Woman's Journal*, the widely circulated periodical affiliated with the American Woman Suffrage Association (AWSA). In the April 24, 1886, issue, the column includes notices about the activities of Elizabeth Cady Stanton, Frances Willard, and Frances Ellen Watkins Harper, among other professional and political women. What is striking about this juxtaposition is that each of these women was primarily associated with a different political organization or reform movement. Elizabeth Cady Stanton was president of the National Woman Suffrage Association (NWSA) and Frances Willard was the nationally popular leader of the Women's Christian Temperance Union (WCTU). Frances E. W. Harper was a well-known abolitionist and race-reform lecturer and later the vice president of the National Council of Negro Women, as well as a prominent leader in the WCTU and a worker for AWSA. Nonetheless, all three activists frequently lectured in support of women's political enfranchisement. Such interdependence persisted into the first decades of the twentieth century, known as the Progressive Era, when women from a variety of socioeconomic groups responded to America's rapid urbanization and industrialization by not only supporting woman suffrage but by also establishing settlement houses, organizing labor strikes, and generally working to improve urban living conditions. Furthermore, to call these characters "feminist activist heroines" points to the tension between the characters' radical behavior as activists and their conventional portrayal as white, middle-class women who are formulaically good and pure and who are immersed in the expected heterosexual romance plot.

Because I am interested in how these novels contribute to our understanding of nineteenth-century feminist history, I read them alongside contemporary documents such as speeches, letters, journal entries, and letters. I am equally concerned, however, with their aesthetic contributions to American literary history. The activist writers I discuss quite consciously appealed to contemporary literary tastes when they wrote stories about activist heroines. For example, authors writing in the 1870s composed sentimental and sensation novels that nevertheless debunked many generic expectations, such as that of the heroine's passivity and dependence on others, while simultaneously upholding readerly expectations that she would be white and middle class. Late nineteenth-century authors were writing realist texts that, in some cases, effectively undermined the racist myths perpetuated by reconciliation literature, a popular genre that symbolically reunited the white South and North after the Civil War by idealizing antebellum race relations. And, writers from the 1910s tapped into both the nation's Progressive fervor and its xenophobic anxieties to write persuasive "middlebrow" narratives that appealed to a wide readership but that did not sacrifice the authors' literary aspirations.

While each text is clearly responding to the conventions of its particular historical moment, there is one narrative element that is always present, though its treatment changes considerably over time. Every author writing feminist activist fiction must confront the almost inescapable fictive trajectory for heroines: the heterosexual romance or marriage plot. In *Writing Beyond the Ending*, Rachel Blau DuPlessis sees the nineteenth-century heterosexual romance plot as driven by the tension between "love and quest" in which quest is always subordinated to love. DuPlessis acknowledges that twentieth-century authors are sometimes able to transcend the limitations of this plot, but her overarching contention is that this narrative structure is inherently conservative. In the nineteenth-century at least, the status quo of gendered roles is maintained at all costs, even if it means killing off the heroine at the end. Karen Tracey, however, takes a more moderate stance in her recent book, *Plots and Proposals: American Women's Fiction, 1850–90*. Tracey argues that "novelists used their heroines' power of choice among suitors to give those characters some agency within the restrictive ideology of marriage" (29). In many nineteenth- and twentieth-century feminist activist works, the choice of whom to marry is crucial and hinges on political as well as personal considerations; giving their heroines the ability to choose a husband acceptable to them, therefore, allows these works to reenvision the relationship between husband and wife as more intellectually and socially equal as well as more activist. Novelists' preoccupation with the heterosexual romance plot reflects a corresponding concern with "real life" marriage among feminist activists. For example, in a private letter to Susan B. Anthony dated March 1, 1853, Stanton confides, "I feel this whole question of woman's rights turns on the point of the marriage relation" (56). Given the social expectation and the economic imperative of marriage for most middle-class white women as well as the woman's rights movement's primary focus on this subset of women, it is not surprising that stories about feminist activists would often be told as heterosexual romances, nor is it surprising that these narratives would take an activist role in redefining what heterosexual romance means.

Yet because the formation of a community of like-minded reformers—both male and female—is at the heart of most feminist activist fiction, a variety of other characters are also prominently featured and politically important in these novels. The "oppositional communities" in which the feminist activist heroines who serve as the central protagonists in these works interact and the love born of shared political fervor that bonds feminist activists and other members of these communities to each other are therefore interrelated components that suggest the ways literary conventions are appropriated and transformed by those who would portray politically active women.

The communal element in these texts is crucial because it reveals the importance of organized reform activity in political movements. In her essay, "Feminist Communities and Moral Revolution," Ann Ferguson defines an oppositional community as a "network of actual and imagined others to whom one voluntarily commits oneself in order to empower oneself and those bonded with others by challenging a social order perceived to be unjust, usually by working on a shared project for social change" (372). Ferguson elaborates on this definition in another essay by stressing not only the personal empowerment of the members of this community but their political activism as well: "These are networks of people who share a critique of the existing order and who choose to identify with and engage in some material or political practices to express this critique" ("Can I Choose?" 121). Because members join voluntarily after conscious deliberation, oppositional communities are examples of "existential communitarianism." Existential communitarianism differs from traditional communitarianism in that it "does not valorize status quo norms of communities of birth or residence" ("Can I Choose?" 121).

Oppositional communities are both personally and politically imperative if one is to challenge the status quo. According to this model, the first step toward social transformation is an individual's desire to effect change when she realizes the injustice in which she is implicated or by which she is oppressed; this realization is the "development of self-consciousness" or the "existential moment." However, because the self is relational, one cannot maintain this process of "reconstitutive interests" alone ("Moral Responsibility" 128). Moreover, in isolation one is almost sure to succumb to the pull of "status-quo social interests" ("Feminist Communities" 380) that "allow for easy bonding with others in one's cultural milieu" (371). Therefore, if one is to maintain one's commitment to altering the moral landscape of her world, one must find (or convince or imagine) others who share the same goal. Ferguson claims that for the reconstitutive desires of individuals to have an effect on a political level, "they must be collective and ethico-political, since [. . .] [they] connect to status quo interests [. . .] [that] are reinforced by material and economic structures that institutionalize power and inequality. To alter or eliminate them is thus a collective task" ("Can I Choose?" 117). In other words, an oppositional community is "an interrelationship in which the whole group creates more energy to change the world in its joint support of each individual than any one individual would have on her own" ("Feminist Communities" 375).

The lesson from Ferguson's model of an oppositional community is that one cannot maintain an oppositional stance in isolation; one must find other likeminded reformers with whom one is bound by sympathy and avoid entering into relationships in which an irreconcilable conflict between personal affection and political desires might arise. Only in such a reciprocal environment can a community with strength enough to defy convention thrive. Reading fictional depictions of feminist activism against Ferguson's ideal allows one to understand how they negotiate the important dialectics between the individual and the community as well as between the personal and political realms. A crucial component of these negotiations is what Ferguson calls "revolutionary love":

> [R]evolutionary love [is] the effect of a social relation only possible with a group of friends constituted to fight for social justice. In such a community the distinction between egoism and altruism does not really apply, since each individual gains something important, namely, a reconstitution of his or her sense of self—for example, as a feminist activist or as antiracist or anti-imperialist. For members of a dominant group, revolutionary love develops by developing friendships with particular others in subordinate groups as well with others in one's social groups of origin who are interested in challenging their role as dominants. ("Feminist Communities" 382)

The confluence of "altruism" and "egoism" is important because it suggests that this sympathetic, affectionate bond, while self-fulfilling, is also outwardly motivated; those bonded together by revolutionary love are joined by both personal and political affinity.

The other important aspect of this type of love is that it not only links members of "subordinate groups" to each other but also bridges the gap between those who are cultural subordinates and those who are "dominants." Therefore, revolutionary love, which is both personal and political, which bonds people who are alike and who are different, provides a useful lens through which the female-to-female relationships in the texts, as well as the male-female relationships, can be viewed. The concept of revolutionary love offers a different way of interpreting the fictional feminist activist's interaction with the women in her world as well as the heterosexual romance plot in which she is usually enmeshed. For example, the ties of "revolutionary love" among women that reach across lines of class and race—or fail to do so—yield insight into how much potential there is for genuinely radical transformation in these narratives. Along those same lines, the importance placed on female community in many of the texts de-emphasizes but does not often decenter the heterosexual romance narrative at the heart of most of them.

Ferguson's ideal of "revolutionary love" also helps one articulate the way feminist action fiction expands the notion of "romance" that is traditionally associated with the heroine. Relying on the heterosexual romance plot is in many ways a conservative, limiting maneuver on the part of the authors but it is not pure capitulation to the status quo. The romance narratives in these texts frequently become conversion narratives as well, with the male protagonists almost always being converted to a sympathetic position on woman's rights and other tenets of reform politics. In this way, the romance hinges not only on the conventional womanly virtues of the feminist heroine but also on the unconventional behavior of her male counterpart, and many of these heterosexual relationships can be deemed "revolutionary romances" because of the personal and political sympathies between the male and female characters. At the same time, the attributes that make the hero open to conversion are often traits associated with race and class privilege: chivalry, rationality, and education. Clearly, what drives these novels is a tension between conventional and unconventional ideas about gender, race, and class. Consequently, while these texts significantly expand the realm of acceptable behavior and narrative possibility for certain characters, they fail to create truly revolutionary alternatives to the dominant social narratives of the time because their representation of the woman's rights movement is in many ways a reflection of the real-world movement that was dominated by white, middle-class women.

Making an argument that meaningfully connects the literary history and the formal properties of feminist activist fiction is not an easy task; however, the work of theorist Frederic Jameson and feminist literary scholars Rita Felski and Lisa Hogeland provide invaluable models for thinking about such a connection. In the *Political Unconscious*, Jameson posits that a cultural text, such as a novel, "constitutes a symbolic act, whereby real social contradictions, insurmountable in their own terms, find a purely formal resolution in the aesthetic realm" (79). So one could say that nineteenth-century feminist activist fiction, insofar as it constituted a "symbolic act," sought to resolve what often seemed like the irreconcilable ideologies of its actual historical moment and of its vision of future reform. In other words, these narratives served as a "bridge" between the state of gender norms at the time and the next step toward feminist liberation. Because the connection was symbolic, however, one might suppose that activist writers found it difficult to wholly relinquish their conservative reality and imagine a thoroughly alternate society. Along those same lines, these narratives often take on an almost allegorical cast, resolving competing claims to power by various marginalized groups in a way that is satisfactory to their author and audience but that glosses over the complexities of this conflict in the real world. For example, a book that positions a feminist activist heroine as its protagonist and an ethnic minority politician as its antagonist can at once portray the liberation of white women and the containment of ethnic men.

Felski's *Beyond Feminist Aesthetics: Feminist Literature and Social Change* and Hogeland's *Feminism and Its Fictions* follow Jameson's lead in treating narrative as a "symbolic act" that nevertheless has ideological consequences in the real world and illuminate how one might recognize the links between history, narrative, and feminist reform. Felski asserts that "to develop a more adequate theorization of the relationship between feminist politics and literature it is necessary to move beyond the bounds of textual analysis to consider the status and effects of the women's movement as a force for change in the public realm" (163). She delineates two ways in which feminist activist narratives influence the formation of actual reform movements: "First, [. . .] the construction of symbolic fictions constitutes an important moment in the self-definition of an oppositional feminist community. [. . .] Second, it has become apparent that the process of identity formation in feminist literature is crucially indebted to a concept of community. The individual subject is viewed in relation to and as a representative of a gendered collective which self-consciously defines itself against society as a whole" (154–55). Felski's claims about late twentieth-century feminist literature are equally valid when applied to nineteenth- and early twentieth-century stories about feminist activists. These novels were not only the means by which activist writers came to self-knowledge about what their reform goals were, but they also served as prototypes of oppositional communities their authors hoped to see emulated by their readership. Furthermore, reading these narratives could help bring others to self-knowledge, which in turn could lead to their joining a community that "self-consciously define[d] itself against society as a whole."

Focusing on consciousness-raising (CR) novels written in America in the 1970s, Lisa Hogeland builds on Felski's observations about literature's importance to female community formation. Hogeland observes that the primary goal of consciousness-raising activities is to analyze "personal narratives in order to shift the terrain of their interpretation from the personal to the political" (23). The idea that private, individual experience has larger, more pervasive political implications is also explored in nineteenth- and early twentieth-century fictional representations of reform and in fact perhaps plays an even more crucial role in these earlier texts given the pervasiveness at the time of separate spheres rhetoric. According to Hogeland, literature is instrumental in making these "big picture" connections for its readers, and the CR novel is particularly useful because it emulates for its readers the process by which one's consciousness is raised: "The 'overplot' of the CR novel traces a similar trajectory, as the protagonist moves from feeling somehow at odds with others' expectations of her, into confrontations with others and with institutions, and into a new and newly politicized understanding of herself and her society" (23). Nineteenth-century feminist activist texts do not necessarily adhere to the particulars of this conventional narrative pattern, but they almost always show the heroine becoming increasingly aware of the broader political implications of her private actions (for example, her choice of friends, occupation, and husband). They should also help the reader come to a similar awareness about her own life and hopefully encourage her to act on this awareness by making yet another choice: to join a feminist oppositional community.

Jameson's, Felski's, and Hogeland's insights inform my exploration of how narrative patterns in novels and stories about first-wave feminists change over time as activist fiction engages in an ongoing dialogue with the development of real-world feminist oppositional communities. My first chapter focuses on two novels written by activists at a pivotal organizational moment for the woman's rights movement, Elizabeth Boynton Harbert's *Out of Her Sphere* (1871) and Lillie Devereux Blake's *Fettered for Life* (1874). Juxtaposing the sentimental narrative of *Out of Her Sphere* with the more sensational text of *Fettered for Life*, I argue that the authors' respective generic choices reflect a corresponding difference in their beliefs about why gender reform is needed and how it might be achieved. Yet there is also a striking similarity between the novels; at a moment when the woman's rights movement was consciously distancing itself from race activism, each contributes to this effort by drawing both subtle and explicit attention to the whiteness of its characters.

I then turn to two works published in 1892, Frances Watkins Ellen Harper's *Iola Leroy* and Hamlin Garland's *A Spoil of Office*. These texts expand the literary vision of feminist activism by demonstrating the fluidity among and shared concerns of different organized reform movements. *Iola Leroy*, written by a politically active author, is a novel influenced by the tenets of the racial uplift movement as well as those of the temperance and suffrage movements, and the title character is a strong feminist who creates radical change and whose activism helps unite a community. Hamlin Garland's novel is largely about the Populist movement, which sought to improve conditions for midwestern farmers. However, the heroine, Ida Wilbur, is a public speaker who lectures for woman's rights as well as those of the farmers. It is her presence that converts the protagonist, Bradley Talcott, to a more progressive view of politics, and her voice that speaks the most persuasive arguments for reform. Like *Out of Her Sphere* and *Fettered for Life*, these more comprehensive reform narratives depict both the confluence of and the antagonism between different marginalized groups as they advocate for fairness.

In the third chapter, I return to narratives written specifically about the organized suffrage movement, taking up two works that were published right before the ratification of the Nineteenth Amendment and one that was published immediately after. The first, Majorie Shuler's *For Rent—One Pedestal* (1917), is an epistolary novel; the second, *The Sturdy Oak* (1917), is a composite novel edited by Elizabeth Jordan; and the last is a short story cycle by Oreola Williams Haskell called *Banner Bearers: Tales of the Suffrage Campaigns* (1920). I argue that these formal choices enable the authors to represent the lives of their feminist activists with greater complexity and thereby do justice to the new, more modern reality of the early twentieth-century woman suffrage movement. In addition, these novels cater to twentieth-century Americans' attraction to spectacle and ironic wit in order to charm their mainstream "middlebrow" readership into supporting suffrage. They also tap into their audience's seemingly contradictory impulses to garner their support. On one hand, they appeal to their enthusiasm for liberal, progressive reform; on the other hand, they exploit their xenophobic nervousness.

All these works were written, at least in part, to advance the cause of a particular political movement or movements with a feminist impulse. James's *The Bostonians* (1886), however, the subject of my concluding chapter, is not overtly sympathetic to reform. But still I read it as part of the larger tradition of feminist activism in literature that I have developed in the preceding chapters, showing how it presents its own version of an oppositional community and speculating about its impact on a reform-minded readership. The heterosexual romance plot and other generic conventions that James and other writers of the time use to depict feminist activism, the relationship that can be seen between real-world feminist oppositional communities and their literary counterparts, and the tradition of feminist activism in American literature of which these texts are representative illuminate the role of feminist activist fiction in American culture and politics.

CHAPTER ONE

"True Christian Philanthropy"; or, a Release from the "Prison-House" of Marriage

Fictional Representations of Feminist Activism in the 1870s

A piece in one of the early volumes of Elizabeth Cady Stanton and Susan B. Anthony's journal, *The Revolution*, quotes a passage from a book by Professor D'Arcy W. Thompson:[1]

> There is an extremely beautiful fairy tale, exquisitely handled by our Poet Laureate, of a sleeping princess awakened by a true lover's kiss. The story is thus far true in its suggestions, that warm and reciprocated love throws a superlative charm into the life of man or woman; but it is false if it suggests that woman has no duties or responsibilities of weight anterior to wedlock, and no subsequent duties and responsibilities disconnected with her new condition. ("Education of Girls")

The anonymous author of "Education of Girls" cites this passage because she sees it as "a hopeful sign that the attention of so many of the best men and women throughout the civilized world is turned to the subject of women's education" ("Education of Girls"). Its inclusion in a leading woman's rights journal suggests its pertinence to suffragists and other feminist activists trying to convince women to join their ranks, and no doubt the author agrees with Professor Thompson that matrimony and its attendant domestic duties are not a woman's only calling or even her highest one. The author also might have thought the professor's remarks were notable because she likely believed, like many feminists at the time, that fictional narratives, such as the fairy tale of the sleeping princess, played a persuasive and primary role in the conventional education of women by modeling for females the single-minded pursuit of matrimony from the time they were old enough to hear bedtime stories.

William Leach notes that mid-nineteenth-century feminists like Stanton were concerned about the pernicious influence of romantic fiction about heterosexual love, the genre many women read once they were too old for fairytales, and urged writers to pen stories that presented a more honest version of marriage:

> Feminists reproached [...] novelists for offering women false ideas of love as well as for broadcasting unrealistic conceptions of the outside world. Stanton, for example, searched for realistic fictional depictions of woman's condition and thought she found one in Fanny Fern's *Ruth Hall*, which went far "to prove" she said, that the "common notion" dispensed in novels "that God made woman to depend on man" is a "romance and not a fact of everyday life." She exhorted other women to imitate Fern and "divest themselves of all false notions of justice and delicacy and give the world full revelations of their suffering and miseries." (114)

What is implicit in both Professor Thompson's critique of fairy tales and Stanton's of romantic fiction is the idea that if these traditional stories contribute to the perpetuation of gender norms, then a different kind of storytelling could have the opposite effect. Revisionist stories about marriage that make room for Thompson's "disconnected duties" and Stanton's "revelations of [...] suffering" could be powerful tools for reeducating American women. In the 1870s, two feminist activists, Elizabeth Boynton Harbert and Lillie Devereux Blake, attempted just such a reeducation by writing novels that appropriated the marriage plot to show their readers that it was not the only story that could be told about a heroine.

These novels were written at a crucial time in America's woman's rights movement, its first decade as an autonomous, organized reform community. Although the movement's conception in America is marked by the Seneca Falls Convention in 1848, most women involved in political reform before the 1870s were more active as abolitionists, and their work for woman's rights sprang loosely and organically out of the antislavery conventions that were held throughout the country. However, after the Civil War the focus for many of these feminist activists shifted, and they founded organizations such as the National Woman Suffrage Association (NWSA) and the American Woman Suffrage Association (AWSA) that were specifically devoted to gender reform.[2] In the

1870s then, the woman's rights movement was in the early stages of becoming what Ann Ferguson has identified as an oppositional community. Ferguson also identifies one of the main barriers to the proliferation of woman's rights communities: "Connecting to an oppositional community is at some level an act of rebellion or resistance" (372). Many members of the population to whom the woman's rights movement most appealed for supporters—white, middle-class women—had internalized an abhorrence of rebelling or resisting their social roles as "true women."[3] Therefore, to build an oppositional community, feminist activists had to find a way to overcome this resistance to rebellion.

Ferguson argues that for people to be empowered enough to attempt such a rebellion, they must be fortified by participating in "imagined communities with unseen others [. . .] that allow [them] to reconstitute [themselves] as promoters of care and justice for these others as an ethical responsibility" ("Feminist Communities" 380–81). A potential activist must feel strengthened by a supportive group of like-minded reformers and, equally importantly, she must feel an "ethical responsibility" to help others improve their situation, not just a desire to improve her own. In using the phrase "imagined communities," Ferguson invokes Benedict Anderson's influential work by the same name. Anderson shows how such a community can come into being, starting in one's mind, and though he is tracing the rise of the nation-state and its members' sense of connection, his lessons are valuable for a smaller group seeking a communal identity: "It is *imagined* because the members of even the smallest nation will never know most of their fellow members, meet them, or even hear of them, yet in the minds of each lives the image of their communion" (15).

Anderson attributes this "image of their communion" in part to the increased circulation of printed texts, specifically newspapers and novels, which "provide the technical means for 're-presenting' the kind of imagined community that is the nation" (25). Specifically, Anderson says a novel creates a sense of community in two ways. First, the characters are "embedded in 'societies'" that represent fictionally what a community looks like (25). Second, the characters are "embedded in the minds of the omniscient readers," making those readers feel personally connected to that fictional community (26). For those writers hoping to draw readers into their imagined feminist oppositional community, however, there is a challenge. Not only must they write novels that initiate the reader into a community, but they must also convince the reader that she wants or needs to be part of this community.

There were significant limits to the imagination of those agitating for gender reform in the last quarter of the nineteenth century. Although Harbert's reliance on the model of the abolitionist reform novel *Uncle Tom's Cabin* and Blake's titular comparison between enslaved African Americans and white women attest to the legacy of race reform in the woman's rights movement, events immediately after the Civil War initiated a systematic disassociation from that legacy. For a short time in the 1860s, abolitionists and woman's rights advocates were united in the American Equal Rights Association (AERA), but this alliance quickly fell apart. The bone of contention was the Fourteenth and Fifteenth Amendments, which would give African American males the rights of citizenship, including enfranchisement, but that would also require the word "male" to be inserted into the Constitution for the first time as a qualification for voting. The dissolution of the AERA provoked a backlash; the AWSA and the NWSA distanced themselves from the cause of racial equality and very deliberately defined the concerns of their movement as being solely about gender reform. Thus, at the very moment they were consciously constructing an oppositional community, they were also consciously disavowing race reform. Louise Michele Newman quotes Susan B. Anthony as saying, "I have but one question, that of the equality between the sexes—that of the races has no place on our platform" (4).

By opportunistically drawing lines between the "woman question" and the "race question," the woman's rights movement ended up erasing the particular concerns of African American women and other women of color. This erasure is evident in both *Fettered for Life* and *Out of Her Sphere*. Although *Fettered for Life* does pay attention to questions of class, the characters in it and *Out of Her Sphere* are disturbingly monochromatic. In fact, in both their subject matter and modes of persuasion, these novels not only reflect the (often unspoken) understanding that the changes feminist activists pushed for—reform in marriage laws, greater educational and professional opportunities, and enfranchisement—would only most immediately benefit a rather narrow subset of the population; they also give their tacit approval to this arrangement. Thus, although "woman's rights" ostensibly included all women, the reality is that the reform concerns expressed in these novels were heavily weighted toward improving the conditions of white, middle-class women.

In attempting to persuade this primarily white, middle-class female audience of the necessity for gender reform and to convince them to work toward it, Harbert and Blake were forced to confront the greatest cultural barrier to gaining middle-class support for woman's rights: the sacrosanct doctrine of separate spheres and its concomitant vision of marriage, both of which are reiterated over and over in countless popular novels of the time, including two of the most popular, Susan Warner's *The Wide, Wide World* (1850) and Maria Susanna Cummins's *The Lamplighter* (1854). Both novels were best sellers and were reprinted numerous times, and *The Lamplighter* in particular is famous for having tried the temper of Nathaniel Hawthorne, who singles it out in it his notorious tirade against the "damned mob of scribbling women" whom he believed dominated the American literary marketplace with their stories of female self-sacrifice.[4] In each case, an orphaned heroine learns the virtues of Christian submission and conformity and is rewarded with a husband and home. As Joanna Dobson points out, the advice given to the heroine of *The Wide, Wide World* at the beginning of the novel is an apt summation of the ethos of this type of domestic fiction: "Though we must sorrow, we must not rebel" (Dobson, "The Hidden Hand" 223; Warner 12).[5]

If, therefore, women used to the lessons of domestic fiction were to be encouraged and empowered to rebel, they would have to read novels that offered a compelling alternative to this conventional narrative. Both Harbert and Blake approach this challenge by self-consciously invoking several well-known literary traditions: the heterosexual romance plot, and in particular the conventions of genres like the domestic fiction of Warner and Cummins; the sentimental reform novel, best exemplified by *Uncle Tom's Cabin*; and the ubiquitous sensational novels, made famous in England by Wilkie Collins, but equally popular with both writers and readers in America. The authors use these traditions to gain sympathy from their audience while simultaneously criticizing the ways the traditions had been employed in the past. Both novels thus confront their literary and historical milieu and position themselves both within it and in opposition to it. Nevertheless, the ways in which these novels achieve their shared goal are markedly different, and this difference testifies to the contradictory nature of woman's rights ideology during this transitional time in the movement. Harbert's *Out of Her Sphere* models for its readers an imagined oppositional community founded on the rhetoric of expediency, which argues that the unique moral superiority of the "true woman" dictates women's political participation. On the other hand, *Fettered for Life* constructs a vision of opposition informed primarily by arguments of justice that are derived from political notions of individual rights.[6]

The racial assumptions that underlie these reform models, however, undercut in serious ways the liberatory impulse in suffrage rhetoric generally and Harbert's and Blake's novels in particular. As Louise Michele Newman observes, "[o]ften [. . .] [suffragists] made universal claims about man, woman, and the race that they clearly intended to apply only to whites. Regardless of whether they used racial modifiers, ideas about race difference were always present, even if race functioned as an absent present, as it so often did" (57). In *Out of Her Sphere* and *Fettered for Life*, race is certainly an "absent present," not only because their authors rely on abolitionist sentiment yet nevertheless erase "race" as an overt category of analysis, but also because they rely on unspoken yet potent cultural assumptions about white women to communicate the racially exclusive nature of their message. For example, both authors assign, to varying degrees, three symbolic roles associated most often with white women to their characters: white woman-as-moral-arbiter, white woman-as-civilization, and white woman-as-victim. In her book, *White Women's Rights*, Newman argues that in the mid-nineteenth century, "white women began to assert themselves as the rightful, natural protectors of uncivilized races (the protector of black men, not the other way around) and used this racialized responsibility to assert their rights as *white* ('*Saxon*') *female* citizens" (57). This role as protector confirmed the white woman's unique moral power and also aligned her with the more civilized (and thus more suited to govern) white race.

Vron Ware, in *Beyond the Pale: White Women, Racism and History*, agrees with many tenets of Newman's analysis, claiming that throughout much of Western history, the "white woman is a symbol of Civilization" (14). As such, she is often implicitly or explicitly compared to women in nonwhite societies to highlight her relative privilege (or sometimes her lack thereof) because, as Ware observes, "the position of women in a society indicates the level of civilization it has achieved" (14). A variation on the comparison between "civilized" and "uncivilized" plays out in the final cultural trope employed by these authors and identified by Ware: "white woman-as-victim" (4). According to Ware, "[t]he threat to women's safety stems from the idea that women are more likely to be victims of male aggression and less likely to be able to defend themselves [. . . .] The images of vulnerability and defenselessness involved in many discussions about women's safety in the city often feed on racist assumptions about who are the victims and who are the perpetrators of crimes against women" (7). After the Civil War, it became common for white men to justify lynching on the grounds that the black man had raped a white woman, which by and large was a lie. The idea that black men posed a special threat to white women is not explicitly voiced in Harbert's and Blake's novels, but it would certainly have been present in the minds of their readers, informing their understanding of which women were most vulnerable.

Elizabeth Boynton Harbert, according to contemporary accounts, was "versatile to a rare degree" (Hanaford, *Women of the Century* 55).[7] Her wedding announcement, published in the *Cincinnati Journal* in 1869, describes her as "the well-known and talented lecturess" who nevertheless found time to "[make] her beautiful wedding dress of white satin and tulle as well as much of the delicious wedding cake" herself. The juxtaposition of these two details reveals the core of

Harbert's feminism. She, unlike many of her contemporaries, did not see any conflict between her political activism and her domestic and familial duties. In a speech given a few years later, she tells the Illinois State Legislature:

> What we desire does not contravene [a woman's] duties as a daughter, with holiest, tenderest memories clinging around the sacred name of "Father," as a wife receiving constant encouragement and cooperation from one who has revealed to me the genuine nobility of true manhood, as a mother whose heart still thrills at the memory of the first "Mother" greeting from our little son, as a sister watching with intense interest the entrance of a brother into the great world of work. I could not be half so loyal to "woman's cause" was [sic] it not synonymous with the equal rights of humanity [and] a diviner justice to all. [. . .]
>
> And now, yielding to none in intense love of womanliness; standing here 'neath the very dome of the old capitol [. . .] as a native born, taxpaying citizen, I ask equality before the law.[8]

Here, we see Harbert insisting that there are no conflicts between a woman's familial, domestic duties—her responsibilities as moral arbiter—and her right to "a diviner justice" from society and "before the law." However, it is also telling that she identifies herself as "native born," a term which aligns her with the white, ruling class of men to whom she appeals. Thus, she relies on their understanding of what "womanliness" means to petition for her rights.

Between her wedding and this later speech, Harbert wrote *Out of Her Sphere*, a loosely autobiographical story about a "well-known and talented lecturess" who embodies (and yet transcends) many of the feminine characteristics of heroines found in novels like *The Lamplighter*. Like her heroine, Harbert began agitating at an early age, after she was denied admittance to Wabash College in her hometown of Evanston, Illinois. However, Harbert's response to this rejection was less lady-like and more controversial than her heroine's. She organized a performance in which she and twenty-three other young women in her town acted in a comedy entitled "The Coming Woman," burlesquing their rejection. Their purpose was to raise money to purchase the nucleus of a town library, but their performance was so popular that they exceeded this modest goal. In addition to the library, Harbert and her friends bought a town flag, a church organ, and Evanston's first fire truck. Convinced, then, at an early age that women could successfully intervene in society, Harbert embarked on a career to improve opportunities for them even as she maintained a belief in their unique attributes and responsibilities.

Popular fiction was one aspect of American cultural life Harbert believed required changing. In the final chapter of *Out of Her Sphere*, which the author disingenuously claims "has no connection" with the rest of the book, Harbert reflects on some of the causes for the current interest in gender reform. One of these causes, she claims, is women's realization that literature over the centuries had painted a false portrait of them:

> Women, who really believed that men admired weakness and silliness, peeped into the papers [. . .] and discovered such pleasant paragraphs as, "Frailty, thy name is woman;" "Weak as a woman;" or some writer excusing the waywardness of some man of genius, because his wife was too ignorant to be the congenial friend of so gifted a man. In fact, they discovered that they were invariably designated as an extravagant, silly, vain portion of the race; that in endeavoring to please everybody they had failed to please anybody, and so decided that the safest, surest, and best way was to endeavor to please God and themselves, and to trust to the result. (173)

Far from being unrelated, this mythical account of the beginning of the woman's rights movement is crucial to understanding Harbert's project in the rest of her novel. By creating the character Marjory Warner, the author is attempting to replace what she sees as a false, damaging portrayal of women in literature with a truer one. She is a new kind of true woman, one who defies false social conventions and whose morality leads her naturally to the woman's rights movement, which is identified by one character as "a true christian philanthropy."

It is perhaps not surprising, then, that in creating this strong heroine who defies the literary tradition of female weakness, Harbert invokes (albeit somewhat critically) another literary tradition, that of the sentimental reform novel. This genre, which is most fully realized textually and culturally in Harriet Beecher Stowe's *Uncle Tom's Cabin*, appeals to the emotions of readers to bring about political change. In *Uncle Tom's Cabin* in particular the author writes to convert her white readers into abolitionists by creating a sympathetic bond between them and the fictional slaves through the things they have in common, like familial (and especially maternal) love and devotion to Christ. Ample textual evidence suggests that Harbert had *Uncle Tom's Cabin* in mind while writing *Out of Her Sphere*. For example, when young Marjory does something inadvertently mischievous, her father calls her "Topsy," an allusion to the slave child who misbehaves frequently in Stowe's novel, until Christian influence and a mother's love reform her. An even more overt reference can be found in the final chapter, when the narrator cites Stowe as one of the most accomplished American women authors and reminds the reader of her cultural impact: "Harriet Beecher Stowe has written 'Uncle Tom's Cabin.' God willed, she wrote, Lincoln signed, and the slaves are free" (173).[9]

Some of the formal qualities of *Out of Her Sphere* make an even stronger case for Stowe's influence on Harbert. Both novels have an intrusive, didactic narrator; while this type of character is not uncommon in nineteenth-century literature, both Stowe and Harbert employ her to make direct appeals to the reader's sympathy, and especially her assumed maternal compassion and moral superiority, in order to bring about political change. Stowe's narrator challenges the reader to consider what she would do "if it were your Harry" being sold into slavery; similarly, in Harbert's novel, the narrator wonders "how many mothers seated by girl-children, watching with tenderest love the first, feint indications of genius, taste, or individuality, do not [. . .] hesitate ere they attempt to crowd the little soul into the straight-jacket woven by the old tyrant Custom" (30). Both novels remind the reader of the maternal imperative to protect her children—in one case, an African American male, in another, a white female—even if it means defying the law and social custom.

The concluding chapter of *Out of Her Sphere* is also reminiscent of *Uncle Tom's Cabin*. Stowe ends her text with a section entitled "Concluding Remarks" that breaks from the fictional tale in order to answer questions about the veracity of its depiction of slavery and to make a final, direct appeal to the sympathies and reform impulses of the "men and women of America" (441). Harbert attempts to convert her readers in a comparable way in her final chapter, "A chapter which has no connection with our story." Ostensibly, this title is to remind the reader that it is not part of the fictional narrative of Marjory's life. It is clearly ironic, however, because the persuasive rhetoric here expands on the novel's attempt to make readers into woman's rights activists. Like Stowe, Harbert begins this final chapter by assuring her reader that, although imaginative, her story is grounded in fact: "You, that have kindly followed Marjory through her varied life, until she was the mistress of a beautiful home, may deem the picture purely imaginary, hence I ask permission to state some facts, and invite you to one more hour with other American women, who have been guided 'out of their spheres'" (170). Just as Stowe provides proof with factual accounts of slave life, Harbert describes the lives of current feminist activists such as Lucretia Mott, Julia Ward Howe, and Stanton; in this way, the book draws a connection between its fictional heroine and the lives of her real-world counterparts. Harbert hopes that by showing that the leaders of the woman's rights movement are, like Marjory, loving, devoted, pious wives and mothers as well as activists, the reader will extend her sympathy for Marjory to them.

Novels like Stowe's—and Harbert's—appeal to their readers' Christian ideals and rely on the assumption of women's moral superiority as well as their domesticity to elicit the emotional reaction that is critical to the genre's success. Amy Schrager Lang notes that these novels ostensibly question the implications of sentimental conventions by insisting that the awakening of one's emotions they bring about has a political purpose, but as she points out, they are limited by the rigidly defined "gender distinction inherent in [them]." Sentimental reform fiction "identifies the home as the repository of Christian virtue and places in it women admirable for their self-denial and submission" and "[t]o this extent [. . .] rationalizes the status quo" (33). The confinement of women to the domestic realm in sentimental reform fiction ultimately creates an inescapable paradox for it: "For one thing, the values of the home—self-denial, generosity, disinterested virtue—are dysfunctional in the larger world. For another, since the identity of the woman at home is subsumed in the identity of her husband and since her moral qualities are contingent upon her dependent state, the system of values she embodies, however admirable, cannot readily be translated into public form" (35). Given the rigid spatial and gendered demarcation on which sentimental reform rhetoric is founded, it is clearly problematic to use this type of appeal to pursue even white women's public, political rights. Instead of undermining the culturally imagined barriers between home and society, Stowe's emphasis on feminine morality, according to Lang, forcefully reifies them in her novel.

However, as Frances Willard argues in her 1890 speech "A White Life for Two," the way to circumvent the correlation between white women's assumed moral superiority and their confinement to the domestic realm is by "restructuring the ideal of womanhood" to accommodate a broader range of influence (324). The traditional "ideal of womanhood" prescribed by mid-nineteenth-century American culture has been classified by Barbara Welter as the "Cult of True Womanhood." Willard's restructuring does not seek to do away with the traits associated with the ideal of true womanhood, which Welter persuasively argues are purity, piety, domesticity, and submissiveness, but rather to demonstrate how the nurturing influence they imply has relevance in the public world of politics, business, and in the case of Harbert's novel, the pulpit. Of course, Willard's title, "A White Life for Two," clearly has racial implications as well as gendered ones. The overall gist of her speech is that (white) men must be held to the same sexual standard—strict monogamy after marriage—as their wives. As Newman observes, Willard here conflates moral differences with racial and religious differences, suggesting that only white Christian men and women are considered moral human beings (66). This conflation is germane to Harbert's fictional portrait of the true woman. If only white women are "true women," then the "restructuring the ideal of womanhood" that Willard and Harbert advocate will only affect (and thus benefit) a small portion of American females.

Nevertheless, in her restructuring Harbert revises an important function of the traditional sentimental heroine, that of wife. Lang argues that the stereotypical heroine of the genre "is characterized by her commendable, if utterly disabling, submission to God and husband" (36). In the story of Marjory Warner, Harbert takes "husband" out of the equation, creating a heroine who, as a white woman sincerely invested in her role as moral arbiter, believes that her socially unconventional beliefs and actions are God's will and who refuses to compromise her Christian duty in exchange for marriage and a home. In effect, Marjory grows up to be the woman Harbert envisions in her final chapter, a woman who "endeavors to please God and [herself]" before other people and who can use her belief that submission is a woman's duty to effect change in the political, public sphere without the benefit of male mediation. Of course, in one way her agency is still circumscribed by self-denial and an acceptance of the idea that women are by nature submissive. Nevertheless, in another way, her submission to God's will requires her to rebel against societal standards, compelling her to support woman's rights.

Frances Willard's commitment to "restructuring the ideal of womanhood" and Harbert's fictional attempt to fulfill it are both examples of one type of woman's rights ideology, what Aileen Kraditor calls "arguments of expediency."[10] Rather than challenge the notion that women are inherently different from men, feminists like Willard and Harbert embrace this difference and use it as justification for their entrance into the public sphere, arguing their political activity is merely an extension of their natural domestic and familial roles. Arguments of expediency were powerful in convincing women who believed in their more conventional roles to nevertheless behave in unconventional ways. This paradox is embodied in Willard's life. She was the nationally popular president of the Women's Christian Temperance Union (WCTU),[11] and although she promoted the sanctity of the home and the marriage tie, she remained single her entire life, traveling across the country to convince women to work politically for temperance and the elimination of other social ills, in part by demanding the vote.

One sees clearly this blend of orthodox and unorthodox ideology in a speech Willard delivered in 1876 advocating "home protection," a euphemism for female enfranchisement, arguing that voting was not a woman's right, but her duty. As Willard tells her audience, "God has indicated woman, who is the born conservator of the home, to be the Nemesis of home's arch enemy, King Alcohol. [. . .] [I]n a republic, this power of hers may be most effectively exercised by giving her a voice in the decision by which the rum-shop door shall be opened or closed beside her home" ("Temperance and Home Protection" 223). Willard does not challenge the conventional doctrine of separate spheres but bases her activism on it, arguing that women are ideally suited to politics because of their higher moral nature and domesticity. Like Harbert, Willard was from Evanston, Illinois, and the two carried on a lifelong correspondence, which seems to have been influential in forming Harbert's ideas about gender and particularly her fictional portrayal of feminist activism.[12]

To gain her reader's sympathy for the "restructuring [of] the ideal of womanhood," Harbert creates a heroine who embodies flawlessly the virtues to which all "true women" aspire (and in which a middle-class white audience would be invested) but whose exercise of those virtues is inhibited by a restrictive society. Aware of the limitations in Stowe's model of sentimental reform, Harbert engenders a heroine who can engage actively with the ailing world she hopes to help. To this end, she creates in Marjory a character who is reminiscent of and yet pointedly different from Stowe's angelic character, Little Eva. As a child, dark-haired Marjory is likened to the dark-haired speaker of the poem "Earth Angel" who laments that she may be "too brown" to "dwell with angel's [*sic*] fair" but who wants to be "one on earth" and "serve [the Lord] everywhere" (24). Later in the novel, Marjory's best friend, Daisy Warner, says of the future feminist activist: "I like her better than the girls in the Sunday-school books, I think; but I don't think she will die very young, 'cause she likes to play hide-and-seek, and she does get a little spunky sometimes; but she says her prayers a good deal. But *she* don't want to be a boy. She says she intends to do whatever God wants her to, and *be a girl*; thinks may-be she will preach" (34). Marjory, like Little Eva, "says her prayers a good deal" and is kind and generous to those around her, but unlike Eva, Marjory is too full of life and energy to follow Eva's well-known footsteps into an early, self-sacrificing grave. In *Sensational Designs*, Jane Tompkins argues that Eva's dying is the best known example of an innocent child's death in nineteenth-century literature and that it is frequently invoked as a trope for the notion that "the pure and powerless [die] to save the powerful and corrupt" (128). Harbert's novel, however, opts for an active rather than passive model of redemption. Marjory will not "die very young" like the other heroines in Sunday school books; rather, "she thinks she will preach," thereby taking charge of her own destiny and at the same time giving her life to help others.

It is important to note, however, that Marjory is able to pursue an active path toward redemption (and then later an activist path) in large part because she is, like Little Eva, not only figuratively but also literally "pure," i.e., white. Ironically, images of blackness and allusions to slave life and confinement, symbolizing the social obstacles she must overcome, first make us aware of her whiteness. Marjory's alignment with the earth-angel who is "too brown" to "dwell with angel's [*sic*] fair" (24) suggests a more "down-to-earth" (and thus effective) approach to moral reform, but it also suggests Marjory's initial limitations; she is bound to an imperfect world. She laments that her hair "grows blacker and blacker" every day so she "can't be an angel anyhow" (23), and when her father calls her "Topsy," the allusion to Stowe's character momentarily aligns her with not only mischief, but also with enslavement. However, Marjory's association with these images implies that she will be capable of transcending inhibiting obstacles if given the opportunity, and furthermore, that her literal whiteness is one of the things that will help her.

The poetic epigraph to the fourth chapter (in which Marjory laments her black hair and the impossibility of being an angel) demonstrates this point:

> "O, lift your natures up;
> Embrace our aims, work out your freedom. Girls,
> Knowledge is now no more a fountain sealed;
> Drink deep, until the habits of the slave,
> The sins of *emptiness, gossip,* and *spite,*
> And *slander, die. Better not be at all*
> *Than not be noble.*" (21)

Here, the juxtaposition of the word "girls" with "slave," which semantically suggests that the girls are white and the slaves black (and most likely, male), intimates that while white females are in an analogous condition to uneducated slaves, they can transcend this condition through the path of "knowledge."[13] Now that it is not a "fountain sealed," the path is open for them to uplift not only themselves but others. Similarly, when the narrator asks, "how many mothers seated by girl-children [...] hesitate ere they attempt to crowd the little soul into the straight-jacket woven by the old tyrant, Custom, which renders them custom-made articles instead of God's free angels?" she aligns the girl-children with a different type of enslaved person, the mental patient; the figurative strait-jacket, the narrator insinuates, will prevent them from achieving their potential as moral arbiters, as "God's free angels." This second analogy is as suggestive as the one comparing girls to slaves. Many woman's rights advocates pointed out that white women who could not vote were therefore classed with "lunatics and felons," and this was as much of an outrage to many of them as being a white woman who could not vote when African American men could. What underlies this anger, as well as these textual comparisons, is the notion that white women are more "fit for self-government" and more capable of helping the body politic than any of these other groups, and thus, they should have greater freedoms, including the opportunity to vote.

Marjory's later experiences demonstrate how white women's current legal, social, and political situation hinders them; not only are they unable to maintain the integrity of the domestic sphere, but they are also incapable of exercising fully the moral suasion and "feminine" talents that would allow them to become "God's *free* angels" (emphasis added). For example, when Marjory's father dies early in the story, she is taken away from her mother and sent to live on a farm by her legal guardian, Uncle Thomas, because, according to Marjory, "board was cheap" (16). Marjory is forced to endure a painful separation from her remaining family until her mother "can settle things," because the law does not automatically grant women custody of their children, even if the father dies. This temporary domestic rupture foreshadows Marjory's major disappointment, being denied access to a formal education that will prepare her for her "calling" to preach. Marjory voices the novel's message about the need for gender reform as she laments her rejection from college:

> Yes, mother, I know I'm wicked [for praying bitterly to God to let her die because society disapproves of her unconventional choices], but *being a girl*, it does not matter. Men like a touch of wickedness, they say, and all I have to do in life is to *catch a husband*, since that is a girl's peculiar work. Why did God send me into the world with this intense desire to preach His beautiful Gospel? Why has he given me this intense desire for education, and then bound me hand and foot? Ah! He has not done it. My heart tells me that my Heavenly Father has not made a mistake. The fault is the world's. But, mother, with God on my side, I will succeed yet; but, oh! this world is a hard place for girls. (40)

Here, conventional gender expectations for middle-class women are represented as being at odds with "true" Christianity. It is not God who desires silence and passivity from them, but the world. Furthermore, Marjory suggests that marriage could be detrimental to fulfilling one's greater moral duty; if one only aspires to find a husband, then she is concerned with pleasing a man, not God. This sentiment is echoed by other characters who seem to represent the authorial viewpoint, like Marjory's mother, who muses, "I really wonder if God gives little girls such desires without designing that they should be heeded?" (30). The underlying message for the reader is that inhibiting women from exerting their moral influence and pursuing the roles outside of marriage to which they feel "called" is not only wrong but, from a Christian perspective, sinful.

This construction of feminist sentiment radically recasts the roles and abilities of "true women" as individually empowering but it is founded on the very conservative expectation that "true women" ought to be self-sacrificing and dutiful. This paradox is clear in Marjory Warner's subsequent development. Marjory's desire to be a preacher, while firmly grounded in conventional expectations of woman's piety, is, to say the least, controversial. One of the strongest biblical arguments used against feminist activism comes from Paul's injunction that women be silent in the churches; female preachers are all but unheard of in most nineteenth-century Christian sects, which rigorously preserved the patriarchal hierarchy of the church.[14] The narrator challenges this objection by insisting that if the church will adhere to Paul's command then it should "banish at once every woman from [its] Sabbath-schools since they not only speak but teach." "Do not," she implores them, "intrust [sic] your children to the care of teachers who are deprived of the benefit of spiritual consultation" (32).

Marjory's calling may be unorthodox for a woman, but the novel makes it easy to accept the unconventional choices that she makes by linking them with her sense of responsibility toward others and specifically, her family. Marjory's brother wants to be an artist and he "wept as bitterly as [Marjory] because [. . .] with a widowed mother and a sister dependent upon him, he must [instead] adopt some profession which would insure him a competency" (41). The imposition of gendered expectations thus adversely affects both males and females in this story, and he is forced to "give[] up his cherished idea, and adopt[] an irksome profession" (41). When Marjory learns how her forced dependence is also keeping her brother from his "calling," she finds the courage to educate herself and defy society's expectations. Marjory tells her mother "[I]t seemed to me that I could not tread the thorny path for my own sake, but *I can for my brother's*. Ah, God has given me something to do—save my brother for art, and once out of my sphere, I will find my pulpit" (41). This other-centered rationale for activism is a common refrain in nineteenth-century rhetoric; in fact, in a contemporary speech, Willard uses almost the same words when explaining how she entered the public world of reform: "For my own sake, I had not the courage, but I have for thy sake, dear native land" ("Temperance and Home Protection" 226). Marjory's resolve, then, is the same as Willard's, but it is fictionalized literally as "home protection"; her independence will "save" her brother as well as herself, and by extension it will save her "native land," by making the middle-class nuclear family, conceived as the basic unit of American "civilization," stronger.

It is an organizing irony of the novel that Marjory's most conventionally feminine impulses give rise to her most unorthodox actions. One of the most unusual ways that irony manifests itself is in Marjory's desire "to buy a little girl" (22). As a young child, Marjory decides that her mother will need someone to stay at home with her when Marjory leaves to preach. To this end, Marjory tries to make money to buy the baby by sewing rags together to sell. While this plan is treated as childish fancy, when Marjory is a bit older, she does adopt an orphan child, Christine, who fortuitously escapes from the theater and shows up amid a group of Marjory's friends on Christmas Day. Clearly, adopting this "Kissmus child" (as Christine calls herself) and becoming a mother without physical conception aligns Marjory with the Virgin Mary.[15] Other characters remind Marjory that taking on the responsibilities of parenthood might harm her chances of marrying, but she becomes indignant because she is tired of the suggestion that marrying well should be her only goal in life. Thus, Harbert creates a heroine who chooses to be a mother out of love and concern for the child—"I want to take this poor, little, homeless child," she states, "and give her home, happiness and love" (71)—but who has the freedom to be independent outside the marriage bond.

This pattern repeats itself when Marjory decides to let an invalid man who cares about her live with her and her mother, despite the gossip this decision generates, because it is the moral, nurturing thing to do, and again when she decides to become a lecturer for woman's rights because she feels compelled to speak the "truth" and challenge the social dictates stifling her and her female peers. Marjory considers her reform work, like her preaching, to be not only consistent with but also inspired by her Christian faith; thus, being a feminist activist becomes synonymous with being a moral arbiter. The night before her first lecture she prays, "Oh! Father, for the sake of these little ones of thine; for the sake of the toiling and suffering, help me, give me strength and courage to speak the truth. My prayer tonight, is simply this, 'Father, guide, for Jesus' sake'" (95).

Given the emphasis on domesticity in the novel, it is perhaps not surprising that Marjory's family is the germ of the oppositional community that coalesces around her. When Marjory determines to help her brother by becoming a preacher, she does not make this choice alone; the entire family commits to defying society's restrictions. Marjory enthusiastically appeals to her mother: "We will support ourselves. Ah, there are three of us, and with each other's love we can defy the prejudices of the world" (41). Marjory's mother and brother, and later her little girl, never waiver in their support of her feminism, and the entire family is happier and more harmonious because of it. At one point, Marjory says that everyone she knows tries to persuade her to abandon her unusual activities, "excepting [her] own dear mother" (71). Later, Marjory's brother, now a promising artist, claims that his sister is his "idol" because she "actually earned enough money while [he] was in college, to support mother and herself, so that [he] could devote [himself] to painting"(99). While Ferguson stresses choice over birth as the crucial way of entering an oppositional community, in Harbert's novel, the two are inextricably linked; given the emphasis on familial relations for the true woman, it is important in Harbert's model of a reform community that personal affections and political beliefs do not cause conflict in the domestic realm. At the same time, if we consider the unspoken racial dynamic in this conception of oppositional community formation, we see how it privileges the white, middle-class family as the primary unit of American society, and thus we see how positive reform in its structure would solidify its position as such. Furthermore, making familial connections central to oppositional community formation prevents those who do not live in these traditional, middle-class families from joining, thereby negating both their potential to influence gender reform as well as their potential to benefit from it.

Marjory's oppositional community does not begin and end with her family, however. Her activist work as a lecturer and writer converts several other characters, many of whom are prejudiced at first against "strong-minded women." For example, during her public lectures, Marjory's persuasiveness as well as her propriety brings many of her listeners into the folds of the feminist oppositional community. When Marjory lectures in "fashionable Saratoga," the narrator describes her appearance on the stage from the perspective of an audience member: "The audience glanced at the soulful face; then at the delicate lavender silk, covered with a filmy, delicate, black shawl; at the small hands and little feet; and ere she had spoken one word, she evoked the applause of the large audience *by the power of womanhood alone*" (126). The narrator lingers over Marjory's delicate appearance, as she often does in the book, to stress the compatibility between femininity and gender reform. Many surprised, converted audience members greet Marjory after she delivers her "earnest, womanly" speech. Her cousin, previously mortified by Marjory's public appearances, says that she is "delighted" because the speech "did not seem a particle bold" (127). Marjory is also congratulated by a "good, motherly, but ignorant woman" and a "grey-haired old clergyman." These two well-wishers remind the reader that gender reform and Christian belief go hand-in-hand; the more charitably-minded government that would come from women's political involvement would benefit poor people and satisfy church leaders that its government was heeding the Christian call to help the most needy. Perhaps most telling are the young, wealthy girls who claim they are now supporters of woman's rights after seeing Marjory's reception because, as one of them tells her friends, "Girls, its [sic] all a humbug about the boys not liking strong-minded women. I tell you, they treat her as though she was an empress. If a girl is pretty and lady-like, everybody will respect her, and the fact is, I'm converted" (129). Although Marjory's example stresses that in Harbert's view a woman should not be solely concerned with attracting a husband, these affluent young converts are important members of Marjory's oppositional community. Their presence is intended to reassure Harbert's white middle-class female readers, who would presumably fear that men would shun them for behaving unconventionally. As long as women maintain their "womanly" respectability, the young converts suggest, their political activism will only increase their attractiveness. More importantly, confronting society's hindrance of their moral work will help them be more fully realized "true women."

These convertees are, however, in the minority; the other members of Marjory's "inner circle" (with the noted exception of her family and her liberal benefactor Warren Huntington) are either uninterested in feminism or actively opposed to woman's rights ideology. For example, the females closest to Marjory serve as contrasting models of young white womanhood and are not initially an integral part of her reform community. While Daisy claims she would never want to vote, she has not given the matter much thought and her opposition seems a matter of indifference. Marjory encounters a more complex form of resistance, however, in Maude Johnstone, a young girl whom she meets at the home of Warren Huntington. The narrator ironically labels Maude "heroine number two" in the novel, highlighting the fact that she is a "type" of fictional character. As such, she embodies all the flaws the novel attributes to women who have been acclimated to current gender norms in part by reading popular fiction, and her vocal disapproval of woman's rights reform is presented as proof of her selfishness and "unwomanliness."

Harbert uses Maude to expose the weakness and vanity of conventional literary heroines. The title of the chapter in which Maude is introduced, "A Girl of the Period," alludes to Eliza Lynn Linton's essay of the same name, which was published in England in 1868 and caused quite a controversy on both sides of the Atlantic. In it, Linton offers a satiric account of the shallowness, vanity, and "fastness" of the young generation of British women; Harbert's Maude has similar flaws, which are revealed in the subsequent chapter. Harbert opens the chapter with a quote from William Thackeray's *Vanity Fair* that presents an opposing (and according to Harbert, misguided) interpretation of the actions of many young women, both real and fictional: "[V]ery likely the heroic female character which women admire is a more glorious and beautiful object than the kind, fresh, smiling, artless, little tender, domestic goddess whom men are inclined to worship; yet the latter and inferior sort of women must have this consolation, that men do admire them after all, and in fact I am inclined to think that to be despised by her own sex is a very great compliment to woman" (45). The narrator counters with the claim that Maude, who indeed "has always been admired and loved by men," has been "disliked by women [. . .] [n]ot solely because men admire her, but because she is not lovable or lovely to women" (45). Harbert's novel exposes Thackeray's "little tender, domestic goddess" as a façade. Maude is "artfully artless"; she is bored and unfriendly in the company of other women, but "in the presence of young men, she is everything that is modest, brilliant and fascinating" (45).

The narrator is quick to point out, however, that it is not Maude's fault that she is deceptive and self-centered. She is the "legitimate outgrowth of the teachings of society," which tells her she must find a rich husband, and her antifeminist sentiments (she claims to have "all the rights she wanted") are part of this single-minded pursuit. The narrator even goes so far as to say that Maude has modeled her behavior on the work of "the novelists who were admitted to be the most faithful portrayers of human nature," and she laments that if Maude succeeds in her plan to marry a rich husband "the world will applaud," thereby underscoring its false priorities (46). For the reader, the juxtaposition of Maude's shallowness and single-minded pursuit of matrimony with Marjory's earnest attempt to be useful is an uncomfortable one, especially when the reader considers that Marjory's actions might prevent "heroine number one" from finding a happy marriage of her own.

According to the novel, the threat posed by Marjory's "adopt[ing] this independent course" is that she "will sacrafice [sic] to it love and a home" (41) and so end up lonely. The novel presents the difficulty a feminist activist like Marjory faces in reconciling her public work with a loving marriage as the unfortunate result of a narrow-minded society prejudiced against an ultimately liberating transformation. Therefore, the reader sees that not only do middle-class women need to become useful activists but also that middle-class men need to learn how to love these new women. Warren Huntington describes these ideal new husbands as "true men": "[T]rue men have faith in manhood; because he [sic] knows that he would protect his mother or sister at the polls just as effectually as he does at the post-offices, in rail-road cars, or on the streets. A true man would not thus thrust aside a *grand idea*, nor desire to have a right yield to expediency" (38). In Harbert's imagined world, the process by which "true men" are transformed is the same as that by which true womanhood is restructured. Men who support female political participation and gender reform are presented as the more fully realized embodiment of the ideal of the chivalrous, noble, and honest man. Underscoring this definition of the "true man" is the supposition that men who do not support reform are cowardly because they are not willing to take care of women at all times and are small-minded and selfish because they would deny women their right to vote in order to maintain the status quo.

Like Harbert's restructuring of true womanhood, however, her conception of a new, "true man" relies on unspoken notions about the race and class of its subject. As Huntington points out, were women to get the vote the true man would "protect his mother and sister at the polls" just as he now protects them in post offices and on the streets (unlike the "boys" Huntington criticizes)(38), intimating that the characters inhabit a rather violent political landscape. Newman provides enlightening historical context for this intimation: "A new understanding of politics as a competitive and corrupt *business* emerged [after the Civil War], reflecting white elites' general fear and distrust of immigrants, blacks and working classes [. . . .] The ballot, previously considered a privilege granted to white men in recognition of their moral virtue and economic independence, was reconceptualized as a tool used by a morally reprehensible leadership to dominate servile and racially inferior classes of men" (59). Undoubtedly, this "general fear and distrust" is what motivates Huntington's understanding that women will need protecting at the polls, because politics, no longer the bastion of the white elite, has become so corrupt. Such distrust marks Harbert's "true man" and "true woman" as members of the white upper class.

Therefore, for America to reach what Harbert considers its ideal state, these true men and women must both open their minds to new possibilities. As the narrator advises her reader, "Educate girls for womanhood—not wifehood. Educate them as responsible beings before the law, human and divine; and, at the same time, educate American men to admire such womanhood" (75).

In the course of the story, Winthrop Wright, Marjory's childhood friend and adult love interest, undergoes just such an education. As a very young man, he instinctively admires Marjory's originality and ambition, but his stereotypical ideas about woman's rights activists put him on his guard. When Warren Huntington suggests that Marjory will probably grow up to be a "strong-minded woman," Winthrop disagrees: "'Oh, no sir, indeed she won't. [. . .] You mistake, I said she did not want to be a man, and you know all these strong-minded women do'" (35). "Strong-minded" is a derogatory term used to describe feminist activists and other unconventional women, but as with other well-known phrases such as "out of her sphere" and even "true woman," Harbert appropriates the term in the service of reform. Huntington observes that Winthrop has gotten his ideas "from the newspapers" and he advises the younger man to help himself by revising his opinion: "If you want to be a complete success, try to win a strong-minded woman" (38). However, Winthrop replies, "I'll never do it," revealing that his education has barely begun.

Marjory and Winthrop seem hopelessly at odds at this point because he cannot accept her feminist activism. His equivocation because of her "strong-mindedness" extends into his adult life, when he waivers in his desire to propose after finding out she has embarked on a career as a woman's rights lecturer. This revelation changes his mind, even though he says she "has been the best friend of [his] life" (97). Marjory will never waiver in making her work as a lecturer a priority, because she believes it is her Christian duty; therefore, her marrying is contingent on her being able to pursue this calling. We learn of this contingency from one of Marjory's diary entries, which she begins, "'At times my woman's heart shrinks from entering this new work, lest it should lead me away from home and love; but then I know my soul would never recognize her king in any one who would love me less, for duty performed" (100). Marjory concludes the entry with a quote from Margaret Fuller: "The woman in me kneels and weeps in tender rapture; the man in me rushes forth, but only to be baffled. Yet the time will come, when, from the union of this tragic king and queen, shall be born a radiant sovereign self" (100). This passage is a rare moment in the text that acknowledges that a truly reformed notion of "true womanhood" would recognize the balance of "female" and "male" traits in women. While Fuller believed in an essential femininity and masculinity, she maintained that every human had characteristics of both sexes. This quote's placement right after Marjory's observation about her ideal companion suggests that the marriage she envisions would, by extension, also be a more balanced, equal relationship than was the norm. Nevertheless, her noting that her soul "would never recognize her king" in a man that would love her less for performing her duty conflicts with the idea that she desires a "sovereign self," highlighting the problem of reconciling the conventional gendered assumptions that underlie expediency arguments with a substantial revision of marriage and society.

Winthrop's inability to accept Marjory's vision of a marriage that does not impinge on her duty creates a seemingly irreconcilable conflict in the center of the text. In their first interview after Winthrop learns of Marjory's lecturing, he asks her what she intends to do about her work after she marries. Marjory replies that she does not plan to travel constantly and live more or less separately from her husband. In fact, she claims, "I want to share his labors, be interested in his business, and know his friends. I want to preach, and I hope to marry—well, say an editor—then in our cosy [sic] sanctum we could sit together and he write his editorials, and I could write my sermons" (118). After hearing Marjory's wishes, Winthrop believes they are incompatible with his own, and he tells her: "'Confident that after knowing you I can never love another woman, I yet feel that I could not satisfy you, and that you could not yield to me the intense love my nature demands, and so, darling, good-bye'" (118). Although it is Winthrop, not Marjory, who verbally rejects the possibility of their marriage, there is much textual evidence to suggest that Marjory would never have consented to the marriage that Winthrop would have wanted at this point, which would apparently have her sacrifice her work in order to yield to him all her attention and affection.

This proposal is aborted, but Winthrop will try again; this storyline situates the novel within the genre Karen Tracey has labeled the "double proposal plot," which "can be identified by the heroine's rejection and acceptance of proposals from the same suitor." These narratives, Tracey argues, "deploy two specific opportunities created by the double-proposal device: the opened space between rejected and accepted proposals and the inherent contrast between rejected and accepted marriage conditions" (4). According to Tracey, "[t]ypically, the first proposal does not result in marriage at least in part because something is wrong with the hero-to-be. If the heroine were to marry him the first time, she would sacrifice herself to a marriage that would inhibit her individual growth and subject her to a dominating husband. It is not enough that the suitor 'loves' the heroine passionately; he needs to be reformed, humbled, or otherwise transformed so that when the heroine does accept him the marriage will be egalitarian" (23).

After he leaves the room "blind to his own mistake" (118), Marjory realizes that Winthrop would have to change for her to accept him; she holds little hope at this point, however, that it will happen. According to the narrator, in the aftermath of this scene, "Marjory sat still as a statue, quietly, calmly, icily accepting her fate. Recognizing that her work, if performed, must be wrought alone, since not yet did even the best of men fully understand how intense love and intense womanliness, could be united with self-reliance and consecration to the public good" (118). Unlike other heroines in this situation, Marjory's "heart did not break"; she understands that "she had much to live for" (119) in her work. Her ability to master her grief and to sing the next day to cheer others around her is misinterpreted by Winthrop, who wonders if it is "possible that her intellect has dwarfed her soul" (119). Winthrop's misinterpretation calls to mind Professor's Thompson's observation; most people cannot imagine a "normal" woman who accepts responsibilities outside the primary heterosexual bond.

Far from dwarfing her soul, this break in their romantic attachment allows Marjory to realize more fully her feminist potential. Tracey argues that the postponement of marriage in the double proposal plot opens up a narrative space for the heroine's independent development as well as the hero's by "shift[ing] [the heroine's story] to a post-courtship bildungsroman or sometimes *Künstlerroman*" (23). The trajectory of *Out of Her Sphere*'s plot is consistent with this pattern; only after Winthrop and Marjory "drift apart" do they achieve significant success in their chosen fields. Winthrop becomes an accomplished editor while Marjory becomes an author and travels both domestically and abroad as a lecturer for woman's rights, gaining widespread recognition and converting many people to her feminist cause. However, the narrator alerts the reader that "both of them are fully conscious that something is needed to render their lives complete" (130), which is, of course, their reconciliation and marriage. In order for this reunion to come about, Winthrop must come to accept Marjory's vision of an egalitarian marriage that would allow her to fulfill her duties as a woman's rights lecturer and eventually, as a preacher. Winthrop is finally converted as he reviews Marjory's recently published book on feminist reform for his magazine: "Again and again, he read some of the best passages, and then putting the little volume aside, [. . .] he now determines to ignore all prejudice, to bid her write, lecture or preach,—to perform her entire duty—and yet to accept his love; to be his wife" (131).

From this point on, the story moves rapidly toward a resolution of all lingering conflicts. Marjory reaps the benefits of her unwavering devotion to her duty, and the narrative builds to the author's utopian vision of a happier community founded on "the restructuring of the ideal of womanhood." In the final chapters, Marjory receives letters from both Maude and Daisy, and while very different in content, each letter attests to its author's conversion to feminist reform and affirms the bonds of an imagined community among reformers, a community necessary to bringing about change. Maude writes to Marjory for help, because she has learned from hard experience that marrying for money is a dangerous prospect for a woman; her husband has died and has left her child in the custody of its grandparents, and Maude asks Marjory's assistance in helping her escape to Europe. Once again, we find parallels to *Uncle Tom's Cabin*; Marjory says that she will violate the law and help Maude, "just as [she] would have assisted a fugitive slave-mother, flying from those who would sell her" (152). Maude's husband was Warren Huntington, and his callous disregard for his wife's feelings also resonates with the lessons of *Uncle Tom's Cabin*: even a seemingly kind character will take advantage of those subordinated to him. In this scenario, Marjory is aligned most closely with Stowe's character Mrs. Byrd, the senator's wife, who says that "obeying God never brings on public evils" (77). Unlike Mrs. Byrd, however, Marjory is in a position to help Maude escape herself, instead of having to depend on her husband, as Mrs. Byrd must do to help Eliza, reiterating once again the necessity of white women's active, rather than passive, roles in bringing about Christian-minded reform. For her part, Maude is chastened by her experience and, once it is safe for her to return to the United States, enters "the list of woman suffrage advocates"; "by telling the story of her own wrongs, [she makes] more converts than she could have done by eloquent appeals, and unanswerable logic" (152). Maude, like Harbert, understands the strength of sentimental appeal.

This scene is, however, one of the most overt examples of how such a sentimental appeal, while effective in gaining support from its white audience, nevertheless relies on racial notions that prohibit nonwhites from being full participants in Harbert's imagined community. The dynamic between Mrs. Byrd and Eliza in *Uncle Tom's Cabin* is replicated in the relationship between Marjory and Maude and reflects what Newman calls a "white abolitionist ideology of liberation and uplift." This ideology "created two interdependent roles delineated along racial lines: for the enslaved black woman, the role of a helpless debased victim; for the free white woman, the role of an empowered sanctified uplifter" (62). Clearly, Marjory is the "empowered sanctified uplifter" here, and she is even more powerful than Mrs. Byrd because of her active and activist role. At the same time, while Maude is associated with Eliza, she is literally a white, American woman, and thus, she has the option of returning to the country and joining the ranks of white feminist activists. Therefore, the possibility of Marjory and Maude bringing about moral and gender reform is dependent on their status as white and native-born.

Daisy, meanwhile, is liberated by "frontier suffrage."[16] She writes to Marjory from her new home in Laramie, Wyoming (in presumably an all-white settlement), to tell her childhood friend of her newfound happiness. She has started her own business and hired a woman who could not get other work to take over her housekeeping duties (Daisy is depicted as an inept domestic worker throughout the novel). Daisy's upward mobility, which allows her to hire a housekeeper, supports another common woman's rights argument: improving the condition of more affluent women will also improve that of laboring-class women by giving them access to more appealing, better-paying jobs. Once again, Harbert underscores the role of the middle-class, white woman as both a moral and a civilizing influence; from her relatively privileged position, she is able to help those women who are socially below her also have a "better" life.

Daisy also tells Marjory how voting gives her the opportunity to ride to town with her husband, an enjoyable outing that only takes her away from her children for a few hours. The point here is to counter the antisuffragist argument that chaos in the home would be the inevitable outcome if women were allowed to vote—both Daisy's and Maude's stories testify once again to the compatibility between "feminine" virtues such as maternity and domesticity and woman suffrage, at least for white, middle-class females. Furthermore, these letters imagine a network of feminists across the country and across the world who, though not physically proximate to each other, have benefited from reform, a feat meant to give hope to readers who would support feminist activism but who feel isolated from actual reform communities and activities because of either geographical distance or domestic responsibilities.

For Marjory, the ending of her story is the happy one the reader might expect, but it embodies the same mix of commitment to radical change and adherence to conventions that marks the story as whole. Winthrop proposes and their marriage becomes a partnership; they work together in Winthrop's office at his newspaper, just as Marjory envisioned. Soon, she finds a congregation, a group of "poor weary women, who never attended church," but who ask Marjory to "preach for them a little" because they feel she "[is] interested in them" (168). Marjory's charity to the poor is a conventional "womanly" activity; she is still a moral influence, but the fact that she is in charge is unprecedented. Marjory is finally in her sphere, the church, but the roles are reversed; the wife is the preacher in her pulpit, while her husband is the willing helpmeet ("Will you assist me, Winthrop?" she asks him after the women entreat her to preach to them, and he readily agrees he will [168]). As the feminist activist heroine, she has accepted the challenge that Harbert's narrator issues to all "true women": "American women, while such things exist [as intemperance and poverty], will you not with influence, voice, pen and the ballot, assist the true fathers of the republic in their endeavors to save its sons? [. . .] Mothers of the republic, when your sons ask for bread, will you give them a stone? When the good and the true ask for co-operation, sympathy and assistance, can you bestow upon them only indifference, prejudice, and that selfish assertion, *you* have all the rights *you* want?" (68). Like Stowe, Harbert implores women to use their influence as mothers to help America live up to its promise of happiness and freedom for everyone. However, in contrast to Stowe, who argues that women's influence will be most effective if it is indirect and limited to the domestic realm, Harbert supports a more direct means of influence, the "voice, pen and the ballot" whereby by women would extend their womanly morality into the public world of politics. Harbert's ideal certainly represents a substantial revision of separate spheres ideology and sentimental appeal; nevertheless, Harbert, like Stowe, is still bound by notions of femininity and maternity that are associated with the white middle-class. Hence, while she imagines a world of committed, white female reformers, she cannot conceive of an egalitarian interracial oppositional community.

If *Out of Her Sphere* likens its feminist activist heroine to the morally superior white mothers-turned-abolitionists who people *Uncle Tom's Cabin*, Lillie Devereux Blake's *Fettered for Life* (which was published just three years after *Out of Her Sphere*) likens its heroines to slaves who are bound and need liberating, an analogy made explicit in the title, which equates the marriage bond with the shackles of slavery. This analogy, which rests on a problematic appropriation of the slave's experience but nevertheless was often an effective suffragist device, was employed as early as 1848, when Elizabeth Cady Stanton presented the Declaration of Sentiments to the first Woman's Rights Convention in Seneca Falls, New York.[17] Stanton relied heavily on arguments based on the natural rights of American citizens, arguing they should be extended to white women, just as many abolitionists argued they should be extended to slaves. Although Lillie Devereux Blake was not at Seneca Falls, when she joined the woman's rights movement in the early 1870s she aligned herself with Stanton and others who argued from the radical position that, just as citizens should be "colorless" for legal and political purposes, they should also be thought of as "sexless." This analogy denies the relevance of gender when determining a person's legal position and rests on "arguments of justice," the other strain of what Kraditor identifies as conflicting woman's rights ideologies, founded on Enlightenment ideals of a human being's inherent natural rights.

The differences between Blake's book and Harbert's are extensive and stem directly from the authors' varying perspectives on the importance of femininity and domestic relations for white, middle-class women. In *Out of Her Sphere*, the heroine is a rearticulation of the attributes of the true woman employed in the service of Christian-minded feminist activism, the oppositional community that forms is an organic outgrowth of her unconventional view of her familial responsibilities, and the vision at the end is firmly grounded in Christian ideals and the expectation that the middle class will be charitable to the poor and morally influence the rest of society. A woman's sphere becomes limitless, but it is still a peculiarly feminine space, and the feminist reform community, while expansive, is still restricted by class and racial barriers. Harbert attempts to persuade her audience by appealing to what she takes to be a shared understanding between them of the merits of femininity and Christianity as well by assuming a racial and class affinity. In contrast, the heroines in *Fettered for Life* pursue feminist activism not primarily to aid others but to fulfill their ambitions and, importantly, protect themselves. The resulting model of an oppositional community, far from being grounded in familial relations, is one based on a shared experience of gender oppression that makes women's family life unhappy or abusive and thus that often sets family members against each other. Thus, the community consists of women banding together to resist the oppression of this power. The fate of the central heroine is ostensibly a harmonious marriage; however, not only is there is textual evidence to make one doubt this prediction but the one character who seems destined for significant success is the one who chooses activism over marriage. Ultimately, this book seeks to recruit feminist reformers by making its readers aware that as long as women are denied their natural rights, they will lack legal and financial resources to protect themselves.

In *Fettered for Life*, unlike in *Out of Her Sphere*, women reach out across class lines to fight their subordination, but both novels share a vision of gender reform and oppositional community formation that is informed by their authors' (and characters') race privilege. In *Whiteness of a Different Color*, Matthew Frye Jacobson argues that, from the early days of the republic, "the idea of citizenship had become thoroughly entwined with the idea of 'whiteness' (and maleness)," and he attributes this connection to assumptions about who was "fit for self-government"—white men—and by extension, about who was "human" enough to be endowed with natural rights (25). Thus, when white women began seeking more equality under the law, including the vote, they often based their right to it on their racial affinity with those in power. According to Newman, "[t]he feelings of racial superiority that Anglo-Protestant women nurtured concerning their own ancestry, heredity, and evolutionary history led them to insist that they shared the white man's inherited capacity for self-government"(64).

This insistence became even more pronounced and more vitriolic as the nineteenth century progressed, first because of the mid-century wave of Irish and other immigrants (whose male population could vote after residing in the United States for one year), and then because of the passage of the Fourteenth and Fifteenth Amendments after the Civil War, which made African Americans citizens and gave African American men the right to vote, respectively. Many white suffragists, including Stanton and Anthony, felt especially betrayed by the passage of these amendments, which they believed gave intellectually and socially inferior men legal dominion over them as well as made it harder for women to gain the vote, because of the insertion of the word "male" into the Constitution in relation to the franchise. Thus, Stanton increasingly incorporated a racist strain of rhetoric in her suffrage arguments. In 1869, she said, "Think of Patrick and Sambo and Hans and Ung Tung [. . .] who do not know the difference between a monarchy and a republic, who can not read the Declaration of Independence or Webster's spelling book, making laws for Lydia Maria Child, Lucretia Mott, or Fanny Kemble" ("Address" 254).[18] On another occasion, Stanton went so far as to suggest that giving African American men the vote before giving it to white women would "create an antagonism between black men and all women that will culminate in fearful outrages on womanhood, especially in the Southern states" (qtd. in Davis 76).

While *Fettered for Life* does not overtly take part in this racist agenda (at least as it is aimed at African Americans), Blake was certainly a participant in and product of this group of feminist activists; she was a member of NWSA, Stanton and Anthony's suffrage organization. This context is important to bear in mind because although the story seems to advocate natural rights for all women, only white women are depicted as wanting (or needing) these rights. Further, Stanton's claim that the "antagonism" created by enfranchising African American (and other ethnic minority) males leads to white women's political, and by extension, sexual vulnerability forces us to consider the absent presence of racial prejudice in the images of vulnerable, abused, and powerless white women in the novel. Blake's efforts to expose the inequality of gender relations and to encourage her readers to fight this inequality are praiseworthy, but they are grounded in a racist understanding of who deserves equality.

As the leaders of NWSA, Stanton and Anthony began a journal, *The Revolution*, that, despite its occasional racist discourse, also tackled many controversial feminist issues in bold, radical ways. Blake seems to draw heavily on the articles and opinions in this journal in forming her own controversial fictional reform community; there are many characters and scenarios in her novel that embody the abstract ideas and problems raised in the journal. Stanton's editorials on the problems of spousal abuse and the need for changes in the divorce laws appear to influence the graphic depiction of domestic violence in the novel, and other topics such as dress reform, drunkenness, prostitution, and political corruption are "brought to life" in the pages of *Fettered for Life*. Another connection can be seen in the depiction of the central heroine, Laura Stanley, who seems inspired by an article from the journal, "Women in Art," which discusses the "recent exhibitions of the National Academy of Design" (the school Laura attends) that "have contained evidence that American women can attain high positions in many of the departments of art" (236). However, there are crucial differences between the journal's approach to these issues and Blake's; the journal's style is rhetorical and argumentative, which likely alienated a number of would-be supporters. Blake's imaginative rendering, on the other hand, personalizes the characters; the reader feels an intimate connection with those who suffer from social, political, and domestic evils. Just as importantly, Blake is free to depict possible solutions to them.

Blake's fictionalization of physical violence and criminal corruption suggests that her book is influenced by a popular mid-nineteenth-century genre, the sensation novel. This genre developed in both England and America in part as a backlash to what was perceived to be the excessive propriety of much sentimental domestic fiction. In his essay "What Is 'Sensational' about the 'Sensation Novel'?" Patrick Brantlinger defines the genre's "special structural qualities" as "a unique mixture of contemporary domestic realism with elements of the Gothic romance, the Newgate novel of criminal 'love life', and the 'silver fork' novel of scandalous and sometimes criminal 'high life'" (30). Brantlinger also contends that the best sensation novels are those "with a secret" (30), yielding sordid tales of murder or attempted murder, physical violence, blackmail, and deception that span both the upper and lower classes, and Blake's novel fits the bill. Furthermore, according to Anne French Dalke, sensation novels were known for their portrayals of sexual lasciviousness and seduction and in particular, the figure of "the female seducer [who] is both sexually and economically powerful" ("Hawthorne and Melville" 196).

Textual evidence in *Fettered for Life* suggests Blake knew the sensation novel well and is consciously but critically introducing components of it into her novel. Dalke discusses several American sensation novels in "'The Shameless Woman Is the Worst of Men': Sexual Aggression in Nineteenth-Century Sensational Novels," including George Lippard's *The Monks of Monk Hall* and *New York: Its Upper Ten and Lower Million*. According to Dalke, "the passionate woman *par excellence* of *Monks*" who "traffics her body for money and power" is named Dora Livingstone (298). It seems hardly a coincidence that the body of one of Blake's characters, Flora Livingston, is also "traffic[ked] for money and power"; however, in Flora's case, it is her parents who benefit, by betrothing their daughter to an affluent patrician. Also striking is the similarity between another of Blake's characters and one of Lippard's in *New York*, Frank van Huyden. Lippard's Frank is a female "who has a masculine name" and who "appears in male costume" (297). She uses this disguise to seduce previously chaste men, and her fate is to "die finally on a raft in the ocean, where two of her victims stab her bosom [. . .] and drink her blood to save their lives" (297).

Blake's Frank Heywood is also a female character who disguises herself as a man, but she uses her male costume to help women who are powerless in society. Furthermore, this Frank also finds herself on a raft in the ocean, but rather than having her life taken, one of the women whom she has helped gives up her life to save Frank. The differences are crucial, to say the least, and attest to Blake's revisionist intention. Blake is not interested in titillating her audience with misogynist stories of the immense power of sexually deviant women. Rather, she wants to show how powerless most women are because of their sex. In this way, *Fettered* seems part of a larger body of fiction that Lyn Pykett describes as women's sensation novels "that depict marriage and the family as problematic institutions for women and men" (45). While I would argue that *Fettered* is more complex than a pure sensation novel, Blake's judicious use of the genre's sordidness makes it possible for her to harness its shock value to bring about political conversion.

Blake clearly believes that both sensational and sentimental fiction aggravate the problems with these institutions through their unrealistic portraits of women's roles in marriage and their social (and sexual) freedom. Part of her revisionist impulse, then, is to undercut this literature's power. For example, Mrs. Bludgett, an abused wife who is the victim of horrifically graphic violence, ironically finds her escape in popular fiction that glorifies just such violence, which she claims affords her her "only pleasure" (16). Her favorite works, "Headless Lover, or Beauty's Last Temptation, a Tale of Love and Despair" and "Berenice the Beautiful," are clearly reminiscent of sensation novels such as Joseph Holt Ingraham's works *Frank Rivers: or The Dangers of the Town. A Story of Temptation, Trial and Crime* and *Eleanor Sherwood, the Beautiful Temptress* (Dalke, "Shameless Woman" 296). Likewise, Flora, the upper-class character who suffers mental abuse from her husband that is ultimately as lethal as the physical abuse Mrs. Bludgett receives from hers, writes poetry about love describing an experience that sharply differs from her miserable situation: "Silvery sweet the joyous swaying / Of wedding bells, that far out fling / Their melodious rapture" (307). These literary works mock the misleading nature of popular romance narratives and maudlin poetry that belie the unhappy reality of most marriages and women's subordinated role in them.

A more explicit critique comes from Dr. D'Arcy, a woman doctor and feminist activist who observes, "Just so long as our literature is pervaded with the thought that women are inferior, so long will our sex be held in low estimate" (254). The doctor then lists several contradictory stereotypes about women found in literature and ends with the exasperated exclamation, "The amount of such trash that one finds is really aggravating!" (255). This observation is very similar to the one Harbert's narrator makes in the final chapter of *Out of Her Sphere*, and one can argue that, like the earlier novel, one of the most important ways *Fettered for Life* converts its readership to feminism is to provide an alternate fictional landscape, one that models a politically active heroine who is independent and talented and who develops egalitarian relationships with men and other women.

Blake, like Harbert, criticizes literary forms and notions even as she appropriates them in order to bring about real-world change, rendering her own version of the feminist activist heroine in the process. Like Marjory, Laura Stanley has the traditional attributes of heroines in sentimental novels, such as beauty, purity, and goodness. However, unlike Marjory's, Laura's piety and morality are not explicitly discussed at length, and thus the presence of the Cult of True Womanhood is not as strongly felt in *Fettered for Life*. At the same time, Laura does not in any way resemble the "female seducer" found in so much sensation fiction. Instead, her distinctive features include intelligence, plain-spokenness, good health, and physical fitness. At one point, Laura says that she is always "unromantically well," suggesting that her general well-being distinguishes her from other romantic heroines (108). Perhaps her most important attributes, though, are her artistic talent and her desire for financial and social independence, a desire that sets the story in motion. As Grace Farrell observes in her afterword to the novel, "Lillie Blake reversed the protagonist's sex in an archetypal fairy tale of a youth who goes out into the world to seek his fortune and—like [Virginia] Woolf long after her—imagined the consequences" (382).[19]

While Laura Stanley is not a sentimental heroine like those found in *The Lamplighter*, *The Wide, Wide World*, or even *Out of Her Sphere*, she does have fictional precursors in American literature, most notably the eponymous heroine of Catharine Maria Sedgwick's *Hope Leslie* (1827) and Capitola Black in E. D. E. N. Southworth's *The Hidden Hand* (1859). In both cases, the heroine is (like Laura) an outsider; Hope Leslie moves to America from England and Capitola Black is an orphan living on the streets of New York City, disguised as a boy, when her soon-to-be-benefactor discovers she is an heiress and takes her back to Virginia to live. Even more importantly, each is a gender-subversive heroine who was, nevertheless, quite popular with contemporary American reading audiences. Hope Leslie befriends several Native American characters, even defying the stern Puritan authorities in the book (including John Winthrop) by helping some of them escape colonial confinement. Throughout the story, she is guided by her conscience, refusing to bend to social pressure. Similarly, Capitola Black takes care of herself as a young child and as a young woman refuses to have her spirit quelled by her guardian, Old Hurricane. She also defies authority on several occasions and saves a friend from an unhappy marriage and herself from rape.

Mary Kelly notes that Hope is motivated by "concepts such as reliance upon self, independence and autonomy," which "challenge the premises upon which sexual hierarchy was constructed and promote rebellious behavior" (xxv). Likewise, Joanne Dobson says that, because Capitola disguises herself as a boy when she is a teenager, she has "a confidence born of autonomy, ability and pride. Cap's masculine socialization [. . .] allows her to develop the saving characteristics of self-reliance, irreverence, and active, rather than passive, courage" (xxxi). In Laura Stanley, Blake continues this tradition of independent, self-reliant heroines and transforms it by making the situations Laura faces more perilous and by demonstrating that even her originality and autonomy are not enough to overcome all the obstacles she faces (as they are for the more successful Hope and Capitola). In this way, Blake draws on the gender subversion of these earlier novels but makes even more explicit the connection between her heroine's personal independence and her need for (and legitimate claim to) political rights.

Similar to Hope Leslie, who relocates to the New World, and Capitola Black, who envisions herself as a "damsel errant in quest of adventures," Laura, a recent college graduate, moves to New York to "seek her fortune" as an artist. Laura announces early in the book, "I always had 'ideas,' I cannot see why a daughter should hang on her father for support any more than a son. I have been educated so that I can earn my own living, and I intend to do it" (40–41). Laura has considerable artistic talent, and she takes great pleasure from painting. Laura's feminism is motivated primarily by her need for self-fulfillment, which she believes is her right as a human being, in contrast to Marjory, whose other-centered feminism is inspired by Christian ideals. Laura is not saving a brother for art; she is the artist. In fact, the only time her art is discussed in terms of benefiting others is in a specifically political context. Dr. D'Arcy says that Laura can help bring about "the civil and political equality of women" by devoting herself to her art: "This country has not yet produced a really great woman-painter, why should you not achieve a triumph for yourself and your sex in that art?" (64).

Laura *is* similar to Marjory in that she refuses to let marriage interfere with her feminist ambitions; however, for Laura, this refusal stems from a belief in her natural right to self-fulfillment. When Laura proclaims that she hopes she will not always be an art teacher, a friend misunderstands her, thinking she means that she hopes to marry and give up working. Laura replies indignantly, "No, I do not! [. . .] Of course I may marry some day—why shouldn't I? But I do not intend to allow that to interfere with my profession, I hope I shall not always be obliged to give lessons, but when I can sell my pictures for good prices, it will not be necessary" (71). Laura's priorities are telling; she talks about marriage casually, clearly considering it tangential to her career, which she insists on pursuing. Also, her desire for personal recognition and success, as well as for money, clearly reflects a self-interestedness that contradicts the tenets of true womanhood and suggests the heroine's (and the author's) unequivocal belief that the right to the "pursuit of happiness" extends to middle-class females.

In order to impress on her readers the obstacles facing women in this pursuit (and to shock her readers into doing something about them), Blake depicts New York City as a hostile, patriarchal world. This concentrated, dangerous urban landscape also attests to the sensation novel's influence on Blake; these novels are almost always set in crowded, busy cities. The unchecked political power of men has corrupted every facet of contemporary life, creating a city teeming with sexual predators, dissipated saloon-goers, abusive husbands and fathers, not to mention facile, condescending men whose pride is undeserved and whose pomposity is unbearable. On her first night in town, Laura appeals to a policeman to let her sleep in jail after being insulted and propositioned when she tries to find a hotel in which to stay. On her second night, Judge Swinton (a character who pursues Laura lasciviously and ruthlessly throughout the text) conspires with Mr. Bludgett (a political crony who is often drunk and beats his wife mercilessly) to compromise the young heroine by trapping her in Bludgett's house. These opening scenes are harbingers of the pervasive masculine threat Laura feels later in the novel: "The surging throng around [Laura] seemed so many enemies, any one of whom would wound her or hunt her. Among all these strong, pushing, busy men, there seemed no place, and no hope for a woman to expect justice or mercy" (183).

The political corruption in the novel is just as sinister as the physical and sexual threats are. Swinton, Bludgett, and others conspire to maintain control of the political machine in New York in order to protect their financial interests, which include saloons and alcohol sales. Their corrupt dealings eventually result in Bludgett's murdering a political opponent and Swinton's arranging the murderer's acquittal, a scene that is immediately followed by a satiric description of a political meeting in which Judge Swinton accepts his party's nomination to Congress, proclaiming his devotion to the "duties of the hour" and "the responsibilities of the high position to which he aspired" (339). The juxtaposition of these two scenes impresses on the reader the moral decay that lies underneath the genteel surface of politics. However, it is not only the underworld of politics that is corrupt; one of the most heartless, domineering, and dangerous men in the novel, Ferdinand Le Roy, is also one of the wealthiest men in New York. Here, Blake employs the sensation novel's technique of roaming among various classes to show how corrupting unchecked power can be, suggesting that this pervasive problem can only be solved by allowing educated, ethical women enough power to fight it.

This "surging throng" of threatening white men bears witness to women's relatively greater vulnerability to sexual assault and political manipulation. But given that it was the post–Civil War myth of the black rapist, a myth exacerbated by Stanton and others who saw African American men voting as an analogous threat to white womanhood, that gave rise to the trope of white woman-as-victim, the "surging throng" is also a displacement of white anxiety about black men. *Fettered for Life* depicts white, native-born men as the primary aggressors, but since in the "real world" outside the novel, images of sexual predators were often racially and ethnically inflected, the reader's response to Laura's danger would hinge on not only her knowledge of these racial stereotypes but also her belief that white, middle-class women are particularly vulnerable to sexual assault.[20]

In a similar way, the political corruption in the novel is ethnically coded. As I noted in my discussion of *Out of Her Sphere*, after the Civil War many white, affluent people reconceived politics, which they had formerly regarded as an honorable republican activity, as "a morally bankrupt realm of activity, in which men of 'lower races' manipulated voters through patronage and bribery" (Newman 59). While it is impossible to determine the country of origin of most of Blake's characters, because she generally uses symbolic instead of stereotypical names, this threat of political danger (linked to sexual danger by Stanton and others) would have contributed to Blake's readers' outrage that white, educated women were powerless against the manipulation depicted in the novel.[21] Furthermore, if the reader were a white middle-class woman, her perception of herself as especially vulnerable to such dangers would have been reinforced as well, and she would have been even more inclined to support woman's rights.

Within such a sexually and politically dangerous setting, *Fettered for Life* carves out an oppositional community of women who literally must work together to protect themselves and each other and whose intimate relationships are formed across lines of class and "respectability," if not race. The women whom Laura befriends during her adventures form a diverse group that, in spite of their differences from each other, is bound together by both choice and necessity. It includes Dr. D'Arcy and Frank Heywood (neither the reader nor Laura realizes Frank's true identity until the end of the story; however, he/she is part of the sympathetic web of women from the beginning). There's also Mrs. Moulder, a critical embodiment of the passivity and submission expected of a model wife, who, although not as affluent as Dr. D'Arcy, Frank, or Laura, is still middle-class; she befriends Laura after taking her in as a boarder. Many members of the community, however, are in even more dire financial and personal circumstances than Mrs. Moulder, including Mrs. Bludgett and also Rhoda and Maggie, both wage-earning women who have fallen victim to male sexual predators. Although they are seamstresses by trade, currently, Rhoda works in a saloon and supports Maggie, who is dying of consumption. On the other end of the social spectrum, there is Flora Livingston, Laura's college friend who is just as confined and unhappy in her affluence as Maggie, Rhoda, and others are in their deprivation. What links these characters together is the book's contention that (native-born, white) women, regardless of class or position, are vulnerable as long as they are denied equal legal and social recourse. The marriages of Flora and Mrs. Bludgett are both intolerably abusive, although the women live in very different social circumstances, and both die as a direct result of their husbands' cruelty. Also, Laura and Flora, both members of "respectable" society, are sexually harassed or physically threatened by the same men, Judge Swinton and Ferdinand Le Roy, whose sexual dominance ruins the reputations and lives of Rhoda and Maggie.

There are two minor female characters in *Fettered for Life*, however, whose presence reminds the reader of the way this oppositional community is circumscribed by race and ethnicity. The first is Biddy Maloney, a poor Irish woman who asks Dr. D'Arcy for advice about her son Patrick. In stereotypical Irish idiom, Biddy says to the doctor, "He was as good a b'ye, was Pat, as a mother would ax for, [...] but he's tuk to bad company these last two months, and he's goin' on very bad intirely. Gettin' dhrunk, ma'am, savin' your presence" (30). Biddy wants Dr. D'Arcy to "git some great gintleman to spake to [him]," and while Dr. D'Arcy consents, it is clear that this relationship is not reciprocal (32). Dr. D'Arcy helps Biddy but does not draw her into the community of women who interact throughout the book. Clearly, Biddy is in a subordinate, "uncivilized" role, and her son Patrick is the stereotypically "savage" immigrant male with dangerous political power. This subordination is reinforced by her brogue, which marks her as different from most of the other female characters. Biddy is one of the people whom Dr. D'Arcy, as an affluent white woman, is empowered to help, but she is not depicted in the novel as a character who is worthy (or capable) of pursuing feminist goals or whose vulnerability merits much attention in the text.

The other female character who is not included in the community of feminist activists in any meaningful way is Aunt Phoebe, Maggie's "mammy," who appears briefly after Dr. D'Arcy and Frank help Maggie and Rhoda travel to the South so that Maggie can see her mother again. Like Biddy, Aunt Phoebe talks in stereotypical dialect; on Maggie's arrival, she exclaims, "De Lord bress my precious honey, pickaninny! is you done come back to ole mammy?" (224). Aunt Phoebe is a faithful former slave, common in much popular fiction of the 1870s, and even though the Civil War freed her, she has stayed to care for Maggie's mother, Mrs. Bertram, who is also ill. Only after both Maggie and her mother die does Aunt Phoebe return to Richmond to live with her son. Interestingly, Aunt Phoebe is perhaps the only female character who does not seem to have personal problems that stem from her vulnerability; she is completely other-centered, and when she leaves Rhoda at the train station, she too disappears from the community. The depiction of Aunt Phoebe underscores the implicit whiteness of feminist activist communities in two ways. She is not portrayed as being imperiled (and therefore in need of rights), and so she does not "threaten" the white readership with the notion that African American women will also demand greater political freedom. Her presence also reminds the reader of Maggie's white, aristocratic past, which makes her eligible for inclusion in the novel's feminist community.

The exclusivity of the novel's feminist oppositional community notwithstanding, many of the white characters who become part of it benefit from the support it provides. For example, storytelling becomes a way for these women to bridge their personal differences and learn to depend on one another. We see this effect early in the novel, when Mr. Bludgett takes a friendless Laura to his home so Judge Swinton can pursue her in private, forcing his wife (whom he has abused into submission) to keep her there. However, she and Laura begin talking, and Laura shows Mrs. Bludgett kindness, sympathy, and interest, saying to her, "I should like to hear all your story. [. . .] We women ought to stand by each other, and care for each other" (18). Mrs. Bludgett, though hesitant, admits that she does not think her husband's actions are always kind or good, but she does not question his right to control her. She also admits that, before they married, she had a decent job as a shop girl, and she misses the freedom of her single days. Laura continues talking to Mrs. Bludgett and helps prepare the evening meal; such friendliness emboldens Mrs. Bludgett to defy her husband and warn Laura that she needs to escape (although Laura does not realize she is in danger, Mrs. Bludgett does). Laura leaves with Frank Heywood, who, after hitting Mr. Bludgett, takes Laura to Dr. D'Arcy and thus introduces her to the feminist community. Mrs. Bludgett, meanwhile, is beaten by her husband for this act of defiance, but she gains the trust and friendship of Laura and Frank and thereby is initiated into the feminist oppositional community as well.

Such a request to "hear all [one's] story" is repeated throughout the book, and it often leads to similar types of assistance. For example, Dr. D'Arcy entreats Laura, "[N]ow my dear, tell me all about yourself" (33); the reader then learns of Laura's aunt sending her to college despite her disapproving father and of her mother's helping her to run away from her rural home to the city. Later, Laura convinces a hesitant and reticent Rhoda to tell a respectable girl about life in the saloons with the earnest appeal, "I can understand [. . .] do tell me about it; I should like so much to hear your story" (57). Here, the reader and the characters not only learn about the horrible conditions of this lifestyle from Rhoda but also see in Laura a model of sympathy that defies the debilitating silence imposed on middle-class white women by expectations of propriety. The reader gleans almost all of the information about the various plights of the women in the book from scenes in which one character asks another to tell her story. In this context, Frank Heywood's journalistic efforts to protect women by reporting sexist injustices have implications for organized, public political activity. In one episode, she helps imprisoned women get better treatment by threatening to write a story about their lack of blankets and food; in another, she warns Judge Swinton that she will expose the politician's illicit activities to her readership if he continues to pursue Laura.

Sharing stories is only one way these female characters forge a communal bond; they also learn to depend on each other for support, comfort, and ultimately, survival. The examples of this mutual assistance are ubiquitous. Frank and Dr. D'Arcy take Laura in when she moves to New York, and Dr. D'Arcy helps her find a job and a place to stay. Laura boards with Mrs. Moulder and helps her with her overwhelming family tasks and keeps her company. The most striking examples, however, are when the characters actually save, or attempt to save, each other's lives. Frank saves Laura twice from the judge who is physically threatening her; one rescue is particularly daring because Laura has been kidnapped and chloroformed. Rhoda is also instrumental in saving Laura from the judge; at one point, she refuses a large sum of money he has offered her to conceal his past from Laura. Later in the novel, another minor character summons Dr. D'Arcy to Maggie's sickbed, and Dr. D'Arcy helps both Rhoda and Maggie improve their situation; furthermore, she treats the two laboring-class women as family, not as recipients of her charity: "The manner in which the good lady treated her during her daily visits was balm to Rhoda's poor sore heart. Mrs. D'Arcy was as kind to her as if she had been the cherished daughter of a friend" (165). Frank accompanies the sick girl and her friend on their trip to the South, and when their ship capsizes on the return voyage, Rhoda allows herself to drown so Frank can float on the only piece of driftwood.

This web of concern, action, and sacrifice models an oppositional community that has an air of urgency and immediacy owing to the very real dangers its members confront. These women do not bond together to bring about change based on abstract reform ideology; rather, they literally battle together against an unfair world in need of gender reform. This version of oppositional community formation is different from those based on expediency arguments that define feminist activism in part as "true christian philanthropy," which suggests a hierarchy of assistance; the more privileged women are responsible for taking care of poor women, but the reverse is not necessarily true. The members of the oppositional community in *Fettered for Life*, on the other hand, engage in reciprocal acts of rescue and assistance; they model a community in which white women of different classes who share a common vulnerability as women commit to building a coalition.

The multitude of life-endangering situations and hair-breadth escapes in

Fettered for Life reveals a narrative indebtedness to not only typical sensation novels but also to more mainstream books like *Hope Leslie* and *The Hidden Hand*, which also place their brave heroines (and other female characters) in dangerous (if sometimes outlandish) circumstances. Most pertinent to this study are the moments when Hope and Capitola rescue their friends (and sometimes enemies) from a terrible fate—either death or a bad marriage. In *Hope Leslie*, the heroine twice helps Native American women escape from the Puritan authorities because she believes they have been wrongly imprisoned. The first, Nelema, is accused of being the "emissary of Satan" because she helps cure Hope's tutor, Mr. Craddock, from a snakebite (105). Unwilling to see her wrongly accused (and surely executed if found guilty), Hope masterminds a plot to free her and help her leave the town. Later, Hope and Everell Fletcher (her adopted brother and future husband) devise a plan of disguise and subterfuge to save Magawisca, the novel's other heroine (herself a strong and independent woman who is in essence a prisoner of the Pequod War). Similarly, in a chapter from *The Hidden Hand* entitled "Cap Frees the Captive," Capitola helps her friend Clara Day escape a forced, secret wedding to the villain, Craven Le Noir. Clara, a submissive true-woman-style heroine, is on the verge of committing suicide, but Cap intercedes, disguising herself as Clara until the other woman can escape. In this way, Cap is able to subvert Le Noir's patriarchal imperative that Clara be his legal and sexual property.

The differences between these successful rescue operations and Laura's analogous attempt to save her friend Flora from a bad marriage are quite telling. Flora has been coerced by her parents into accepting the proposal of Ferdinand Le Roy. Days before the wedding, she appeals to Laura to help her in her desperate attempt to get away. Flora leads Laura to the railroad station and tells her, "I would rather do anything, submit to anything, than be his wife" (235). Laura agrees that it is better for Flora to escape than to "wreck [her] happiness for life" (235). Laura, as cool-headed as either Hope or Cap, takes charge of the situation and arranges to accompany Flora to her uncle's home, where she will be hidden and safe. Le Roy, however, pursues them to the train station and overtakes them: "Laura had raised her hand to the iron rail to help Flora; but just as the fugitive girl would have stepped up, a heavy grasp was laid on her shoulder" (240). Flora faints, Le Roy carries her away, and Laura is left helpless and "heart-sick with indignant scorn" (241). Eventually, Flora dies because of her unhappiness and confinement.

This is not the only instance in *Fettered for Life* where female characters try but fail to save each other. By the end of the novel, Mrs. Bludgett, Rhoda, and Maggie are also all dead, and Mrs. Moulder is gravely ill after a miscarriage.

These failures no doubt make *Fettered for Life* a less satisfying reading experience than *Hope Leslie* or *The Hidden Hand*, but Blake has a more overtly somber message to convey. Independence of mind and a free spirit are not enough to defy the status quo, even if an oppositional community can offer support and some measure of assistance. Instead, Blake insists that only systemic gender reform would have made it possible for all her characters to have saved themselves and/or others. In fact, only those members deeply engaged in political activism—Dr. D'Arcy, Frank Heywood, and Laura Stanley—survive. In this way, the book intimates that the white, middle-class female reader's very life might depend on her entering the ranks of feminist activists and reminds her that she has an elemental right to "life" in addition to "liberty and the pursuit of happiness."

Fettered draws a rigid boundary between the oppositional female community and the oppressive society of male dominance. This division is seen in almost every household in the story, where domineering fathers and husbands are pitted against their female dependents, demonstrating the perverse effect that gendered conventions and white women's legal status have on familial relationships. However, Frank is an important liminal figure who because she "passes" as male is able to cross this boundary at will, thereby serving as a persuasive example of a female's inherent "personhood." Frank's character, like Laura's, seems inspired by Capitola in *The Hidden Hand*. Cap disguises herself as a boy when she is a child living on the streets of New York because as she says, "while all the ragged boys I knew could get little jobs to earn bread, I, because I was a girl, was not allowed to carry a gentleman's parcel, or black his boots [. . .] or do *any*thing that *I* could do just as well as *they*" (44). In addition to economic opportunity, Cap's disguise provides her with protection; she admits, "Well, being always exposed, sleeping out-of-doors, I was often in danger from bad boys and bad men" (45).

Frank encounters a similarly hostile environment when she arrives in New York: "I was insulted, refused work, unless I would comply with the disgraceful propositions of my employers; in short, I had the experience which so many young women have in the great city; poverty, temptation, cruelty" (366). While Frank's experiences seem clearly modeled on Cap's, the differences are significant. In Southworth's novel, these cross-dressing adventures are introduced, in part, for comic effect; the humor as well as the fact that Cap is a child seem to render the implications of the threats less serious. Furthermore, this episode only serves as a brief "back story" in Capitola's adventures; it is not long before her gender identity (along with her money and the protection her wealth affords her) is restored. Frank, on the other hand, is a young woman of twenty, a sexually vulnerable age, when she moves to New York and her disguise, which she maintains throughout the novel, is an integral part of her feminist activism. Blake's revisions of *The Hidden Hand* work to foreground the seriousness and urgency of gender reform.

Nevertheless, Joanne Dobson's observation about Capitola seems equally apt when applied to Frank: "An aberrant gender socialization is, significantly, [her] salvation" (xxxi). Frank is able to survive and flourish, in part because her disguise allows her to attempt many "masculine" activities, which she performs admirably. Her talent as a journalist earns her a job as a travel writer; the "spicy" stories she sends back are literary manifestations of a freedom of movement and expression she would never have had as a woman. The reader first encounters Frank when she saves Laura from Mr. Bludgett and Judge Swinton; in this scene, she is brave and cool-headed, the knight in shining armor rather than the damsel in distress: "[T]he young reporter who had stood by, with his face very pale and his lips pressed tightly together, now drew back and with wonderful vigor and scientific dexterity, planted a quick blow directly under the big man's right ear" (24). Frank's actions here undermine arguments those opposed to gender reform made about women's inability to interact effectively in the public sphere. "Blake's use of the gender switch," Farrell notes, suggests that "gender itself is a surface detail" (394).

At the same time, Frank is a model of the ideal "man" who believes in gender reform and who uses his masculine privilege to help the oppressed, engaging in acts of "revolutionary love" instead of abusing that privilege for his own gain. Early in the novel, Frank tells Laura, "Very few men do realize the scope of woman's needs. [. . .] [T]hey think that the agitation of woman suffrage is only the work of a few discontented souls. They do not understand that the demand for political equality is but one of the public utterances of a great dumb cry, that goes up from millions of hearts" (54). However, the fact that the male character who is most sympathetic and enthusiastic about feminist reform is, in the end, a woman, suggests that Blake is skeptical of men's ability to fully empathize with the woman's rights movement because they have not experienced firsthand the unfairness of women's legal oppression.

This skepticism about men's ability to be feminist activists is evident in the novel's heterosexual romance plot, which involves Laura and Guy Bradford and that is, perhaps not surprisingly, complicated by Frank's presence. The three appear to be embroiled in a love triangle for most of the novel. The names of Laura's two ostensible suitors are revealing. Guy is, in fact, an average "guy" who, if not violent and dangerous like most of the men in the story, seems rather unremarkable. He is most often described as "earnest" and "honest" and "eager," and his relationship with Laura lacks the intimacy that she shares with the female characters she befriends. She and Guy in fact seem to do little more than blush and stammer in each other's presence. Guy does profess support for woman's rights, having been raised by a progressive couple; however, he himself is not an activist, and his notions about gender are more conventional than Laura's. He tells Laura on their first meeting, "Indeed, you will find me as warm an advocate of the equality of the sexes as you could wish. I am no reformer, it is true; I am only a hard working business man, but I have been brought up in the right way on these points by my parents" (68). "It seems," he states in elaborating on the "right way" he was raised, "to me a very one sided government, which refuses to my mother and sister all voice, while it professes to honor goodness and purity" (68).

Guy is a proponent of suffrage as long as it does not muddy the societal distinctions between masculinity and femininity, and later, we learn that he would not necessarily encourage Laura to be an activist either. When she jokingly suggests that she would be an "electioneer" for his mother if she ever ran for office, Guy responds, "I am not quite clear that I should like to have you" (208). In the same conversation, Laura says, "[S]ometimes I feel as if I would like to go veiled like the Turkish women; some of your sex are so rude," to which Guy replies, "I only wish you could wear a veil; that is, provided you took it off for me" (206). While the obvious implication of his remark is that he should like for her to be his bride, it also can be read as suggesting he believes that even if women have the vote, they ought to be confined; likewise, his opinion about Laura's political involvement suggests that he thinks women ought to be acquiescent.

Laura's relationship with Guy is further called into question by the juxtaposition of scenes that depict his and Laura's sexually charged, romantic interludes with some of the most depressing or frightening scenes of domestic life. In one such scene, Laura is overwhelmed by passion and romance after a walk in the park with Guy: "She scarcely ventured to define her thoughts; but the blood in her veins was dancing to some happy tune, and the future rose before her fair with the enchanted 'light that never seems to end'" (209). But this wandering in the "enchanted" romantic realm that the book criticizes elsewhere is short-lived. Laura enters the Moulders' house (where she is a boarder) and "[i]t was [. . .] like a harsh discord after some strain of sweet, soft music, to go down to the dull dining-room [. . .] and descend from the fairy realms in which she had been dreaming to the prosaic realities of common life" (209). What follows is a quarrelsome scene in which the Moulders' son, acting on his assumed superiority to his sisters, is especially mean to them, and a disagreement ensues between Laura and Mr. Moulder. The reader, like Laura, is not allowed to engage in romantic fantasy for long without being reminded of the discordant reality of patriarchal society.

Laura's relationship with Frank, by contrast, is much more substantial, based on shared experiences and an ability to truly communicate with each other. This description of Laura's early encounter with Frank is a harbinger of their intimacy to come:

> [A]mong so many strangers [Laura] felt quite alone, and was heartily glad, when after awhile, Frank Heywood came in. She greeted him with well-pleased cordiality and the two were soon chatting in a corner, like old friends.
>
> The young man had a fund of information on topics in which Laura was interested, and there was about him so absolute an air of purity, that she found herself confiding in him in a way that surprised her when she thought of it afterwards. His handsome melancholy face was very attractive to her, and the tones of his low musical voice fascinated her strangely. (48)

Laura's reaction to Frank *is* fascinating, given his concealed identity. He has both conventional feminine and masculine qualities ("an air of purity" and a "handsome, melancholy face"), and it is clear she is very attracted to him. Furthermore, the reticence and awkwardness that defines her relationship with Guy is completely missing here; at the start, this relationship seems the more promising of the two. Laura insists that the Moulders' oldest daughter chaperone when Guy visits but always sees Frank alone, because "he was so like a brother" (134). That she sees him alone underscores that she feels safe with him in a way she does not with Guy, aligning the latter with the threatening male world of the rest of the book.[22]

If Laura and Frank seem to understand each other perfectly, Laura's relationship with Guy is fraught with misunderstanding. When Guy becomes unjustifiably jealous, the narrator tells the reader: "Laura was amused and annoyed. She could read this big honest fellow like an open book; while to him she was a wonderful being, whose smile was happiness, but whose favor he knew not how to win, he was to her a transparent soul" (196). Guy's feelings for Laura are not founded on a thorough understanding of her character, resulting in *Fettered for Life*'s variation on the "double proposal plot." On the day Guy plans to propose, Judge Swinton anonymously sends him a letter about the dubious circumstances of Laura's first night in New York (which the reader knows she spent in the police station for protection). Guy wants Laura to account for it, claiming that "between us two, who have so nearly looked on each other's hearts, there is no need of ceremony" (292). The reader, of course, is reminded of Guy's frequent miscomprehension of Laura's heart and is not surprised when she rebukes his question: "I declare that you have no right to ask it! Would you give me equal right to question *your* life?" (292). Guy insists that her asking him is "a very different thing" (293). She again refuses to answer him because she is angered by his "distrust and [his] cross-examination," and so he leaves (293). Like Marjory in *Out of Her Sphere*, Laura has not explicitly rejected the proposal of her suitor. It is clear, nonetheless, that Guy's marriage offer is contingent on Laura's answering his inquiry, and her refusal to do so is likewise a refusal to marry Guy on his terms.

This plot line thus enters what Tracey calls the "post-courtship" stage. After Laura refuses Guy, she continues to work on her art and, like Marjory Warner, finds some peace because she has an occupation other than marriage: "If the only man she had ever cared for should be lost to her, she had still her art, and life should not be ruined to her" (361). However, Laura does not change during this period.[23] Rather, in contrast to *Out of Her Sphere*, in *Fettered for Life*, it is only the hero who must undergo change. Although he has all along expressed support for woman's rights, he must acknowledge Laura's autonomy and individual determination before the two of them can understand each other and come to an acceptable agreement about what gender reform really means. Clearly, the question that Guy asks Laura has sexual implications. Her refusal to answer it shows that she believes this autonomy must extend to her right to control her own sexuality and to be held to the same sexual standards as Guy, both of which were much more controversial demands in nineteenth-century American society than the demand for the right to vote. Guy must be converted to Laura's radical position on these issues, accepting her essential "personhood" and revising what he means by the word "equality."

The resolution of *Fettered* demonstrates—guardedly—that such a conversion is possible. Guy returns after several months in Europe and admits that he behaved foolishly, acknowledging his question to Laura was unfair unless he were willing to answer it as well. The novel ends with a second proposal, to which Laura answers, "Yes, Guy [. . .] for I believe you will not ask me to surrender my liberty entirely and will permit me to follow out my own career in life" (379). Although Guy agrees, saying "your obligations to me shall be no greater than mine to you," his previously narrow view of woman's rights might make the reader skeptical that he is in fact changed (379). However, the novel opens up the possibility at least that Guy has been converted to a more liberal view of gender reform by his love for Laura, a personal experience (like reading) that can break down prejudices abstract ideology cannot. If so, then their revolutionary romance provides hope that a cross-gender oppositional community could be a reality, even while men still have such a mammoth advantage in the power differential that results from political inequality.

This potential community, however, is still predicated on the implicit whiteness of its members and the racial privilege that is inherent in many feminist arguments about American women's natural rights as citizens. To make this point clear, it is perhaps useful to return once again to the earlier novel, *Hope Leslie*. In many ways, the bonds that Hope shares with Native American women are much more radical than the cross-racial bonds found in *Fettered for Life*. She and Magawisca are both fully realized, complex, moral characters, and Sedgwick does not shy away from making Magawisca right on some occasions and Hope wrong. Nevertheless, at the end of the novel, Sedgwick has Magawisca leave Boston forever, rather than remain in contact with white society. Judith Fetterley reads Magawisca as Hope's symbolic "sister" and claims that the novel ends inevitably in this sororal banishment, because "[the novel employs] a rhetoric designed to bring privileged white women into citizenship [that] may not do much for their differently raced (or classed) sisters. To put it slightly differently, as long as the rhetoric of equality begins from the ground of the 'brother,' there will be no place in America for 'my sister! my sister!'" ("Rhetoric" 83). When we apply this logic to *Fettered for Life*, we see that the revolutionary romance at the end (and the gender equality that it implies) is only possible because Laura's claim to sexual and political equality with Guy rests on the implicit assumption of her racial superiority. Guy is the white male whose republican (and moral) virtue contrasts with the sordid politicians and sexual predators whose power to incite fear in the reader derives in part from the suggestion that they are ethnic. Similarly, Laura's assertion of her own "natural" rights—to education, a profession, suffrage, and sexual autonomy—cannot be separated from the novel's implication that white women are the most in need of (and deserving of) these rights. Perhaps, then, this marriage of (racial) equals is the appropriate conclusion for a book that models a feminist oppositional community that, while class integrated and somewhat gender integrated, is racially homogenous.

Nevertheless, this rather conventional heterosexual union and "happy ending" seem inconsistent with the novel's virulent criticism of the marriage institution. Farrell claims that this happy ending is "part of a cover plot [...] to reassert the status quo in order to make [the novel] more palatable to the literary marketplace" (399). If Farrell is right, Blake's partial capitulation to the expectations of the heterosexual romance narrative quells the truly unorthodox potential within the narrative. The most obvious example of this potential is the prospect of a same-sex union between Laura and Frank, which the novel indulges at the beginning, before Frank's true identity is revealed; when Mrs. Bludgett and Rhoda see Frank and Laura together for the first time, the older woman tells her friend: "That's as nice a couple as I ever see. [. . .] It would be just like a story, if he should marry her" (59). Of course, the irony is that a marriage between Laura and Frank would be unlike any conventional romance story read by Mrs. Bludgett or anyone else in the nineteenth century, and although the book clearly presents such a coupling as an option, it is careful to enforce the heterosexual norm. Other examples of this capitulation are the deaths of Rhoda and Maggie. Although they are not the only women who die in the story, the sort of death they endure is consistent with that of other "fallen women" in nineteenth-century fiction. Maggie dies a painful, sentimentally described death that is a direct result of her sexual transgression, and Rhoda suffers an equally conventional fate; her "heroic" death, sacrificing herself for Frank, redeems her from her sins.[24]

In the end, perhaps the feminist activist most worthy of emulation is not Laura, but Frank, who has embarked on an independent lifestyle that is fulfilling, even without romantic love. Like other sensation novels, *Fettered* has a secret at its heart; however, in keeping with Blake's feminist revision, Frank's disguise is not an occasion for him to wreak havoc; instead, Blake has him don it so that he can undertake important work for woman's rights. This secret, which is hinted at throughout the text, is finally revealed to Laura (and the reader) at the very end. Frank takes Laura into his confidence during the train ride after Rhoda has saved him and once he confesses his true identity, he elaborates on the productive work his disguise will allow him to accomplish in the future:

> I shall not marry; my work must be father and mother, wife and children to me. I believe that a great newspaper may be conducted only in the interest of truth, of justice and of right. The experiment has never yet been tried as I hope to try it; but I trust that the day will come when I may shape, with my own hands, a paper which shall be a teacher of the people, a guide in the path of virtue, and reform, and this aim must take me from all family ties. I feel myself more than ever consecrated and set apart for this work, since Rhoda's death. (302)

In this plan, too, may be an indirect homage to Stanton and *The Revolution*, which had gone out of print a few years earlier because of financial trouble. Frank's activism will be the culmination of his success in the male world, and as Laura observes, "[I]f there were some trials in the young journalist's life, there must surely be some compensations also" (368). Certainly, Frank has found an effective way to pursue his political goals. As Caroline Levander observes, "By shedding women's clothing and its vocal and sexual constraints, Frank Heywood is able to use his voice to defend women publicly against male oppression" (132).

In addition to providing readers with models of individual activists such as Laura and Frank, *Fettered* also teaches valuable lessons about communal resistance in the real world to those readers who would join a feminist oppositional community. Although Blake seems clearly motivated by arguments from justice, her novel also models how oppositional communities can be formed in spite of philosophical differences and specifically shows how arguments of justice and of expediency can coexist. Guy is not the only character who champions expediency arguments; Dr. D'Arcy expounds them as well. As Farrell observes, "While she appears to be the novel's spokesperson for Blake's own ideology, instead, she speaks the language of mainstream suffrage thought [that argues for woman's unique feminine contribution to politics]" (393). However, there is no compelling evidence that Dr. D'Arcy is the single (or most significant) authorial spokesperson in the book; instead, she is one of several characters who espouse varying arguments for woman's rights that all seem to carry the same authorial weight. Blake thereby promotes natural rights ideology without sacrificing the efficacy of expediency arguments. Nevertheless, in *Fettered for Life*, the presumptive whiteness of their proponents underlies the different arguments proffered for reform. One "difference" that is never set aside is that of race and the role race should play in feminist reform work is never "on the table" in the novel as an issue of contention.

The critical reception of Blake's book has historically been mixed. In an early review of the novel, a writer for *Harper's New Monthly Magazine* says that "the style is spirited and the plot so interesting to the average novel-reader that the story will be popular" ("Editor's Literary Record" 442–43). However, the writer seems to have missed the radical arguments in the book; she describes it as a testament to "the necessity of independence to the development of true womanhood," thereby failing to distinguish it from the more mainstream expediency arguments ("Editor's Literary Record" 442–43).[25] More recently, in *Beneath the American Renaissance*, David S. Reynolds calls *Fettered for Life* "the most comprehensive women's rights novel of the nineteenth-century" (357). On the other hand, one contemporary reviewer for *The Literary World* warns the author about using such a critical, "unwomanly" tone when trying to bring about political change: "It is not politic to make a man angry before you try to convince him" ("Fettered for Life" 87).

It is perhaps not surprising that many readers either misunderstood Blake's position or were offended by it; however, the critical attention that her novel received, especially in mainstream publications, suggests that it was being read and debated by a relatively large readership. Blake's daughter also suggests that the novel was widely circulated; in her biography of her mother, she and her coauthor Margaret Wallace report that it sold "1300 copies" on "the day of publication" (*Champion of Women* 97). Many people likely read the novel primarily because they were tantalized by its sensationalism—the cross-dressing and kidnapping, for example—that place it in the tradition of other popular novels such as *Hope Leslie* and *The Hidden Hand*. In contrast, very little national or mainstream attention was paid to Harbert's book at the time of its publication (unlike its more sentimental precursors, *The Lamplighter*, *The Wide, Wide World* and *Uncle Tom's Cabin*), and it has been virtually ignored ever since. In the end, although Blake's ideology about gender reform may have been less popular with readers than Harbert's, perhaps the more sensational elements of *Fettered for Life* gained it a wider audience and thus allowed it to be a greater influence in the creation of a real-world oppositional community dedicated to gender reform.

Without question, though, both *Out of Her Sphere* and *Fettered for Life* forged a link between a mainstream readership and the nascent, marginal woman's rights movement by appropriating popular literary devices and trends of their day for their own purposes. These works are important literary reflections of the desires, imaginations, and fears that motivated early feminists as they considered what their real-world oppositional community should be. However, while they clearly performed important activist cultural work, they also contributed to a narrow-mindedness about race that would vex the first wave of American feminism from beginning to end. In each novel, it is clear that the primary proponents and beneficiaries of gender reform are white women. Such myopia is a central concern of two novels from the 1890s, Frances Ellen Watkins Harper's *Iola Leroy* and Hamlin Garland's *A Spoil of Office*, neither of which is about the woman's rights movement per se. Because their authors reject single-issue politics, each is able to offer an alternative model of feminist activism and imagine oppositional communities that acknowledge the connections between racism, sexism, and classism in America.

CHAPTER TWO

Expanding the Vision of Feminist Activism

Frances E. W. Harper's *Iola Leroy* and Hamlin Garland's *A Spoil of Office*

In her book of essays, *A Voice from the South* (1892), the African American activist Anna Julia Cooper criticizes the racial bias of the woman's rights movement and challenges it to see beyond the increasingly narrow agenda of woman suffrage:[1]

> The cause of freedom is not the cause of a race or a sect, a party or a class,—it is the cause of human kind, the very birthright of humanity. Now unless we are greatly mistaken the Reform of our day, known as the Woman's Movement, is essentially such an embodiment, if its pioneers could only realize it, of the universal good. [...]
> It is not the intelligent woman vs. the ignorant woman; nor the white woman vs. the black, the brown, and the red,—it is not even the cause of woman vs. man. Nay, 'tis woman's strongest vindication for speaking that the *world needs to hear her voice*. It would be subversive of every human interest that the cry of one-half the human family be stifled. (120–21)

Cooper here highlights the broader implications of the woman's rights movement, pointing out that it is a particular manifestation of a greater principle, that all human beings should have equal rights, protection, and opportunities within their society. And because women span every socio-economic and ethnic group, the cause of woman's rights, she makes clear, is truly the "cause of [all] human kind"; the "Woman's Movement" should not only be attuned to the varying situations of all women—intelligent, ignorant, white, black, brown, and red—but should also be attuned to injustices everywhere.

Ironically, this passage was written at a time when the movement was head-ing in an increasingly conservative, discriminatory direction. In the 1880s and 1890s, the membership and rhetoric of the suffrage organizations became more overtly anti-immigrant, reflecting the class and nativist bias of the American population at large. These organizations also became more prejudiced against African Americans in part because woman's rights activists resented that black men were legally enfranchised while women were not and also in part because of the post-Reconstruction backlash against African Americans in general among the American population. The growing oppression of African Americans was eventually codified in *Plessy v. Ferguson* (1896), the Supreme Court case that legalized the concept of "separate but equal" accommodations for blacks and whites and that eased the way for a series of Jim Crow laws that reinstituted the legal subordination of African Americans.[2] Furthermore, the movement adopted a public policy of catering to its southern members who, like most other white southerners, supported disenfranchising African Americans of both genders. As Ida B. Wells recalls in her autobiography, Susan B. Anthony asked Fredrick Douglass, who had been a staunch supporter of woman's rights ever since the 1840s, not to attend the 1894 convention of the National American Woman Suffrage Association (NAWSA) in Atlanta, Georgia, because she "did not want anything to get in the way of bringing the southern white women" into her suffrage association (230).[3] Here Anthony perpetuates racist segregation and white supremacy by privileging gender over race reform.

Nevertheless, it would be unfair to characterize all those who supported gender equality as racist and classist. While the reform communities devoted explicitly or exclusively to woman's rights were not as concerned with other forms of inequality, many other movements included female suffrage as part of their overall agenda. For example, the National Association of Colored Women advocated woman's rights as part of an agenda that called for cultural and economic advancement for all African Americans. In the West, growing discontent with the conditions of farm life sparked a radical collective movement by agrarians, who often supported woman's rights more heartily than their eastern counterparts. More mainstream organizations, such as the Women's Christian Temperance Movement, supported woman suffrage as a way to infuse "feminine morality" into politics and defeat the liquor interests. These examples and many more suggest the fluidity of reform activities taking place in the United States, as well as the centrality of feminist activism in these efforts, during the first years of what has become known at the Progressive Era in American politics.

American literature of the late nineteenth century manifested the competing impulses of conservatism and progressivism driving the nation's politics. This era was dominated by realism, which William Dean Howells defined as an aesthetic drive toward verisimilitude and moral complexity. The genre took several forms in American letters. Reconciliation literature, whose most famous practitioners were Thomas Nelson Page, Joel Chandler Harris, and Grace King (who published her sympathetic collection of stories about the prewar South, *Tales of a Time and a Place*, in 1892), flourished in the 1870s, 1880s, and into the 1890s. Reconciliation stories were set in the southern United States, and they were realistic in that they sought to capture the particulars of the landscape and ostensibly the language of the region. However, they also dangerously romanticized the South, and in particular, race relations before and after the Civil War. They often employ an African American narrator who speaks in stereotypical dialect and who laments losing the joys of life "befo' the wah." Authors of reconciliation fiction sought to convince northern readers that southern life was harmonious, and thus, they need not worry about "reconstructing" it any more.

At the same time, the late nineteenth century, and the year 1892 in particular, saw a great flowering of progressive, radical writing. This writing took the form of essays, stories, speeches, and editorials and included Cooper's *A Voice from the South*, Charlotte Perkins Gilman's "The Yellow Wallpaper," a feminist short story that chronicles how a woman is driven to insanity by her confinement, and Ida B. Wells's *Southern Horrors: Lynch Law in All Its Phases*, which is a meticulous rebuttal of the argument that African American men were primarily lynched for raping white women and that sparked an international antilynching movement. This same year, Elizabeth Cady Stanton delivered (and published in pamphlet form) her final, most famous speech as president of NAWSA, "A Solitude of Self." In it, she argues that because all humans, regardless of their sex, are individual, solitary beings, they must be allowed the full development of their faculties so they will be able to cope with the many situations they must ultimately confront alone.[4] Stanton's speech speaks to the complexities of feminist activism in America in the early 1890s. It is considered atypical in the breadth and scope of its application; like Cooper, Stanton seems to take a universal stance, addressing the needs of all human beings. However, her arguments were out of synch with the organization that she was addressing, given that it was focusing more and more narrowly on female suffrage and relying almost exclusively on expediency arguments. It is also worth remembering that Stanton herself had not historically been above using racist arguments to further the agenda of woman's rights, thus further complicating her progressive stance here.[5]

Frances Ellen Watkins Harper's *Iola Leroy* and Hamlin Garland's *A Spoil of Office* were also published in 1892. Both novels seem informed by a conviction—like Cooper's—that the woman's rights movement is only part of a larger agitation for humanity's freedom and both criticize the limited vision of much contemporary reform rhetoric; consequently, they contrast narratively and didactically with the woman's rights novels of the 1870s. *Out of Her Sphere* and *Fettered for Life* pit a heroine who is already enlightened at the beginning of the story against an oppressive society; *Iola Leroy* and *A Spoil of Office*, on the other hand, document the growing political awareness of the central protagonist(s), letting the reader experience firsthand his or her conversion to a more enlightened position on equal rights. Furthermore, these gradual awakenings to political consciousness stress a need for an expansive coalition of reformers who advocate equality on many fronts: sexual, racial, economic. Nonetheless, like *Out of Her Sphere* and *Fettered for Life*, Harper's and Garland's novels feature feminist activist heroines who play pivotal roles in calling these coalitions into being.

Harper wrote *Iola Leroy* at the age of sixty-seven, when she was already a veteran activist and widely read author. In her introduction to *A Brighter Coming Day*, an anthology of Harper's writing, Frances Smith Foster describes how Harper was born free into a prominent African American family in Baltimore and educated at the school started by her uncle, the Reverend William Watkins.[6] By the age of fourteen, Harper was already publishing poetry, and by her early thirties she was a nationally recognized abolition and woman's rights lecturer. Around the same time, her first book of poems, *Poems on Miscellaneous Subjects*, was published, selling over ten thousand copies. Harper worked continuously for the next forty years as a writer and speaker for African American rights, suffrage, and temperance. She was a member of the American Equal Rights Association (AERA) with Frederick Douglass and Elizabeth Cady Stanton, and later she worked for the American Woman Suffrage Association (AWSA) and served as the first African American officer in the Women's Christian Temperance Union (WCTU); in 1896 she was elected vice-president of the National Council of Negro Women (NCNW). As her activities and affiliations suggest, Harper worked from a perspective that acknowledged the interconnectedness of racism and sexism.

Although during her lifetime Harper was best known for her poetry, *Iola Leroy* is her last major work and received considerable literary attention from her contemporaries; modern critics too have given it ample consideration. For several years, it was thought to be the first novel written by an African American woman, though recently even earlier novels have been discovered.[7] Nevertheless, the publication of *Iola Leroy* is significant in African American literary history. As Frances Smith Foster notes, because of her prominence, Harper's writing a novel late in life was a risky endeavor: "Harper's gains were considered the gains of her race. [. . .] Were she to fail [in writing a successful, moving book], Harper knew her failure would be cited as evidence not only of her own declining abilities but also of the artistic inferiority of Afro-Americans in general" (Introduction, *IL* xxxiii–xxxvi).

It may be, though, that Harper's secure position as an "elder statesperson" in the African American community enabled her to produce finally a lengthy, sustained narrative. As her heroine, Iola Leroy, observes, "one needs both leisure and money to make a successful book" (262), and the older author had more of both at this age. Harper explains what she means by a "successful book" in the note appended to the novel—it is not, she claims, one that makes money, but one that can "awaken in the hearts of our countrymen a stronger sense of justice and a more Christlike humanity" (282). And she attempts such a book, she notes, because she is convinced that "out of the [African American] race must come its own thinkers and writers" (*IL* 263). Entreating her African American readers to follow her example and document their experience in an effort to change the current national political climate, she writes: "There are scattered among us materials for mournful tragedies and mirth-provoking comedies, which some hand may yet bring into the literature of the country, glowing with the fervor of the tropics and enriched by the luxuriance of the Orient, and thus add to the solution of our unresolved American problem" (*IL* 282). Harper's own fictional contribution to "the solution of our unresolved American problem" is a story, not surprisingly, of feminist activism, a book uniquely concerned with both the circumstances of being an African American woman in the nineteenth century and with her opportunities for active political intervention. She incorporates three elements into the novel that she believes will motivate her audience, white and African American, and transform their world: Christianity, nationalism, and moral responsibility.

The complex, contradictory critical response to Harper's heroine suggests the difficulties she must have confronted in trying to create a politically engaged African American heroine who would be palatable to readers and yet true to her activist imagination. Iola's appearance is one bone of contention among both contemporary and twentieth-century readers. The first physical description of Iola in the text comes from her friend and fellow slave, Tom: "My! But she's putty. Beautiful long hair comes way down her back; putty blue eyes and jis' ez white ez anybody's in dis place" (38). Tom also assures his listener, "ef you seed dem putty white han's ob hern you'd never tink she kept her own house, let alone anybody else's" (38). From Tom's perspective, markers of affluence and whiteness, like light hair and eyes, as well as soft hands, make Iola's enslavement even more tragic. Many scholars condemn Harper for what they see as her seemingly uncritical colorism, claiming that she blunders by inventing a conventionally attractive, domestic "near white" heroine or an incarnation of the "tragic mulatta" stereotype, even as these critics acknowledge Harper's ostensible motivation for creating such a character.[8] For example, Deborah McDowell argues that Harper and other African American writers contemporary with her misrepresent African American experience by offering only "an alternative homogenization" of femaleness still shaped by Anglo-European expectations and that the "ideology of domesticity" that informs their books is "the veritable antithesis of the black woman's reality" (284). Nevertheless, McDowell believes that African American writers were convinced that this characterization was a necessary concession to "a predominantly white readership" that could only identify with a white character (285).

Other critics, while acknowledging the whiteness of Iola's character, focus more on the political gains of depicting her this way. Claudia Tate says that *Iola Leroy* "uses the mulatto's inherent transitional racial and class status to construct emancipatory resocialization" (147). Similarly, Hazel Carby observes that the mulatta was a useful literary device that "mediated an increasing separation of the races" (89). Iola's appearance can perhaps be interpreted as a visible signifier of Harper's appropriation of the true woman ideal for African American women, showing that they, too, are capable of the "lady-like," chaste, self-effacing qualities that heretofore had been attributed exclusively to privileged white women. Many recent critics have also remarked on the "real world" reasons that underlie the novel's insistence on African American women's morality and purity, such as a desire to refute the racist rhetoric of black promiscuity and depravity, a rhetoric that whites invoked to explain why African Americans were so often lynched and raped.[9] Iola, however, is not merely a passive embodiment of the "true woman" ideal; she is a feminist reinterpretation of it, much like Marjory Warner in *Out of Her Sphere*. Unlike Marjory, however, Iola speaks to the dual concerns of sexism and racism in the lives of African American women and encourages women, white and black, to intervene to end both forms of oppression.

Most critics, including myself, thus agree that Harper's representation of her heroine is problematic because it depends on status quo norms of beauty and propriety. So the question is, what does the narrative accomplish didactically and politically by representing its heroine as a light-skinned African American? I would argue that Iola's skin tone and sheltered childhood (she is raised to believe she is white until shortly before the Civil War) open up a narrative space in which a unique paradigm of feminist activism and oppositional community formation is able to develop. First of all, Iola's story is a conversion narrative; her unwitting passing during her childhood sets her up for the gradual enlightenment to the plight of African Americans, male and female, rich and poor, that she undergoes, a process that privileged readers of all races are invited to participate in.[10] At the same time, she provides a strong model of a politically active woman and so could inspire more passive African American readers to engage in the struggle for racial and gender advancement. Secondly, Iola's liminal racial status makes possible an oppositional community whose members chose to unite instead of just being enlisted to join via an appeal to identity politics. This element of choice provides an extremely powerful, persuasive example of communal activism that Ann Ferguson calls "existential communitarianism," in which members are bound not by cultural similarities or demographic proximity but by a conscious decision to join together and an active desire to effect change, thus complicating any naturalized (or exclusionary) construction of the community based on an uncritical affiliation with one's race or gender.

Unlike Marjory in *Out of Her Sphere* and Laura in *Fettered for Life*, both of whom had been politically progressive all their lives and who were always trying to enlighten others, Harper's protagonist begins life unaware of the worst effects of race and gender oppression. As a young girl at a northern boarding school, Iola counters her classmates' opposition to slavery with personal anecdotal evidence. She tells them, "Slavery can't be wrong [. . .] for my father is a slave-holder, and my mother is as good to our servants as she can be. [. . .] I never saw my father strike one of them. I love my mammy as I do my own mother, and I believe she loves us just as if we were her own children" (97). Here, the heroine speaks the conventional rhetoric of noblesse oblige. She carries on in this vein, claiming that "[their] slaves do not want their freedom" and that, according to her father, "slavery is not wrong if you treat them well and don't sell them from their families" (98). Iola ends her defense by inviting her friends to visit her in the winter to see slavery for themselves during what "will be [her] first season out [in society]," exclaiming in a manner typical of her youthful levity that "[w]e will have such gay times, and you will so fall in love with the sunny South that you will never want to come back to shiver amid the snows and cold of the North. I think one winter in the South would cure you of your Abolitionism" (99). Iola's limited knowledge about slavery prevents her from seeing the cruelty and injustice that is pervasive in the system, and thus she uncritically praises conditions in the "sunny south."

Harper's contemporary reader would have recognized in Iola's musings an allusion to the nostalgia for the antebellum South found in the reconciliation literature published after the war. In fact, her description of race relations seems comparable to the reminiscences of Grace King's white heroine in "Bayou L'Ombre: An Incident of War" (published the same year as *Iola Leroy*): "Thicker and thicker," King's heroine recollects about life before the Civil War, "came little episodes of their pastoral existence together; the counter interchanges of tokens, homely presents, kind offices, loving remembrances; the mutual assistance and consolation in all the accidents of life traversed together, the sicknesses, the births, the deaths" (118). By having her heroine paint a similarly rosy picture of slavery and race relations at the outset, Harper clearly positions her novel, and specifically, her heroine, to respond to and undermine the literary tradition of reconciliation stories.

Furthermore, having Iola, whom the reader already knows is destined for slavery herself, speak most of the common proslavery arguments is a powerful tool for refuting those claims throughout the rest of the text. Harper makes it clear that Iola speaks unquestioningly, that she has absorbed her view of slavery from narrow life experiences: "Iola, being a Southern girl and a slave-holder's daughter, always defended slavery when it was under discussion" (97). Iola's attitude reflects what Ferguson refers to as the "self-horizon": "The self-horizon is that part of the person's social and bodily behavior, motives, and their implications that remain unknown to one, because it is either unconscious or invisible," and it remains "obscured from the person's awareness because of the person's social position of privilege or oppression" ("Moral Responsibility" 129). For a person to morally reconstitute herself (as well as her world), she must become aware of her self-horizon through critical self-reflection. Harper models this self-reconstitutive process for her readers by having Iola endure the literal and figurative loss of her privileged position. Her initial opinions on slavery and race, while clearly naive, were also common and widely perpetuated by reconciliation literature, and thus, it is possible that many contemporary readers would have shared them. Harper, therefore, encourages these members of her audience to likewise become aware of their self-horizons through the process of reading the novel.

The first step in Iola's reconstitution of self begins with a plot twist involving her father's death, a traitorous relative, and a legal loophole that results in Iola, her siblings, and mother being remanded into slavery. Iola, who is being escorted back south on a train by one of her relative's associates without knowing why, falls asleep, only to be awakened by her escort's sexual advances. In a vivid scene, Harper juxtaposes the relative comfort Iola has experienced as a white woman with the physical, sexual peril of her future life as a black woman: "In her dreams she was at home, encircled in the warm clasp of her father's arms, feeling her mother's kisses lingering on her lips, and hearing the joyous greetings of the servants and Mammy Liza's glad welcome as she folded her to her heart. From this dream of bliss she was awakened by a burning kiss pressed on her lips, and a strong arm encircling her" (103).[11] Although Iola is still unaware of her new status as chattel, this event marks the beginning of what Ferguson would identify as the "existential moment" in the heroine's development, a crucial first step in the "development of self-consciousness":

> The "existential moment" makes possible the self-reconstitutive function of a self-process. This is the reflexive moment of subjectivity, when the person evaluates and critiques who she is and what she takes as her interests [....] It is a moment of self-understanding [...] [in which one can] reject, expand and reformulate the prudential and moral codes and norms the person has hitherto been taught to interpret as part of herself. ("Moral Responsibility" 127)

Iola has a "reflexive moment of subjectivity" thrust on her when she realizes that her dream of security has been founded on a false notion of racial superiority as well as a false understanding of the master/slave dynamic.

The juxtaposition of the dream's loving maternal kiss and the embrace between Iola and Mammy Liza, one of the family's slaves, with the reality of the intrusive, domineering kiss by which she is awakened and initiated into a world in which she is no longer a master but a slave makes Iola aware of the violence and cruelty of slaveholders as well as the vulnerability and fear felt by slaves. After this awakening, she must reformulate her moral codes because she is now aligned with the race that she has been only too willing to enslave heretofore. Through this realignment, Iola learns firsthand of the injustices that attend the slave system. Therefore, when she is taken to her mother, who explains how and why Iola's social identity has changed, the newly critical heroine laments, "I used to say that slavery was right. I didn't know what I was talking about" (106).

At this point in the story, it would be incorrect to call Iola's alignment with the African American race a choice. However, Iola's "self-reconstitutive process" has only just begun; subsequent events offer Iola numerous opportunities, which she repeatedly rejects, to recoup her social status as white and affluent. One can attribute her refusal to rejoin the ranks of the white upper class to her newly acquired knowledge of racial oppression and the moral duty she feels to fight against it. A wiser, more mature Iola articulates her choice this way: "It was through [enslaved African Americans'] unrequited toil that I was educated, while they were compelled to live in ignorance. I am indebted to them for the power I have to serve them. I wish other Southern women felt as I do" (235). Iola recognizes the interdependence of white and black, affluent and oppressed, and by appealing to the Christian virtues of her educated readership, she makes a compelling case for their political intervention: "I think they [the Southern women] could do so much to help the colored people at their doors if they would look at their opportunities in the light of the face of Jesus Christ" (235). At first glance, Iola's argument here seems very like those made by white feminist activists who claimed for themselves the role of "empowered sanctified uplifter" and cast African American woman in the role of the "helpless, debased victim" (Newman 62). However, Iola's understanding of this mutually dependent relationship is much more egalitarian. She grasps that white women *owe* African American women (and men) their assistance, because the latter have already sacrificed much—their labor, their homes, their humanity—for a system that gives white women their privileged lifestyle.

Iola Leroy, like other novels about feminist activist heroines, uses the conventions of the heterosexual romance plot to advance its political arguments. Among other things, the choice of life partners becomes a metaphor for Iola's choice to be part of an oppositional community fighting for racial and gender advancement. Iola's crucial decision to self-identify as an African American woman comes right before the end of the Civil War, when she is working in a Union Army hospital as a nurse. Dr. Gresham, a white doctor from a highly respected family, falls in love with Iola and proposes in spite of her African American blood. Although Gresham is a sympathetic character who is "noble and generous," he nonetheless has his shortcomings: "[H]e had scarcely ever seen a colored person, and around the race their misfortunes [*sic*] had thrown a halo of romance. To him the negro was a picturesque being, over whose woes he had wept when a child" (110). This "halo of romance" prevents Dr. Gresham from treating African Americans as his unequivocal equals and his offer to Iola makes clear that he would expect her to renounce what he considers her inferior affiliations: "Your complexion is as fair as mine. What is to hinder you from sharing my Northern home, from having my mother to be your mother?" (116). Dr. Gresham's romantic benevolence toward African Americans would have made him an appropriate match for the younger, more naive Iola; however, now that she has seen firsthand the reality of slavery and race oppression, she recognizes the dangerous limitations of his white, privileged perspective.

The proposal from Dr. Gresham compels Iola to make a choice between leading a comfortable life of material wealth in a white community or fighting oppression and violence by joining the African American community. It is a pivotal moment in the text. Harper highlights the significance of the proposal by turning it into a cliffhanger. The first eight chapters of the novel take place when Iola is already enslaved and working in the Union hospital.[12] Chapter 8 ends with Dr. Gresham asking Iola, "And now I ask, will you not permit me to clasp hands with you for life? [. . .] Give yourself time to think over what

I have proposed" (60). The narrative then flashes back to the story of Iola's parents' courtship and marriage. In this flashback, the reader learns that Iola's mother, Marie, had been a slave, but Iola's father, who was white, chose to marry her anyway. The two of them remained in the South as slaveholders and concealed Marie's former identity, even from their children. When Mr. Leroy dies, his cousin finds a legal loophole that allows him to repossess Marie and her children. This embedded narrative is designed to explain Iola's refusal of what seems such a promising offer by demonstrating the high costs of racial "passing." Four chapters later, the text returns to Iola and Dr. Gresham, and her refusal of the life he promises her is tied to the lessons she has learned from her past as well as her newfound commitment to political activism; she is not deciding to be "black" by rejecting his proposal but is rather refusing a restrictive racial designation that denies the complexities of her lived experience and embracing a more fluid conception of race in an environment that does justice to those complexities: "Thoughts and purposes have come to me in the shadow I should never have learned in the sunshine. I am constantly rousing myself up to suffer and be strong. I intend, when this conflict is over, to cast my lot with the freed people as a helper, teacher, and friend. I have passed through a fiery ordeal, but the ministry of suffering will not be in vain. [. . .] In telling you this, do you not, can you not see, that there is an insurmountable barrier between us?" (114).

The "insurmountable barrier" between them is Dr. Gresham's limited understanding of racial oppression and his complicity with the socially arbitrary way that race is designated. He does not mind that Iola has "African American blood," as long as she is willing to repudiate it and represent herself as white. Iola's decision is also motivated by her desire to find her mother after the war: "I should be ashamed to live and ashamed to die were I to choose a happy lot for myself and leave poor mamma to struggle alone" (119). Here, Iola's personal longing for her mother has political implications as well; she would be denying her moral responsibility to all those who struggle, including her mother, were she to deny her affiliation with the race.[13] Once again, Harper appropriates for her heroine a role culturally assigned to white women, that of moral arbiter, but in this case, the political activism that stems from this sense of duty motivates Iola to align herself with the group that needs liberating rather than stand apart from it because of assumed racial superiority.

Several characters in the novel are confronted with a choice like the one Iola faces, and each time the novel reiterates the moral imperative of allying oneself with the group for whom one can do the most good. For example, the man Iola eventually marries, Dr. Frank Latimer, also "belongs to the negro race both by blood and choice," because he has refused to let his white relations make him an heir (238). Robert, one of the first slaves mentioned in the novel (and who turns out to be Iola's uncle), refuses his captain's offer of a white regiment, saying, "I think my place is where I'm needed most" (43). These characters are not repudiating affiliation with white culture per se; rather, they want to be able to freely and productively associate with a broad range of people, many of whom need a supportive community, and that often happens to mean denying themselves the privileges of white society. Harry, Iola's brother, is given a military opportunity similar to Robert's, and in his answer lies perhaps the most significant commentary the novel makes on personal choice and oppositional community formation:

> It was as if two paths had suddenly opened before him, and he was forced to choose between them. [. . .] Since Harry had come North he had learned to feel profound pity for the slave. But there is a difference between looking on a man as an object of pity and protecting him as such, and being identified with him and being forced to share his lot. To take his place with them on the arena of life was the test of his life, but love was stronger than pride. [. . .] His mother and sister were enslaved by a mockery of justice. It was more than a matter of choice where he should stand on the racial question. He felt that he must stand where he could strike the most effective blow for their freedom. (125–26)

As with Iola, his love for his family profoundly influences the decisions he makes. However, the keynote of the passage, and in some ways the novel, is the difference between "looking on a man as an object of pity" and "being identified with him and being forced to share his lot." Here, *Iola Leroy* calls for a commitment to forming an oppositional community willing to bear the material and social repercussions of political activism and affiliation with the oppressed race and it decries the condescending compassion of both whites and privileged African Americans shielded from racism by education and wealth. In this ideal community, whites and African Americans of all backgrounds, having recognized their common humanity, would regard each other as true equals, and racial distinctions would cease to matter except as the source of injustice against which they were fighting.

Of course, there are plenty of characters in the novel who do not possess the physical and cultural attributes necessary for them to be able to "choose" to be African American. Some critics have argued that the concentration on privileged characters reflects a shortcoming of the broader political movement informing the narrative, the racial uplift movement. This movement, founded by Booker T. Washington, called on the black middle class (or as W. E. B. Du Bois called them, the "Talented Tenth") to commit itself to education, self-improvement, and assisting poorer, more oppressed African Americans, and it often appealed to the Christian and patriotic values of its subscribers.[14] The historian Kevin Gaines, who is rather critical of this movement, calls it "a middle-class ideology [. . .] that measured racial progress in terms of civilization, manhood and patriarchal authority" and that was promoted primarily by the "black intelligentsia who took for granted that black elites, as 'representative Negros,' necessarily spoke for the black majority" (129). Carla L. Peterson applies this criticism to *Iola Leroy*, observing that the novel ignores the grueling reality of the "black subaltern" or laborer by depicting a genteel African American community, although Peterson does acknowledge that Harper tries to represent the African American "folk culture" in a way that will be acceptable to her white readership (103).

Certainly, *Iola Leroy* is a product of the racial uplift movement. At the end of the novel, Harper says her literary efforts will not be in vain if they "inspire [African Americans] [. . .] to determine that they will embrace every opportunity, develop every faculty, and use every power God has given them to rise in the scale of character and condition and to add their quota of good citizenship to the best welfare of the nation" (282). However, I would argue that at the same time Harper is very aware of the condition of the "black subaltern" and that her model oppositional community is one that does not ignore the laborer's plight. In "Frances Ellen Watkins Harper in the Reconstruction South," Farah Jasmine Griffin describes Harper's extended visit to the South in the 1870s. Griffin argues that Harper's speeches and essays from this time show that "her values are [. . .] more in tune with the masses of Black Southerners than are those of other Black leaders" (45). This experience seems to have influenced Harper's vision of her novel, which seeks to model an oppositional community in which black elites "cast their lot" with the black "masses" in an egalitarian way.

As we have seen, Iola's and Harry's choice to identify themselves as African American is motivated largely by their love for their immediate family. Nevertheless, in *Iola Leroy*, the process of forging (and in many cases, reforging) familial ties is inextricably linked with a commitment to working for the advancement of the African American community as a whole. Perhaps Robert Johnson's story is the novel's best example of the relationship between family, political activism, and community formation. Robert has been raised as a slave and identifies with this community; nevertheless, his skin color, education, and familial relations connect him to those African American characters who are relatively more privileged. Peterson posits that "Robert in some sense rivals Iola as the novel's center" and that "his function is [. . .] to introduce the reader to the different social groups that inhabit *Iola Leroy* and then to mediate between them, to recognize, comprehend and bridge difference" (107). While Peterson argues that Robert's mediating role prevents him from achieving heroic status in the book, I would suggest that his liminal position indicates that the novel privileges communal life over the individual.

Robert shares traits with members of many of the seemingly disparate groups in the book; he lives on a slave plantation with characters who have been identified by critics as "folk," such as Aunt Linda, Uncle Daniel, and Tom Anderson. These characters are distinguished in the book by their colloquial speech and their immersion in slave culture. Robert, like the other "folk" characters, has always lived as a slave, but unlike Aunt Linda and others, he has been taught to read and speak standard English by his mistress, and she has used him to keep her books. However, as Marilyn Elkins observes, these qualities do not elevate Robert over the other folk; Elkins convincingly argues that *Iola Leroy* does not "privilege standard white speech over realistic black dialect," pointing out that Aunt Linda and Robert are clearly equals in the slave community, despite their varied levels of education (51). Therefore, from the beginning, Robert is aligned with other slaves on the plantation, but he is also different from them. He does not choose to take advantage of the privilege his education and skin color have offered him, and those in his slave community treat him as a valued, loved member, but not as one who is, or sees himself as, better than they are.

At the heart of Robert's desire for freedom is his lingering anger that his mistress sold his mother and sister away from the plantation when he was very young. According to the narrator, after the war, "[t]o bind anew the ties which slavery had broken and gather together the remnants of his scattered family became the earnest purpose of Robert's life" (148). What the reader discovers, however, as the novel progresses, is that Robert's desire to find his mother and sister is not sustained by a wealth of shared memories or experiences, the things that typically bond a family. He tells Iola he would not recognize his sister if he saw a picture of her, and later, when he meets his sister Marie (who is also Iola's mother), the two of them talk for a long time before "they conclud[e] that they [are] brother and sister" (201). Robert's reunion with his mother happens in a similarly gradual, tentative fashion. Robert recognizes her, not by sight, but from the familiar details in the story she tells at a prayer meeting of ex-slaves. In this story, the reader also sees the activist role that the postwar African American church played in reuniting families and helping heal the larger community. Once Robert, his mother, and sister have confirmed their biological relationship, they make sacrifices for each other and take responsibility for each other as if they had always been together. Robert, committed to living with his mother, moves out of a neighborhood in which she is shunned because of her darker skin color, and Marie willingly sends Iola to care for her grandmother, even though Marie would like to keep her daughter at home.

My point here is that choice plays as much a role as biology in the formation of families in *Iola Leroy*, and the intricacies of connections among their members represent the ways an oppositional community bound by genuine affection can become a political and moral force in the world. Robert's mother is clearly aligned with the black "folk" through her speech and her shared memories of life with Aunt Linda, and of course, his sister, Marie, the well-educated, fair-skinned mother of Harry and Iola, is a matriarch of the black "elite" in the novel. Familial love in this novel becomes "revolutionary love," an emotional bond that the characters choose to form and that is at once both politically and personally charged. This sympathetic love not only compels privileged members to "cast their lot" with less privileged members of an oppositional community, but it also serves as the vehicle through which intracommunity differences, such as colorism and class elitism, can be overcome. Ferguson describes the intangible benefits of revolutionary love, calling it "the kind of love that can motivate us to weather [. . .] [the] difficult processes [of community formation] and yet find it all worth the effort" ("Feminist Communities" 377).

Frances Harper is not the only writer in the late nineteenth century who symbolically reconstructs the African American family and community, nor is she the only African American author who deploys the conventions of reconciliation literature in order to undermine its racist message. In 1899, Charles Chesnutt published "The Wife of His Youth," which also explores the complexities of the peculiar dilemmas facing African Americans after the Civil War. In this story, Mr. Ryder is an affluent, conservative, light-skinned African American who is living in the North and vying to be president of the Blue Vein Society, a satirically named club of educated, professional northern African Americans, most of whom share Mr. Ryder's pale skin. The story takes place on the day that he is to announce his engagement to Mrs. Dixon, a widow who "possessed many attractive qualities," most notably those of being "whiter" and "better educated" than Mr. Ryder (105). Before the engagement party, however, an older, southern ex-slave woman named 'Liza Jane, who is very dark and who speaks in an uneducated dialect, stops by for a visit with Mr. Ryder. In the course of conversation, 'Liza Jane tells Mr. Ryder that she has been looking for her husband Sam for decades, and she is confident he, too, has been looking for her; she says, "I'd know 'im 'mongs' a hund'ed men. Fer dy wuz n' no yuther merlatter man like my man Sam, an' I could n' be mistook. I's toted his picture roun' wid me twenty-five years" (110). Ironically, as the reader learns, Mr. Ryder is the Sam Taylor for whom 'Liza has been searching.

'Liza Jane's erroneous belief that she will be able to recognize her lost husband underscores the fragility of familial ties. And her erroneous belief that her Sam was looking for her too demonstrates that the resumption of those ties is not inevitable; family members must choose to be reunited. The reader sees Mr. Ryder struggling with this choice, deciding whether or not he will thwart his current marriage plans by acknowledging this woman, whose appearance and demeanor are so different from his own and those of his friends. In the end, Mr. Ryder does reclaim 'Liza Jane as a member of his family, presenting her to his friends as "the wife of his youth," and they, in turn, fully approve of his decision. In this narrative, Chesnutt, like Harper in *Iola Leroy*, symbolically reunites the extended African American family through the characters' choices and attempts to dissolve the hierarchy created among its members by their different places of birth, educations, and appearances. Unlike Harper, however, Chesnutt does not attempt to undo the hierarchical construction of gender in this community—both Mrs. Dixon and 'Liza Jane are depicted passively and their fates rest in the hands of Mr. Ryder. Also unlike Harper, Chesnutt does not explore the more overtly political implications of this reunited community, nor does he make explicit the reform power this community could have. Thus, Harper's response to reconciliation literature is more radical than Chesnutt's, in that she also challenges the patriarchal structure of mainstream, white society, rather than emulating it in the symbolic African American family, as Chesnutt does. Harper's vision of "racial uplift" is thus a more progressive, satisfying alternative to the gender and racial norms of American society at the time.

Harper achieves this satisfying alternative not only by depicting the maturation of an African American community committed to racial advancement but also by showing how it takes part in a larger spirit of reform informed by other progressive movements, such as temperance and woman's rights. Harper's novel demonstrates the interdependence of seemingly diverse reform ideologies, arguing that all must be addressed simultaneously to bring about radical change in the nation as a whole and the African American community in particular. In *Iola Leroy*, Harper revisits temperance ideology, a topic she paid considerable attention to in her speeches, poetry, and earlier fiction. Debra Rosenthal speculates that in some of these earlier works, such as "The Two Offers" and *Sowing and Reaping: A Temperance Story*, the author does not identify the race of her characters so she can stress "the shared identity between black and white and a common goal of achieving middle-class respectability" (164). By the time she writes *Iola Leroy*, however, Harper's argument is more nuanced, showing the ways temperance is useful in resisting racial disenfranchisement. Aunt Linda laments how alcohol has weakened the African American community, saying,

"I beliebs we might be a people ef it warn't for dat mizzable drink" (160). Instead of blaming the drinkers, however, Aunt Linda notes the social forces that are responsible: "But it does rile me ter see dese mean white men comin' down yere an' settin' up dere grog-shops, tryin' to fedder dere nests sellin' licker to pore culled people" (159). Here, Aunt Linda shows that the real enemy to be fought is not King Rum but the white establishment who would drain the black community of its resources. Robert also links temperance with radical political activity: "The colored man has escaped from one slavery, and I don't want him to fall into another. I want the young folks to keep their brains clear, and their right arms strong, to fight the battles of life manfully, and take their places alongside of every other people in this country" (170). The African American community in the novel does not support alcohol reform merely because it agrees with whites that temperance is desirable; it also pursues a coalition with temperance societies to wrest some power from the controlling white establishment.

Harper's novel is likewise concerned with the relevance of the woman's rights community to the efforts for racial uplift. However, the novel engages in a thorough critique of and reimagining of this reform movement, exposing the often vexed relationship between gender and race at its heart and offering an alternative model of feminist activism that opposes racism as well as sexism. Again, Iola Leroy's choices play a crucial role in this model. Although Robert tells her that "there is no necessity for [her] to work" while she lives with him, Iola prefers to get a job because she believes "every woman ought to know how to earn her own living" (15). The heroine's feminist convictions about economic independence challenge the notion of the true woman's dependent domesticity, aligning her instead with feminist activist heroines like Laura Stanley in *Fettered for Life* and many twentieth-century suffrage heroines, all of whom are committed to being financially self-supporting. Harper's novel, however, demonstrates how much more difficult this goal is for African American women to achieve, in part because of the reaction of white women. Iola receives a hostile reception from the white women with whom she works; when they find out she is African American, they force the manager to fire her. It is significant that this rejection brings Iola to one of her lowest points in the story: "I feel out of heart. It seems as if the prejudice pursues us through every avenue of life, and assigns us the lowest places" (207). Apparently, the racism of white women with whom she feels an affinity as a fellow worker is an especially painful experience for the heroine. Iola is disappointed time and again by white women who ostracize her in her attempts to be independent. She applies for a room in a boarding house run by "Christian women," but they refuse her because of her color. The narrator points out their hypocrisy: "And these women, professors of a religion which taught, 'If ye have respect to persons ye commit sin,' virtually shut the door in her face because of the outcast blood in her veins" (209).

Elizabeth Ammons claims that through these and several other examples "the racism of white women, particularly as it is directed against black women, emerges as a significant supporting theme in *Iola Leroy*" (33). I would add that these episodes are representative of larger patterns of black women's exclusion from female communities in the real world and in particular, from organizations of feminist activists. In the novel, the author directly addresses this racial schism: "It was as if two women were sinking in the quicksand, and on the solid land stood other women with life-lines in their hands, seeing the deadly sands slowly creeping up around the hapless victims. To one they readily threw the lines of deliverance, but for the other there was not one strand of salvation" (232). Harper's critique here is similar to Anna Julia Cooper's, foregrounding how the racism and classism of white women undermine the possibility of forming a radical feminist oppositional community.

In contrast, *Iola Leroy* offers several counter examples of public reform activity African American women engage in that is informed by both race and gender concerns, enacting for the reader ways to publicly intervene to bring about change. Marie anticipates her daughter's feminist activism when, as a young woman, she gives a commencement address entitled, "American Civilization, its Lights and Shadows," in which she speaks on "behalf of freedom for all and chains for none" (75). To achieve her economic independence, Iola becomes a teacher in an African American school, where "she was not satisfied to teach her children only the rudiments of knowledge" but rather "tried to lay the foundation of good character" (147). Here we see Iola's feminist impulse to have a profession and economic independence working in conjunction with her activist commitment to teaching African American children, presumably male and female, how to be informed, ethical citizens. We see this same commitment to education as a form of activism in Iola's most significant moment as a reformer, which comes at the *conversazione*, a gathering of "a select group of earnest men and women deeply interested in the welfare of the race" (246). This gathering gives voice to many of the political concerns actively debated in African American intellectual circles of the time and during it, Iola takes center stage, presenting a speech entitled the "Education of Mothers."

Iola speaks again, more generally, at the end of the gathering: "And is there [. . .] a path which we have trodden in this country, unless it be the path of sin, into which Jesus Christ has not put His feet and left it luminous with the light of His step? [. . .] And never [. . .] will I recognize any religion as His which despises the least of His brethren" (256–57). Iola's feminism here is similar to

Marjory Warner's in *Out of Her Sphere*; Iola invokes the idea of the special sway women can have in the maternal role to bolster her argument for the education of mothers and her speaking on the subject in a public forum embodies the more active, political stance women must take to expand their influence. And by claiming these feminine and feminist attributes for her African American heroine, Harper deconstructs the implicit whiteness often attributed to feminist activist heroines. Furthermore, in drawing a distinction between "true" Christianity as represented by Jesus's example and organized religion that turns its back on the less fortunate, she strategically links religious and political reform. Only by returning to original Christian doctrine, Iola suggests, can the country solve its race problems, and so she implicates as "un-Christian" those readers who are complicit in perpetuating the religious and racial status quo. Her remarks also speak to the strong activist role that the African American church plays in race reform.

One could argue that Iola's acceptance of conventional notions about maternity and Christianity mitigates the radical potential for her feminism here, that the capitulation to cultural norms sabotages the novel's commitment to gender reform. However, as in *Out of Her Sphere*, these types of expediency arguments, rather than merely accepting established sexual ideology, attempt to reenvision gender roles to allow for more active female participation in the public sphere, even though they perhaps blunt the opposition to change (and the possibility of systemic reform) by appealing to widely shared and often conservative ideas about the "natural" differences between the sexes. Furthermore, an African American woman would have had a different relationship to these cultural values, which were often explicitly or implicitly held to belong to white men and women only. Therefore, claiming the right to one's children as an enlightened mother (or father) is an act of empowerment for African Americans who had historically been denied control over themselves as well as their offspring, just as claiming a similarity between Jesus's suffering and that of the former slaves makes a convincing argument for merging radical politics with religious sentiment.

In *Iola Leroy*, Harper does not offer a monolithic view of feminism. Instead, she shows different modes of feminist activism coexisting, suggesting she believes that there is no one perfect form of feminist intervention but rather that a combination of varying strategies is necessary to bring about change. Like Lillie Devereux Blake, Harper seems to have embodied her more controversial notions about feminism in a secondary character. Lucille Delany, like Frank Heywood in *Fettered for Life*, gives life and voice to this more unorthodox perspective, and although she is not the central heroine, the text makes clear that she is worthy of emulation.[15] Lucille, who is twenty-five when the reader is introduced to her, graduated from college and founded her own girls' school, now a large, thriving institution. Because she is dignified and refined, she also defies the white idea that only light-skinned African Americans can be beautiful. According to Iola's brother Harry, "[n]either [her] hair nor complexion show the least hint of blood admixture" (199), intimating that Lucille's dark appearance marks her as distinctly African American and thus impervious to the racist charge that her "white blood" makes her attractive or talented. Lucille is the embodiment of self-reliant womanhood that Iola longs for but never fully achieves. She is also not afraid to speak out in unconventional ways about gender and race, as the following scene from the *conversazione* demonstrates:

> "I agree," said Rev. Eustace, of St. Mary's parish, "with [Iola's] paper. The great need of the race is enlightened mothers."
> "And enlightened fathers, too," added Miss Delany, quickly. "If there is anything I chafe to see it is a strong, hearty man shirking his burdens, putting them on the shoulders of his wife, and taking life easy himself."
> "I always pity such mothers," interposed Iola, tenderly.
> "I think," said Miss Delany, with a flash in her eye and a ring of decision in her voice, "that such men ought to be drummed out of town!" As she spoke, there was an expression which seemed to say, "And I would like to help do it!" (253)

Iola's heartfelt "feminine" emotion is juxtaposed here with Lucille's less demure righteous indignation.

The narrator, however, makes it clear that Iola and Lucille complement each other rather than compete: "There were no foolish rivalries and jealousies between them. Their lives were too full of zeal and earnestness for them to waste in selfishness their power to be moral and spiritual forces among a people who so much needed their helping hands" (200). The two women are linked through a mutual commitment to race and gender reform, and this bond demonstrates that an oppositional community can exist in harmony even if its members have different ideas about how to achieve its reform objectives. Peterson contends, "In developing the characters of Iola and Lucille, Harper sought to construct a feminist agenda that would deconstruct the dichotomy of public and private spheres and thus forge a space for black women's social activism in the Reconstruction Era" (102). Harper also shows that this space can and should accommodate a wide range of feminist reform activity.

Iola's and Lucille's marriages bring closure to the romance narratives in the novel. In strengthening familial bonds and solidifying an oppositional community committed to a sweeping vision of reform, their marriages also contribute to the utopian ending. During one of their initial encounters, Dr. Latimer says to his future wife, "I think, Miss Leroy, that the world's work, if shared, is better done than when it is performed alone" (242). This pairing of duty and love is found throughout *Iola Leroy*, and it figures prominently in the novel's appropriation of the heterosexual romance plot: "In their desire to help the race their hearts beat in loving unison. One grand and noble purpose was giving tone and color to their lives and strengthening the bonds of affection between them" (266). The way that this revolutionary love manifests itself is rather conventional, however, in keeping with Iola's more mainstream ideas about gender roles. The pair moves to the South, where Iola "quietly [takes] her place in the Sunday-school as a teacher, and in the church as a helper" while her husband becomes a successful doctor in the community. Although Iola continues to reach out to the African American community, she does so through traditionally feminine work, attenuating M. Giulia Fabi's assertion that "Dr. Latimer shares Iola's twin ideals of independent womanhood and racial uplift, and his marriage proposal therefore promises to open a utopian heterosexual space of gender equality" (235). The two clearly are in sympathy when it comes to reform ideology, both racial and gender, but their political efforts are still informed by a traditional middle-class ideology of separate spheres that renders Iola's activism subordinate to her husband's. On the other hand, however, given that, unlike its white counterpart, the African American church has a history of political activism, Iola's involvement in this institution suggests that through it, she will still be able to advocate for progressive reform.

Furthermore, several critics provide extratextual evidence to suggest Iola's married life is more "feminist" than it might seem. Jennifer Campbell rightly points out that for African American women, marriage (like parenthood) was considered empowering, because for years they had been denied this legal status. In addition, P. Gabrielle Foreman makes an intriguing suggestion about Harper's heroine by tracing parallels between Iola and the real-life feminist activist to whom her name alludes, the outspoken, controversial journalist Ida B. Wells, who wrote under the pseudonym "Iola" and who, as I noted before, started her famous antilynching campaign the same year that Harper published *Iola Leroy*. Comparing details of Wells's life with the fictional heroine Iola—both wanted to write a "good strong book" for the race, and both were involved in the black activist church as young teachers—Foreman argues that Harper opens up a space of possibility beyond the narrative closure by "positioning Iola to develop into Wells, or in other words, into her more radical homonymic sister" (341).

Within the novel, however, Lucille Delany's romance is the more convention-defying narrative since it does not take the form of a seamless sequence of proposal, acceptance, and marriage. Lucille initially rejects Harry's love because she is afraid that his family will object to her darker skin; Harry, however, assures her that it is not an issue. The conflict is short-lived, but nonetheless it is a realistic representation of courtship and romance, depicting the difficult negotiations that are often necessary to achieve revolutionary love. Not surprisingly, then, it is Harry and Lucille's marriage, more than Iola and Dr. Latimer's, that can be described as a "utopian space of gender equality." At the end of the novel, the two head "a large and flourishing school," and Lucille continues working full-time as an educator, "her chosen work, to which she was too devoted to resign" (280). While Iola and Frank's marriage is a union that has the potential to accomplish many wonderful things in their community, Harry and Lucille seem to marry their work with their love in an even more balanced partnership. Nevertheless, both couples attest to the power of revolutionary love to transform families and societies.

Both young couples live within a network of family and friends who have, by the end of the novel, developed into a strong oppositional community. All the major characters, both "folk" and "intelligentsia," move to the South after the Civil War because their reform work is most needed there. Robert has purchased a large piece of land and leases small portions to industrious African American farmers at a fair price; Uncle Daniel, Aunt Linda and her husband John Salter, and Grandmother Johnson (Marie and Robert's mother) are exemplary citizens, supportive of the efforts for racial uplift in the community. However, through the example of Dr. Latimer, the novel stresses that true reform work should not be limited to race issues: "[H]e is a true patriot and a good citizen. [. . .] He is a leader in every reform movement for the benefit of the community; but his patriotism is not confined to race lines" (279). At the end, then, Harper restates a major theme of the book, echoing Anna Julia Cooper's claim that "the cause of freedom is not the cause of a race or a sect" only. The novel inspires its readers to answer Dr. Latimer's plea at the *conversazione*: "[I]nstead of narrowing our sympathies to mere racial questions, let us broaden them to humanity's wider issues" (260). This utopian optimism is fitting for a novel set during Reconstruction, a time of hopefulness for newly freed slaves; the reader is, nevertheless, aware of the sobering reality that awaits Iola, Dr. Latimer, and their community: the failure of Reconstruction, the institution of Jim Crow laws, and the widespread practice of lynching. Harper, it might be argued, reminds her audience of the nation's previous enthusiasm for race reform and impresses on it that it is not too late to agitate for equal rights for all human beings. *Iola Leroy* demonstrates that injustice stemming from racism and sexism will always be pressing a national concern because it undermines the tenets of democracy and Christianity on which, in Harper's view, America was founded.

Hamlin Garland was also concerned about the attenuation of democratic ideals in late nineteenth-century America, and like Harper, Garland voiced his worries in both speeches and fiction, achieving fame as an accomplished writer and enthusiastic political activist and lecturer. However, in 1892, when Garland published his own novel about reform and feminist activism, *A Spoil of Office*, he was, unlike Harper, just embarking on his career. Garland had written one well-received book, *Main-Travelled Roads* (1891), when he was hired by B. O. Flower, editor of the progressive journal the *Arena* to write a serialized story about the recent agrarian revolt in the Midwest, a movement known historically as Populism.[16] Consequently, Garland toured the Midwest, including Kansas, Nebraska, and Iowa, to gather material for his work, and in the process he became an avid supporter of the farmers' cause, enlisting as a traveling lecturer for the movement. During this tour, Garland saw firsthand the poverty and disenfranchisement of the galvanized agrarian community, and he spoke out against those who he believed monopolized the land and the modes of transportation, creating an unfair business environment that resulted in the farmers' perpetual economic hardship.

Garland views this economic hardship, however, through the lens of a fiction writer. In an essay published in the *Arena* in 1893, "The Land Question, and Its Relation to Art and Literature," Garland articulates the relationship between art and reality: "We all [artists] dream of somehow touching this great, strange, wallowing, hydra-headed something called 'the public' and waking its better nature into life. We dream of playing upon its heartstrings as a lute, and all the time we passively acquiesce in conditions which keep all the devilish and sordid passions of our audience as an impenetrable barrier between us. We stand mournfully regarding the blind and suffering monster, and do nothing to help it rise" (167). Garland warns that the complicity of many of his fellow artists will not only perpetuate the unfair disparity of opportunity in the country, but it will also harm their own aesthetic endeavors: "The cause of art is the cause of humanity. The dignity of the drama depends upon the comfort and leisure of the common man. The whole social order must undergo change before American art will become the jubilant and wholesome art it should be" (174–75).

Ultimately, Garland tells his audience that only their political involvement will bring about this "jubilant and wholesome" era: "You too must become reformers. You too must stand for equal rights, with all that the fearless leaders of present-day thought have made that phrase mean" (175). In an article published in the *Forum* a year later, Garland explains how the novelist in particular can use his or her work to usher in this new social order.[17] To do so, he or she must be a writer, "who stands for individuality and freedom; who puts woman on an equality with man, making her a human being; who stands for a pure man as well as a pure woman; who stands for an altruistic and free state where involuntary poverty does not exist; who teaches the danger and degradation of lust and greed, and who inculcates a love for all who live, teaching justice and equal rights" ("Productive Conditions of American Literature" 694). These are undoubtedly lofty goals for any writer, and Garland's enthusiasm and unbounded optimism perhaps betray a youthful naïveté about the potential for altruism and sweeping social change. Nevertheless, Garland attempts such an idyllic reform project in *A Spoil of Office*, which anticipates many of the criteria the author outlines in this essay written two years after the novel.

Garland seems to have regarded *Spoil* as a patriotic endeavor meant to promote the individual freedom of all his fellow citizens. A contemporary reviewer for the *Atlantic Monthly* applauds the nationalistic impulse of Garland's story, even though he believes the author is too young to do it justice: "In theme [...] the book is magnificent. He who will embody in a noble fiction, as Mr. Garland has here tried to do, the career of a Western farm-hand, from the time of his early struggles for an education to the time of his election to the national legislature, will achieve, as nearly as any one, the great American novel" ("New Figures in Literature and Art" 843). To be sure, *A Spoil of Office* is a classically American "rags-to-riches" story in the Franklinian tradition, a celebration of the individual who relies almost exclusively on his own resources to rise in the world. However, Garland's story ultimately reminds the reader more of Walt Whitman (one of Garland's favorite authors) in that the rise of the protagonist, Bradley Talcott, is attributable to his growing awareness not only of his individual talent but also of his connection with and responsibility to the many other citizens he encounters. Thus, the hero's success is measured not primarily in terms of material wealth but in terms of his commitment to broad-based political reform. Although Garland's subject matter is very different from Harper's, he, like her, understands that discrimination against a certain group never takes place in a vacuum; it is always part of a larger system of oppression. Also like Harper, he creates a central character whose political conversion occurs through a series of "existential moments." Finally, and perhaps most pertinent to this study, Garland chooses, like Harper, a politically committed female character to serve as the narrative catalyst for change in his novel.

The argument that *Spoil* is an important literary representation of organized reform activity, written in an attempt to persuade readers to join that reform community, is not exactly new. Recently, critics like Quentin Martin and Keith Newlin have tried to reclaim Garland's early fiction in general, and *A Spoil of Office* in particular, from the scholarly dismissal it received from a previous generation of critics skeptical of overtly political art. Indeed, Martin praises the novel for the very reason earlier scholars like Eberhard Alsen criticize it—an unabashed commitment to its reform ideology. According to Martin, *Spoil* is worthy of critical consideration because it "illustrates and analyzes, as no other novel comes close to doing, crucial intellectual movements in American life, specifically the birth and ideological core of the Populist movement" ("'This Spreading Radicalism'" 31). I likewise agree with Martin, who contends that Bradley's transformation (and perhaps the reader's) hinges on "the recognition that the interests of the farmer are and must be linked to the interests of other exploited groups" (33). However, the crucial point on which my analysis differs from that of Martin and others is in my assessment of the heroine, Ida Wilbur, and her role in creating this coalition of reformers.

Ida has received dubious recognition at best ever since William Dean Howells first passed judgment on her. Howells (to whom *Spoil* is dedicated) wrote to Garland privately, "It was *brave* of you to take a Woman's Righter for a heroine; but Nettie Russell [a minor, more conventional female character] was worth a lot for her human nature" (emphasis added, qtd. in Alsen vii). Even Martin, who seems determined to resurrect critical respect for the novel and promote its radical message, claims that "the characterization of Ida and the description of her and Bradley's romance" are some of the "major drawbacks of the novel" (31). Howells is certainly right that Garland was "brave" in creating Ida, but his disapproval of her is not justified. Ida might be the most unconventional representation of a feminist activist of the ones I consider, and it is this unconventionality that makes the novel's relatively radical vision of an oppositional community possible. Although Ida plays a traditionally feminine narrative role, that of "muse" for the male hero, she is unusual nonetheless in that her words and actions act as a powerful catalyst for progressive political change, on both an individual and a communal level. In fact, Bradley's maturation is so intimately tied to Ida's political activity and intellectual guidance that it is almost impossible to talk about his development without reference to her. In his laudatory review of *Spoil*, B. O. Flower observes that the novel "might be separated into four major divisions: The farmer boy; In school; In state politics; In national politics" (48). Later critics such as Martin and Newlin have explicitly or implicitly referred to these turning points in the reform-minded *Bildungsroman*, and they have also acknowledged generally that Ida is an important influence on Bradley's development. However, no one has yet noted that each new stage in

Bradley's life is either precipitated by or in some way dependent on his interaction with Ida.

A Spoil of Office opens on an idyllic summer day in the 1870s at the start of a festive Grange picnic: "At the four corners below stood scores of other wagons, loaded to the rim with men, women and children. [. . .] Everywhere were merry shouts, and far away at the head of the procession the Burr Oak band was playing. All waited for the flag whose beautiful folds flamed afar in the bright sunlight" (3). These local Grange organizations, although avowedly apolitical because they do not endorse either of the two major parties, work together for the economic advantage of the farmers and perhaps more importantly, provide a much-needed social outlet, unifying the agrarian community through its members' shared interests. In his book, *American Populism: A Social History, 1877–1898*, Robert McMath demonstrates the importance of Grange events in encouraging "rural men and women [to bind] themselves together in communities that were as familiar as the churches and lodges to which many belonged, and yet were self-consciously new and purposeful" (124). Garland's version of a Grange event is optimistic, suggesting that it could be the foundation of an oppositional community; however, he also imbues its members with a naïveté about entering the political fray that clearly must be overcome if the farmers are to be a political force. The chairman of this particular Grange organization tells the crowd, "I think that politics will destroy the grange. To make it a debating school on political questions would bring discord and wrangling into it. I hope I shall never see the day" (11).

This communal naïveté mirrors that of Bradley Talcott, who comes to the picnic as a hired man for one of the Grange farmers. As the farmer's driver, Bradley remains on the fringes of the festivities and shows no interest in the speeches made about the movement until he hears the one given by Ida Wilbur, who is introduced as "our State lecturer."[18] Ida speaks about the "poetic side" of the Grange, the communal element: "The farmer is a free citizen of a great republic, it is true; but he is a *Solitary* free citizen. He lives alone too much. His dull life, his hard work, make it almost impossible to keep his better nature uppermost. The work of the Grange is a social work" (13). Although she, too, at this point thinks that the Grange should remain apolitical, she is the first to comment on the importance of community in bringing out one's "better nature," and in the world of the novel, one's better nature is linked to one's commitment to reform. Here, Ida anticipates Ferguson's warning that it is almost impossible to sustain one's progressive impulses in isolation.

By far the most sophisticated intellectual and reformer at the picnic, Ida has a profound and life-changing effect on Garland's hero:

> On Bradley, standing there alone, there fell something mysterious, like a light. Something whiter and more penetrating than sunlight. As he listened, something stirred within him, a vast longing, a hopeless ambition, nameless as it was strange. [...] His eyes absorbed every detail of the girl's face and figure. There was wonder in his eyes at her girlish face, and something like awe at her powerful diction and her impersonal emotion. She stood there like an incarnation of the great dream-world that lay beyond his horizon, the world of poets and singers in the far realms of light and luxury. (14)

This sort of extended description of a woman's physical effect on a man is not anomalous in American literature, as Caroline Levander demonstrates in her book *Voices of the Nation*. Levander presents ample evidence that "American novels devote much space to describing how women's voices sound and what reactions women's speech produces, especially in their male listeners" (2). Levander argues that this device, which directs the reader to fixate on the sound and ignore the content of the female speaker's voice, is most often used to underscore the public/private distinction between males and females and sets in motion "a process by which women have been effectively excluded from the political arena" (34). Garland's novel, however, unequivocally contradicts this pattern. Bradley is certainly taken with Ida's physical presence and the sensation of hearing her voice, but the content of her speech infiltrates his intellect and distracts him, even as he works a few days later: "The centre of his thinking was that slender young woman and the words that she had uttered. He repeated her prophetic words as nearly as he could a hundred times. [...] He began to look ahead and wonder what he should do or could do. [...] His mind moved slowly from point to point, but it never returned to its old dumb patience" (28). On a more visceral level, Bradley has also been moved by the passion for her work that Ida radiates. Having been affected by Ida's words and her presence, Bradley experiences his first "existential moment," when he ceases to accept the norms of society uncritically. Consequently, unlike the "heroes" in the novels Levander discusses, Bradley is inspired to become politically involved himself rather than inhibit the work of the lecturess by whom he is captivated.

During this initial encounter, Ida represents to Bradley a "dream world [...] beyond his horizon." Like Iola Leroy's, Bradley's "self-horizon" obstructs his awareness of oppression and the need for change. Seeing Ida gives Bradley the courage to "better" himself through education, first by leaving the farm and registering at the seminary and then by studying law with the paternal Judge Brown. In these early stages of the narrative, Bradley decides to improve his oratory and debating skills with an eye toward entering politics because "he thought it would please Her best" (66). By almost deifying Ida (thus the capitalized references to her), Bradley seems to reduce Ida to the traditionally passive role of "muse," and one could argue that the novel consequently diminishes Ida's political agency by making her merely the catalyst for Bradley's activism. However, Ida's influence is not of the vague moral or romantic sort; she is instead a political and scholarly mentor, and the fields in which Bradley hopes to acquire a proficiency—lecturing and campaigning—are ones that Ida has already mastered. Therefore, she is a creator and a force in her own right, and Garland significantly transforms the romance narrative by having his hero work not only to impress his love interest, but also to emulate her political example.

In these early stages of Bradley's political enlightenment, the farming community at large undergoes a corresponding nascent progressivism. Finally angered enough by their exclusion from the local Republican committee, the farmers start searching for alternative ways to voice their political opinions. According to the narrator, "[I]t was a singular thing to see the farmers suddenly begin to ask themselves why they should stand quietly by while the townsmen monopolized all the offices" (95). This dawning awareness compels the farmers to break with the larger party and run their own campaigns for local offices in which they defeat the incumbents soundly. Bradley, following Ida's example, tours the county giving several speeches in support of these third-party candidates. The resultant victories reiterate Ida's lesson about the strength inherent in community, and the novel highlights the momentous historical significance of this revelation: "For the first time in the history of the county, the farmers had asserted themselves. For the first time in the history of the farmers of Iowa, they had felt the power of their own mass" (120–21). This narrative optimism cheers the farmers' first foray into oppositional community formation; however, the novel also reminds the reader that this community is still in its infancy: "[The farmers] saw the smaller circle first. They had not yet risen to the perception of solidarity of all productive interests. That was sure to follow" (121). Though they have taken the initial step toward political activism, the members of the farming community, like Bradley, cannot yet see the advantages to a broader reform agenda.

As Bradley's story enters what Flower would call its third stage, state politics, Ida once again serves as the harbinger of progressivism. Her second speech of the novel, "The Real Woman Question," teaches Bradley (and the reader) that he must expand the "smaller circle" of agrarian interests to include gender reform as well. The second meeting between hero and heroine shows that Ida's political commitment has deepened and that she has refined her ideas about justice: "She was the same woman, his ideal and more. She was fuller of form and the poise of her head was more womanly, but she was the same spirit that had come to be such a power and inspiration in his life. As a matter of fact, she had grown also. If she had not, she would have seemed girlish to him now; growing as he grew, she seemed the same distance beyond him" (142). Ida's speech shows that she has grown, not merely beyond Bradley, but also beyond many of her "real-world" feminist counterparts who were increasingly focusing exclusively on suffrage and who had never paid sufficient attention to the wider matrix of oppression, including that based on race and class. In contrast, Ida tells her audience, "It is not a question of suffrage merely—suffrage is the smaller part of the woman question—it is a question of equal rights. It is a question of whether the law of liberty applies to humanity or to men only" (143). Ida's arguments are based solely on natural rights philosophy and fall squarely in the more controversial category of "arguments from justice" that, as we have seen, were taken up by woman's rights activists who wanted to do away with gendered legal distinctions. Ida takes her radicalism one step further when she links women's interest to those of the farmers and other financially disadvantaged groups: "The woman question is not a political one merely, it is an economic one. The real problem is the wage problem, the industrial problem. The real question is woman's dependence upon man as the bread-winner" (143). Certainly, Ida's speech (and Garland's novel) is not the first one to point out the inextricable link between money and sexism; however, at a time when the "woman question" was increasingly defined as political exclusion, Ida's speech refocuses the debate on economics, thereby underscoring the commonality between women and men who are financially impoverished and laying the groundwork for a broader coalition of reformers.

Once again, the novel shows Bradley's horizon growing because of Ida: "She was destined to again set a stake in Bradley's mental horizon. [. . .] He saw women in a new light, and the aloofness of the speaker grew upon him again. He felt that she was holding her place as his teacher" (144). The novel validates Ida's feminist political activity by acknowledging the value of women's perspective as marginalized citizens, much as Anna Julia Cooper does in her collection of essays. Bradley tells Ida that her speech "was right," and that "[he'd] never thought about it before. Women have been kept down. [. . .] The trouble is we men don't think about it at all. We need to have you tell us these things" (148). Bradley's narrow range of experience has prevented him from thinking critically about others' oppression. When he speaks these words, his and Ida's "minds seem[] to come together [. . .] as if by an electrical shock" (148). This first moment of mutual attraction is crucial in the development of the heterosexual romance plot; however, Garland once again refuses to rely on easy gender stereotypes to further it. Instead of stressing her femininity, the narrative describes her looking at Bradley "precisely as one man looks at another, without the slightest false modesty or coquettishness. She evidently considered him a fellow-student on social affairs" (6). Deemphasizing the physical differences between the hero and heroine suggests the possibility of a revolutionary love based on a sustained intellectual exchange and a growing sympathy for humanity. Nevertheless, their connection is described in explicitly physical terms, as an "electrical shock," suggesting that, far from being a passionless, cerebral bond, their love for each other (and by extension their shared sympathy for those in need) is emotional and visceral as well as intellectual.

Ida responds to Bradley's new feminist sensibility with words that prove not only prophetic in the hero's development but that also bear on Garland's revision of literary notions about romantic love. "One radicalism," she says, "open[s] the way to the other. Being a radical is like opening the door to the witches" (148). The reference to witches here is a possible allusion to a poem written by Mary E. Wilkins (Freeman) called "Love and the Witches." Garland would certainly have known this poem, since she published it in the June 1891 installment of *Century* magazine, a volume that also contained Garland's story, "A Spring Romance." In Wilkins's poem, a "little fearful maiden" (line 1) has barred her door tightly against the witches that "by the house had flown," but she quickly opens it when Love "comes a-singing at the door," because as she tells him, "I have watched for you this many a day" (6, 8, 17–18). When she does, her house is invaded, because, as the speaker laments, "Poor little maid, she'd let the witches in with Love" (23–24). Freeman's poem is undoubtedly about how seductive romantic love can be, and also about how potentially dangerous it is to open one's self up to its attendant emotions and passions. *A Spoil of Office* does indeed seem to equate romance with radicalism, acknowledging that both can create a powerful longing in a person—in one case for love, and in the other for justice and social reform—but also that they can make a person vulnerable to pain and alienation. This connection between radicalism and romance is literalized quite clearly in Bradley and Ida's "revolutionary romance," and the characters' subsequent development demonstrates that their growing need for each other is of a piece with their increasing desire to make the world a more just place. At the same time, the final chapters of the novel also show how this longing isolates them from mainstream society, even as it draws them (and by extension, their oppositional community) closer together.

Given this warning, it is perhaps not surprising that, as soon as Ida opens Bradley's eyes to gender discrimination, he becomes more and more attuned to other forms of oppression as well. Specifically, Bradley grows more sensitive to the racism surrounding him and to which he was formerly oblivious. Early on in the story, when Bradley goes to visit Ida at her hotel, the clerk takes his card and "[gives] it to the insolent little darkey who served as 'Front'" (146). Here, the narrative voice seems closely aligned with Bradley's perspective in its uncritical use of these racist, derogatory terms. However, soon after Bradley is elected to the state legislature, he notices that the young African American boy tending him in his hotel "was not allowed to ride in the elevator" (206). The narrator tells us, "For the first time in his life [Bradley] had met the question of caste" (206). Although the narrator still calls African American men "darkeys" at this stage in the novel, after his epiphany Bradley increasingly pays attention to details such as the young man's "badly broken shoes," which he notices are nonetheless "highly polished" (207). While the narrative does not return to the "question of caste" until the fourth stage of the novel, the reader can already see Bradley's "self-horizon" regarding race being challenged. Likewise, Bradley sees young women in the capitol building lobbying for jobs and making themselves vulnerable to politicians who would take advantage of their need in economic and other ways. Rather than merely condemning the women for "this unwomanly struggle for office," however, Bradley now sees that it is "the need for employment which really forced these girls into such a contest" (219). In both cases, Bradley (and the reader) learns that racial and sexual stereotypes are inaccurate, and that the subordinate status of white women and people of color results from poverty and a lack of opportunity rather than personal defects.

At their second meeting, Ida also impresses on Bradley the need for communal action and coalition politics to fight against economic, sexual, and racial injustice. Ida is the first character to see beyond the "smaller circle" of farming interests, and she recognizes that other reformers must do the same. According to the heroine, the Grange is failing because "the farmer can't seem to feel his kinship. [. . .] He must come some day to see that to stand by his fellowman is to stand by himself. That's what civilization means, to stand by each other" (149). Ida predicts that the Grange "must include more or fail" (151); she therefore intuits two of the crucial elements of oppositional community formation that Ferguson articulates. First, Ida recognizes how hard it is to sustain a defiant stance against the status quo in isolation; the farmers will fail if they do not realize their own interdependence. Furthermore, Ida sees that a particular interest group, such as the organization of farmers, is ultimately more successful when it develops "affinities and political affiliations with those in other identity positions who share critiques of the dominant order" (Ferguson, "Feminist Communities" 372). The agrarian revolt initiated by the Grange will be doomed if it does not correct its myopia; it must "include more or fail."

As *A Spoil of Office* moves into the final stage, national politics, the reader learns how the current political climate stifles the formation of coalitions that have the potential to bring about significant change. Bradley is elected to be a Democratic representative to the U.S. Congress and there he discovers how difficult it is to maintain an oppositional stance in mainstream politics—his increasingly radical ideas alienate him from both his fellow congressmen and his constituency. Almost the last fourth of the novel chronicles his increasing disillusionment with organized politics, even as it shows his rapidly maturing sensitivity to many forms of injustice. In Washington, D.C., where he has daily contact with African Americans, he is uncomfortable with the "oppressive courtesy" they show him, and he notices for the first time the complexity of their situation: "The negroes attracted his eyes constantly. They drifted along the street apparently aimlessly, many of them. Their faces were mainly laughing, but in a meaningless way, as if it were a habit. He soon found that they were swift to struggle for a chance to work" (274). By using words such as "apparently" and "habit," Garland's narrator suggests that the carefree demeanor of African Americans is a facade and that in reality, they are desperate to earn a living, just like the women in the state building. *A Spoil of Office* is thus like *Iola Leroy* in exposing the inaccuracy of an outsiders' perception of African American life by intimating the actual conditions of that life. Furthermore, the word "negro" is markedly less racist than the "darkey" used in the first half of the book. During a visit to the U.S. Capitol building, Bradley chooses to sit with the African Americans in the common gallery instead of joining the other representatives in the private gallery. Here, Bradley physically aligns himself with the marginalized people he hopes to help rather than the privileged politicians who are his colleagues, and this physical separation foreshadows the complete break with mainstream politics and status quo interests in which the novel culminates. It also models for the reader an oppositional community that is racially integrated in a relatively egalitarian way.

Until this point, Bradley has worked through the traditional channels of mainstream politics. However, he learns that he must join a community that is not only truly inclusive but also truly oppositional if he is to alter society in a substantive way. Martin calls this "the novel's most important Populist transformation: the formation of a new party," noting that in this ending, "*Spoil*'s romance plot parallels a coalition political plot" (39). After losing reelection to Congress because of his "cranky notions," Bradley determines to leave politics, but once again Ida refocuses him (324). She writes to him of the new organization that has replaced the Grange, the Farmers' Alliance, which she says is "deeper in thought and broader in sympathy," and she assures him, "This order will become political," unlike the Grange (304).

Bradley travels to Kansas on business and hears her speak at an Alliance gathering that counterbalances the more celebratory Grange picnic at the beginning of the novel: "Up the broad street [. . .] came the long procession of revolting farmers. There were no bands to lead them; no fluttering of gay flags; no cheers from the bystanders. They rode in grim silence for the most part, as if at a funeral of their dead hopes—as if their mere presence were a protest" (337). The visible poverty and grim countenances of the farmers underscore their desolate situation and their commitment to reform, garnering sympathy and understanding for the Alliance. The juxtaposition of meetings also highlights Bradley's transformation from naive farmhand to perceptive critical thinker: "[Bradley] wondered if there used to be so many tired faces at the Grange picnics in Iowa. Were the farmers really less comfortable and happy, or had he simply grown clearsighted? He ended by believing in both causes" (342).

Bradley, however, still needs to learn more about the Alliance before he is willing to embrace it, and it takes Ida's final recorded speech in the novel to render the hero completely "clear-sighted." This speech is also juxtaposed with Ida's first in the novel, which she gave when she was much younger; that speech was concerned with the "poetic side" of farming life and she had delivered it standing in the "dapple of shadows," suggesting a certain romanticism (12–13). In contrast, as she speaks for the Alliance, Ida stands in "broad daylight" and her rhetoric is "of the contemporaneous sort" (344). Like the farmers, Ida has given up nostalgia and become modernized. In this final speech, Ida fully articulates the inclusiveness and radicalness toward which the novel has been building from the beginning:

> The heart and centre of this movement is a demand for justice, not for ourselves alone, but for the toiling poor wherever found. [. . .] With me, it is no longer a question of legislating for the farmer; it is a question of the abolition of industrial slavery. [. . .] We're just coming to understand what the fundamental principle of our order means: *Equal Rights to all, and special privileges to none.* [. . .] That means equal rights to women, to the negro, to the Chinese, to the Irish, to everybody that today is hedged in by class prejudice, or by the walls of caste. (346–47)

In Ida's ideal oppositional community, there is no place for the sexism, racism, classism, and xenophobia that was limiting the appeal and vision of a variety of real-world reform communities at the time, including that of the woman's movement; instead, she embraces a genuinely universal notion of equal rights, and the reader sees how affecting such a vision is, not just for Bradley, but for the large group of farmers in attendance, who all gather around Ida and take "her strong, smooth hand in their work-scarred, leathery palms." The farmers' wives are especially moved by her presence. One older woman tells Ida how important her work is: "You've helped us. I reckon life won't seem quite so tough now. We kind o' see a glimmer of a way out" (349). Ida is a feminist activist who has learned Anna Julia Cooper's lesson that "[t]he cause of freedom is not the cause of a race or a sect, a party or a class." She works tirelessly for people less fortunate than she is, becoming what Ferguson calls a "class traitor" through her sympathetic identification with the poor farmers' wives, as well as with African Americans, immigrants, and "everybody hedged in by class prejudice, or by the walls of caste."

In Garland criticism, the historical precursor for Ida's character is almost uniformly assumed to be Mary Elizabeth Lease. According to Walter Lazenby, Garland toured with Lease in Iowa during the year of 1892. However, Garland never claimed that Lease was his inspiration for Ida; rather, it was Vernon Parrington who first proposed (in 1930) that Ida "may have been suggested by Mary Ellen [sic] Lease" (161). That Parrington gets Lease's name wrong, and that most critics have taken his assertion at face value, is indicative of a generally dismissive attitude in *Spoil* scholarship as a whole about feminist contributions to Populism in general, and the feminism in the novel in particular. This carelessness is especially glaring given the meticulous historical research about other aspects of Populism and its relation to Garland's novel critics have undertaken. If one compares Garland's fictional heroine to the description of Lease in MaryJo Wagner's *Farms, Families and Reform* (1986), one finds little resemblance. Wagner claims that Lease was a controversial character who "had a tendency to stretch the truth and exaggerate" (21). Perhaps more damning, Lease was known to be discriminatory and anti-Semitic; Wagner calls Lease's *The Problem of Civilization Solved* (1895) "a racist, outlandish book" (24). Ida, in contrast, is earnest, sincere, and open-minded, committing herself to racial, gender, and economic equality, and her espousal of universal equality is a far cry from Lease's bigotry.

Frances Kaye, in "Hamlin Garland's Feminism," does not refer to Lease but suggests that "Ida was pleasantly liberal, but by no means 'in advance of her time' [Garland's description of her], and would have been completely at home with the WCTU or most woman's clubs" (154). However, the radical natural rights philosophy of woman's rights espoused by Ida, along with her simultaneous commitment to class and race reform, is very different from the mainstream philosophy of expediency promoted by Frances Willard and other clubwomen that implicitly and explicitly favors the needs of white, affluent women. Ida is a more inclusive, radical feminist activist—the embodiment of the optimistic, progressive idealism about equal rights that Garland himself expresses elsewhere—than Garland's contemporary reader would have found in the "real world."

The novel ends idyllically and on a hopeful note, which is fitting for such an extraordinary hero and heroine. Bradley gives up his affiliation with the Democratic Party, pledging himself to the Alliance movement, which plans to launch the independent Populist Party in time for the 1892 election. As Ida leads Bradley through this final political transformation, their relationship undergoes an attendant personal one. When Bradley tells her he is going to work for the Alliance, the reader gets a rare glimpse into Ida's interior thoughts: "She was deeply gratified to think he had entered the great movement, and that she had been instrumental in converting him" (376). Her emotions prompt Ida to grasp Bradley's hand with a "great, sudden resolution" and tell him, "We'll work *together*" (377). While the convergence of political and personal sympathies in the "revolutionary romance" that ends happily is a recurring theme in novels about feminist activists, the ending of *A Spoil of Office* is more controversial—and more promising—than most.

After their marriage, Ida joins Bradley in Washington, D.C., as he finishes up his congressional term, but after a few weeks, she tells him that she must return home to continue lecturing and to encourage the farmers and their wives who depend on her in the Alliance: "Now, we mustn't be selfish, dear; you've got your work to do here, and I've got my work to do there" (384). Bradley responds, "All right, Ida, we enlisted for the whole war" (385). The physical separation of the newlyweds is an unusual and significant twist in the marriage plot designed to advance the cause of political reform. Theirs seems to be a truly equal partnership; neither one's duties nor desires are subordinated to the other person's, and Ida shows an independence and self-reliance rare even for feminist activist heroines. Accordingly, Bradley and Ida's relationship shows that "revolutionary love" defies physical bounds, uniting the lovers even as they are apart pursuing their political goals; their political commitment, though it physical separates them, will keep their marriage emotionally strong. As Barbara Bardes and Suzanne Gossett point out, "In his conclusion Garland takes the most radical position possible about the way in which political action will unite Bradley and Ida" (178).

Other critics, feminist and otherwise, have been less convinced by Garland's "happy ending," and their skepticism seems to result from their assumptions about heterosexual romance. In another article about Garland's feminism, "Hamlin Garland and the Cult of True Womanhood," Roger E. Carp claims that "[i]t is something of a paradox that Garland's ideal marriage of equals is not presented as an enduring relationship," and he cites Ida's returning to the West as proof of this breach (88). The text itself, however, does not suggest that this physical separation means that Ida and Bradley's marriage will not "endure." In fact, Ida reminds Bradley that once his term is over they will be able to work side-by-side for two years. Similarly, Eberhard Alsen argues that the ending is weak because of the "rather implausible self-imposed separation of the newlywed hero and heroine" (95). In both cases, the critics are incapable of believing that the characters' political commitment constitutes a valid reason for their separation, and thus they assume that the marriage is neither viable nor realistic. In Alsen's case, especially, there seems to be a gender bias because it is the woman who insists on the separation so she can continue her work; there are countless stories in which men return to the battlefield, to the sea, or other places of "work" without the separation seeming "implausible." Even Garland's strongest advocate, his editor B. O. Flower, was not entirely comfortable with the novel's ending. In his review for the *Arena*, published in 1892, Flower lamented, "one almost wishes the curtain might have fallen when the lovers reached the station after the night ride from the little Kansas schoolhouse" (which is before their marriage and move to Washington) (50).

As a male writer, Garland would not have felt substantial pressure to conform to gender conventions, and that might explain why he creates such an unabashedly autonomous, revolutionary heroine and such an unorthodox ending. However, reactions such as Howells's and Flower's apparently induced him to capitulate somewhat to mainstream expectations. Five years after its original publication, Garland issued a revised edition of the novel, and in it, he considerably normalizes his heroine. The preface to this new edition obliquely suggests why he might have done so:

> [Maintaining Bradley's point of view as the lens through which one reads the story] has one marked disadvantage, however: it is apt to be misunderstood by the reader who may take the characters, events and theories, judged by the central figure, to be the author's estimate. To illustrate: Ida Wilbur is presented as she appears to Bradley Talcott, and not as the reader would see her, and not as the author would have delineated her had she been taken as the central figure of the book. This explanatory word seemed needed; being given, I leave its working out to the reader. (vii–viii)

Although he is strangely vague and elliptical in this passage, it does seem clear that his depiction of Ida has met with a great deal of disapproval from those readers who, while perhaps progressive in some ways, do not believe such an independent heroine could exist outside of Garland's imagination. Consequently, he distances himself from his own creation, claiming that she is neither "central" to his novel nor objectively drawn, though he never explains to the reader why such a disavowal of his heroine is warranted.

Garland's revisions, however, suggest that he capitulates to his audience's conviction that only a conventionally feminine heroine, relegated to the margins of the plot, is a believable one. The author cut twelve pages of text, primarily, as Quentin Martin notes, Ida's political oratory. Garland also rewrote the ending to make Ida more religious and more passive. After Ida's admonishment, "We musn't be selfish, dear," Garland adds an explanation: "I have been very happy here with you, but there is something of John the Baptist in me: I must go forth and utter the word—the word of the Lord" (374). This analogy seems rather out of place in a book that elsewhere almost completely ignores religion; its insertion seems (rather awkwardly) designed to assure the reader, first, that Ida is Christian, and second, that her political work is subordinate to Bradley's; she has only paved the way for him, as John the Baptist did for Jesus. Another addition, immediately following this exchange, reiterates her subordinate status and is particularly relevant to my argument that in the original version, Ida is Bradley's political and intellectual mentor: "Slowly through years of thought he had grown, till now he was level with her altruistic conception of life" (375). No longer is Ida "holding her place as his teacher," as she does in the original version (144); in this later edition, he has nothing left to learn from her.

Garland undermines his heroine's exceptional autonomy further by having her trade in her activist life for one of married domesticity. After Bradley agrees that the couple has "enlisted for the whole war," he reminds her, "My congressional career will soon end, anyhow" (375). Ida embraces him and responds, "As a matter of fact, you'll work better without me, Bradley, and your public career must not end for many years. You must keep your place for my sake as well as for the sake of the wronged—and also for the sake of—of our children, Bradley" (375). As she says this, "[her] voice grew tremulous" and Bradley "encircled her like a shield and drew her to his knee" (375). In this revised ending, Ida is stripped of almost all her agency and independence, depicted, as Quentin Martin observes, as a "defenseless and childlike woman" who is planning to "stay at home with her husband and raise children like a good wife and mother" (46). In his later autobiography, Garland seems disappointed by the unkind reaction to his heroine and by his own failure to depict faithfully his vision of a feminist activist: "Ida Wilbur was in advance of her time. As I look back on her, I see that she was a lovely forerunner of the well-dressed and wholly competent leaders who followed Susan Anthony's austere generation. I find her not altogether despicable. I knew her type as well as I did that of Bradley Talcott, but

I failed to make her lovable" (154). The author acknowledges that his readers were not ready for such a radical heroine, and one must wonder how much of his political and artistic integrity Garland sacrificed in these revisions to make Ida more "lovable" to his audience.

There is a long-standing critical debate over which of these editions is more artistically satisfying. As I noted earlier, Eberhard Alsen finds the original too overtly political and argues that the revised edition is more "universal" and thus more accomplished. Quentin Martin, on the other hand, finds the original to be the superior version because of its complex, convincing delineation of Populism. It is also difficult to determine which version was the most widely read; the original was published when Garland was considered an up-and-coming western writer, and it was both serialized in the *Arena* and published in book form. However, in 1897, Garland was a more established author, and as such, he most likely had a greater following of readers. It is clear, however, which version is more feminist in its message and more significant in the tradition of American feminist activist fiction. In Garland's first text, Ida's political talent and her progressive commitment are unparalleled and her relationship with Bradley is boldly original; she represents what, as one character says, "a woman can do if y' give 'er a chance" (349).

Just as Garland's original Ida is, in many ways, a utopian figure, whose actions do not need to bend to "real world" expectations of propriety, it must be acknowledged that the oppositional communities fictionalized in *A Spoil of Office* and *Iola Leroy* are in some ways ideals rather than realistic depictions. While Harper's and Garland's novels are products of what Garland calls the "spreading radicalism" of the 1890s, progressivism had many critics and was not itself a wholly radical movement. In *Uplifting the Race,* Gaines shows that many middle-class African American advocates, including Anna Julia Cooper, were against the Populist movement, because they saw "organized labor as a threat to social peace" (135). Gaines says that Cooper was specifically anti-immigrant, seeing "confrontation between labor and capital as evidence of foreign subversion" that threatened African American job security (145). At the same time, the Populist movement was not immune to racism, as the example of Lease suggests. According to McMath, the "issue of race was the most vexing problem for Populist success [. . . .] In the Northwest [the Populists] championed the exclusion of Chinese workers and the South exploited African Americans" (172). Ultimately, the Populists also refused to support a woman suffrage plank; thus, like "other Americans of their time," McMath observes, they had "a myopic view of equal rights, one still distorted by racism and sexism" (210). Nevertheless, as artists and activists, Harper and Garland imagine oppositional communities that are optimistic and idyllic in their openness and inclusiveness, and both authors find strong feminist activist heroines essential to this vision. In this way, they give their readers, male and female, an ideal to which they can aspire, even if their counterparts in the real world fall short.

Even if Harper's and Garland's visions are utopian, they nevertheless rely on realistic descriptions to conjure them up. Unlike the sentimental portrayal of Marjory Warner in *Out of Her Sphere* or the sensational world of kidnapping and disguise in *Fettered for Life*, the communities in *Iola Leroy* and *A Spoil of Office* reflect the authors' adherence to the realism of late nineteenth-century American literature. Harper and Garland, however, put the conventions of literary realism to work for their political cause, just as Harbert borrows the conventions of sentimentalism and Blake the conventions of sensationalism. Harper's use of dialect, a common element in realist fiction, not only reflects the actual voices of her folk characters but also dispels stereotypes of ignorance or imbecility often associated with those who speak in vernacular English—characters like Aunt Linda, Uncle Daniel, and Tom Anderson are fully realized, complex characters who act courageously and who make among the most perceptive, persuasive arguments for reform in the book. Likewise, Garland's detailed descriptions of the vast agrarian landscape, as well as his minute delineation of the farmers' impoverished lives, impresses on the reader the justness and urgency of their cause. In these realistic depictions of idealized reform communities, the difference between the actual and the imagined collapses somewhat, making it easier for the reader to see how to traverse the distance between "what is" and "what is possible." As we shall see, twentieth-century feminist activist writers respond to the changing literary landscape as well, writing "progressive middlebrow" fiction that gives voice to both the artistic and political aspirations of their modern society.

CHAPTER THREE

Making It New

Middlebrow Literary Culture and Twentieth-Century Suffrage Fiction

When Harriot Stanton Blatch returned to the United States from England in 1902, she found her fellow suffragists mired in "the doldrums," a self-described stagnation that had stymied the movement since the mid-1890s.[1] According to Blatch's memoirs,

> The suffrage movement was completely in a rut in New York State at the opening of the twentieth century. It bored its adherents and repelled its opponents. Most of the ammunition was being wasted on its supporters in private drawing rooms and in public halls where friends, drummed up and harried by the ardent, listlessly heard the same old arguments. Unswerving adherence to the cause was held in high esteem, but alas, it was loyalty to a rut run deeper and deeper. (*Challenging Years* 98)

Blatch proposed a number of ways the movement might escape from this rut. Perhaps her most notable suggestion, inspired by the more militant British suffragism in which she had been immersed for years, was that it should infuse itself with an element of spectacle. Noting the ineffectualness of traditional attempts to convert the public through education and "the same old arguments," Blatch conceived of the idea of a suffrage parade because she believed people are "moved to action by emotion, not by argument and reason" (129). The success of this plan, she advised, would depend on a lively performance: "The enemy must be converted through his eyes. [. . .] [He] must hear music, as must each [parade] marcher, music all the time" (180).

According to Ellen Carol DuBois, a leading suffrage historian, Blatch thus led the way to a more up-to-date, publicity-driven campaign for suffrage by introducing methods she learned in England, "especially tactics that sexually integrated public space, such as open-air meetings and parades" ("Harriot Stanton Blatch" 168). These tactics particularly appealed to working-class women, both immigrant and native-born, because they "drew on the militant tradition of the labor movement, and its protest tactics, such as outdoor rallies, [and] were suitable to a constituency with little money" (169). Similar tactics had been used by socialists in Europe for years, and in order to capitalize on some of the immigrant population's familiarity with them, the suffragists "issued propaganda in Yiddish, Italian, and other immigrant languages" (169).[2] Suffragists like Blatch also "were pioneers in the political uses of new media technologies such as movies, commercial radio, and telephones, and in the strategic deployment of public opinion" (169). Both strategies widened considerably the movement's influence, enabling it to reach people in all social strata. This push toward modernization invigorated suffrage advocates and diversified the movement's appeal, causing the ranks of supporters to swell in the first decade of the twentieth century, so that by the second, the suffrage movement was "thoroughly respectable, and in the large cities smart, fashionable" (Schneider and Schneider 169).[3]

The larger social and literary milieus of America were undergoing profound change at the same time that the advocates of woman's rights began trying to address a wider audience and started exploring different ways of getting their message across. Technological advances not only changed suffrage strategies; they also changed the complexion of almost every American's life. Automobiles and airplanes exponentially increased the population's mobility, and this mobility was one of many factors contributing to the shift toward urban living. By 1919, almost half the country was concentrated in the twelve largest cities, and rapid industrialization had irrevocably hampered the widely agrarian economy of the past. This industrialization was part of a worldwide trend, and in European countries as well as in America, people now found themselves working and living in metropolitan areas. To help support this burgeoning economy, immigrants from all over the world were recruited to expand the country's workforce. Such a meteoric rise in population, both immigrant and native-born, overtaxed the infrastructures of large cities, which were ill-equipped for such growth. Consequently, unsafe, unsanitary living conditions were rampant, resulting in tenements and other overcrowded, low-income residential areas. By the beginning of the twentieth century, it was clear that new laws and other reforms would be needed to ameliorate the problems with factory and tenement life as well as to address ongoing gender discrimination. What followed was the period known as the Progressive Era during which there was vigorous social debate about how best to redress these ills.

Dramatic changes were also taking place on the artistic and literary scene, both at home and abroad. Ezra Pound's exhortation to "make it new" sums up modernism, with its emphasis on innovative styles and subject matter. Writers perhaps in part invented such devices as stream of consciousness, multiple narrators, and linear discontinuity as a means of reflecting what they took to be the new reality of most Americans' lives, which had become increasingly complicated and fragmented. At the same time, however, these innovations were likely also supremely liberating. In calling on artists to "make it new," Pound expresses impatience with prevailing literary conventions and what he sees as the naive, outdated ideas that underlie them. His impatience seems analogous to Harriot Stanton Blatch's frustration with "the same old [suffrage] arguments." Clearly, Pound, like Blatch, did not believe the customs of the nineteenth century would work in the twentieth.

In many ways, however, the modernist and suffrage movements seem very far removed from each other. Certainly, traditional cultural and literary criticism has drawn a rigid distinction between a "high" modern aesthetic and "low" popular, progressive politics. As Marianne DeKoven remarks, "Modernism, with its notoriously resistant complexity and its rarefied religion of art, is often thought of as the antithesis to representation of the threat/promise of radical political and cultural change: in fact, it is thought of as a retreat from, or rejection of, the failed, degraded, violent world of twentieth-century politics" (175). DeKoven persuasively challenges this polarization; she not only complicates the binary of art and politics but also other oppositions at work in both the political and artistic realms, such as high/low, critical/popular (and following Andreas Huyssen's lead) male/female.[4] In fact, critics such as DeKoven, Huyssen, Bonnie Kime Scott, and Suzanne Clark have generated a large body of scholarship that broadens considerably our understanding of the interplay between gender, literature, mass culture, and politics in the modernist period. This interplay is manifested in the formal properties of twentieth-century suffrage novels, properties that reflect the political and social developments in the movement. As Clark claims, "In the matrix of American modernism as it emerged in the years before World War I [...] the older discourse of progress and reform mixed confusedly with the new revolutionary forms, also associated with political revolution in the mind of participants" (33). The tactical innovations in the suffrage movement were responsible for creating a large community and solidifying its strength, whereas the formal innovations of the "high" modernist movement in some ways foreground society's discontinuities and differences. However, Clark's claim about the revolutionary ideas of the progressive 1910s "mix[ing] confusedly" with the revolutionary forms (though quite often reactionary politics) of the modernist aesthetic opens a space in which to consider the literary achievement of those writing about feminist activist heroines in the first two decades of the twentieth century.

A number of scholars, including Joan Shelley Rubin, Lisa Botshon, and Meredith Goldsmith, have recently begun charting such a space between "highbrow" aesthetics and "lowbrow" politics by studying what they call the "middlebrow" culture of the Progressive Era, which produced a large flowering of mainstream, accessible literature that, unlike high modernist writing, which was typically published in boutique "little magazines," was widely disseminated in mass periodicals and book-of-the-month clubs. Rubin defines the audience for this genre as "white Anglo-Saxon Protestant readers, male and female, who participated in the civic life of the Lynds' Middletown, shunned the Ku Klux Klan, worried about declining moral standards, and made Dorothy Canfield's novels best sellers" (*Middlebrow Moderns* xv).[5] And though these rather narrow, genteel (if seemingly liberal) concerns led many earlier critics to "associate middlebrow writing with the pernicious aspect of consumer culture" that leads inevitably to conservatism, more recent studies have tried to "disentangle the modern outlook from its customary association with high literary culture" (xii, xi). *Middlebrow Moderns: Popular American Women Writers of the 1920s* (2003), edited by Botshon and Goldsmith, for example, asks us to take seriously the literary and political aspirations of the titular writers, such as Dorothy Canfield, Kathleen Norris, and Edna Ferber, whom Bostshon and Goldsmith describe as "'quasi-respectable' serious yet 'pernicious' authors" who "inhabit a space between the embrace of experimentalism and ambiguity considered characteristic of modernism [. . .] and the critique of the dominant culture [Jane] Tompkins locates in the popular" (10).

Botshon and Goldsmith's collection of essays confirms first that middlebrow literature was "consumed by a majority of readers" (4) and second that as Rubin suggests in *The Making of Middlebrow Culture*, middlebrow writing is gendered, because most producers of it are female and many of the texts depict the lives of twentieth-century women. Furthermore, the contributors to *Middlebrow Moderns* show how middlebrow novels and stories were, as Rubin puts it in her foreword to the volume, "sites for [many] kinds of questionings" (xvi). They "participated and advanced," according to Botshon and Goldsmith, in "the cultural debate over domesticity and women's work, marriage and reproduction, assimilation, consumer culture and capitalism, and the rise of new technologies" (6). From Edna St. Vincent Millay's poetry to Edna Ferber's Emma McChesney stories to Anzia Yezierska's stories about Jewish tenement life, middlebrow literature attests to early twentieth-century Americans' interest in the life of modern woman in all her various forms. Furthermore, a host of lesser-known writers was producing a body of work that Maureen Honey calls "feminist New Woman fiction" for widely circulated periodicals such as *Good Housekeeping* and the *Ladies' Home Journal.* Honey says these stories "share a common concern with women's autonomy as free agents" and "[interrogate] male authority figures who control their female employees, wives, sweethearts or daughters" (87). This literary community of modern women writing about modern women is an important counterpart to the reform community of the suffrage movement, and those writing suffrage fiction situated their works within this larger milieu, modifying the conventions of modernist writing to make the connection between liberatory gender narratives and organized reform activity even more explicit, just as authors of novels about feminist activists from the 1870s modified the conventions of sentimental and sensation fiction.

Jaime Harker has coined a rather specific phrase, "progressive middlebrow," that seems the most appropriate for describing the aesthetic of these suffrage authors. According to Harker, "[T]he 'progressive middlebrow' kept a highbrow concern with serious issues while satisfying both the lowbrow's demand for accessibility and entertainment and its fundamentally ethical judgment of the artistic. It attempted to establish a middle ground in which literature heals, creates community, and saves the nation" (119). Harker's "progressive" designation suggests that these works were written with an activist intent to not only interrogate modern issues but to also intervene in cultural debates and bring about liberal reform. Certainly, the authors of twentieth-century suffrage fiction are dedicated to the serious issue of gender reform and, in many ways, see it as a way to "save the nation." Thus it would have been counterproductive for them to have written in a high modernist style, which Clark claims foregrounded "exile, not community" (71), especially when, as I have argued, coalescing an oppositional community of feminist reformers was paramount in the minds of feminist activist authors.

Nevertheless, as Botshon and Goldsmith observe, some middlebrow writers, while "assess[ing] the interests of a popular audience [. . .] simultaneously tapped into the most important literary movements in the United States" by "experimenting with language" and "stream of consciousness" and making other unusual formal choices (10). Certainly, these early twentieth-century suffrage writers were not oblivious to the self-consciousness about style that marks this period of literary production, even though they were clearly writing for a popular audience. Indeed, it is clear that these authors tried to depict the new, more complicated reality of a growing, increasingly influential woman suffrage movement by making use of the structural deviations—widely found in both popular and critically acclaimed writing of the time—from the single-author, linear narrative of nineteenth-century novels about feminist activists.

Three fictional works about feminist activism particularly demonstrate this point: Marjorie Shuler's *For Rent—One Pedestal* (1917), *The Sturdy Oak* (1917), written by fourteen authors and edited by Elizabeth Jordan, and Oreola Williams Haskell's *Banner Bearers: Tales of the Suffrage Campaigns* (1920). All three were inspired by and are set during the New York campaigns of 1915 and 1917, credited by most suffragists with insuring the passage and ratification of the Nineteenth Amendment just a few years later. Furthermore, each takes an unusual or innovative form: Shuler's is an epistolary novel, *The Sturdy Oak* is a composite novel, and Haskell's book can be classified as a short story cycle.[6]

In each case, attention to form allows the author(s) to express more fully the communal reality of the mature suffrage community. *For Rent* tells the story of two suffrage supporters' friendship through one's correspondence to the other; *The Sturdy Oak* was written by a real-world oppositional community of pro-suffrage authors; and *Banner Bearers*, with its many separate but interrelated stories, accommodates a multitude of activist heroines all united by their feminist agenda. At the same time, these forms give authors the latitude to acknowledge the diverse and at times contradictory individual perspectives that are the building blocks of large oppositional communities. When reading the letters in *For Rent*, for instance, one is always aware that they are only one side of an ongoing dialogue. *The Sturdy Oak* is literally comprised of fourteen different authorial perspectives on suffrage, and the boundaries between the discrete stories in *Banner Bearers* remind one that even though the many characters work together in an oppositional community, each one has a unique experience within that community.

The formal properties of these books draw the readers' attention to what Mikhail Bakhtin has called the "polyphony" of the novelistic form, which is characterized by "a plurality of independent and unmerged voices and consciousnesses" (6). Bakhtin thought this multiplicity of voices, this "fundamental open-endedness" (39), the best literary representation of his belief that "in language, as in the psyche and everywhere else in culture, order is never complete and always requires work. It is a *task*, a *project*, always ongoing and ever unfinished; and it is always opposed to the essential messiness of the world" (Morson and Emerson 139). I would argue that in each case, the structure of these works allows their authors to accomplish a rare feat. They successfully express the notion that those working together for woman suffrage are part of a thriving, expanding oppositional community (to which the reader should belong if she or he does not already) but at the same time acknowledge the ongoing negotiations and dialogues that constantly shape and reshape this massive entity. Thus, without diminishing the communal power of feminist activists, these books show that their communities are, and will always be, "unfinished" and that, though they seem in many ways fully realized, they are an ongoing "task" or "project."

This attention to form also clearly marks a transition in the tradition of feminist activist literature in America. In some ways, the books bespeak the success the movement in general and the literature in particular had had in undermining conventional gender expectations by depicting activist heroines of different ages, occupations, and social backgrounds. The greater freedom of women in turn enables these fictional texts to decenter the heterosexual romance plot, which is so pervasive in nineteenth-century stories about feminist activist heroines, and thereby redefine the importance, even meaning, of romance in their female characters' lives and in certain cases, even posit that "romance" for these heroines is not necessarily limited to love for and attraction to a man.

However, these suffrage texts also demonstrate how mainstream acceptance of the movement blunted the potential for radical social change championed in books about feminist activism from the 1890s like Harper's *Iola Leroy* and Garland's *A Spoil of Office* and show how this mainstream acceptance was predicated on exclusionary racial attitudes analogous to those found in the earlier suffrage novels from the 1870s. Woman's rights activists' frustration in the 1870s over the fact that African American men were constitutionally enfranchised but white women were not led white women, as we have seen, to argue the unfairness of this discrepancy by appealing to racist ideas. As Louise Michele Newman observes, "even before white women drew on evolutionist ideas to assert their own significance to civilizing missions, white women invoked their racial similarity with white men when they insisted on their inherent capacity to vote and their inherent right to the franchise" (58).

At first, this conflict was primarily (though never exclusively) about white women's difference from African Americans; however, as the nineteenth century progressed into the twentieth, the rapidly increasing immigrant population made the discussions about race and racial difference in America more nuanced, not only in the woman's rights movement but in the nation at large.

According to Matthew Frye Jacobson, these nuances had serious political and social implications: "The period of mass European immigration, from the 1840s to the restrictive legislation of 1924 witnessed a fracturing of whiteness into a hierarchy of plural and scientifically determined white races. Vigorous debate ensued over which of these was truly 'fit for self-government' in the good old Anglo-Saxon sense" (7–8). Jacobson calls this hierarchy—which distinguishes between "superior" Anglo-Saxon whites (most often native-born) and other "less civilized" racial/ethnic (but nevertheless "white") groups such as Celts, Slavs, Armenians, Italians, Jews, and so on—"variegated whiteness."

While these groups were still considered superior to those of African descent, they were, nonetheless, considered more savage and barbaric than Anglo-Saxons as well as less intelligent and less moral. This hierarchy was buoyed by scientific racialism (closely tied to social Darwinism), which legitimized the classifying of human beings according to their physical and behavioral traits and that associated these traits with "fixed and unalterable" biological differences, thus leading to the fairly static ranking of these races on a continuum from most-to-least "evolved" (Frye 32). According to many contemporary American intellectuals, it was the influx of these "less civilized" white races (and their subsequent civic participation), along with the presence of newly freed African Americans, that increasingly corrupted and debased national politics in the years after the Civil War and into the 1900s. In an essay entitled "Democracy" (1884), the poet and intellectual James Russell Lowell articulates this widely held belief: "If universal suffrage has worked ill in our larger cities, as it certainly has, this has been mainly because the hands that wielded it were untrained to its use. There the election of a majority of the trustees of the public money is controlled by the most ignorant and vicious of a population which has come to us from abroad, wholly unpracticed in self-government and incapable of assimilation by American habits and methods" (410).[7]

As the immigrant and African American populations grew over the following decades, so too did this angst about the "lower races" dominating American political and social life, until it became palpable even in seemingly open-minded mainstream texts not primarily concerned with immigration. For example, *Roast Beef, Medium* (1913), the first collection of Edna Ferber's popular Emma McChesney stories about a single mother–turned–successful traveling saleswoman clearly falls into the category of "progressive middlebrow literature." Nevertheless, the collection's foreword is rather telling; in it, the author explains her title, which she claims is "not only a food. It is a philosophy." Ferber conveys this philosophy by imagining a symbolic situation: "Seated at Life's Dining Table, with the Menu of Morals before you, your eye wanders a bit over the entrées, the hors d'oeuvres, and things *a la*, though you know that Roast Beef, Medium, is safe, and sane, and sure. It agrees with you. As you hesitate there sounds in your ear a soft and insinuating Voice" (xxix). According to Ferber, this Voice tempts you with exotic foreign cuisine such as "tongue in aspic" and "flaked crab meat [. . .] with a special Russian sauce" (xxix). When you give in to this temptation, however, the "paprika burns [your] tongue" and you have to take a "Moral Pepsin" (xxx).

After such an experience, however, Ferber (and presumably her audience) learns her lesson: "When next we dine we are not tempted by the Voice. We are wary of weird sauces. [...] We look about at our neighbor's table. He is eating of things French, and Russian and Hungarian. Of food garnished, and garish and greasy. And with a little sigh of content and resignation we settle down to our Roast Beef, Medium" (xxx). In many ways, Ferber's anecdote seems benign; she is encouraging her reader to make simple, safe, reliable choices instead of unusual or daring ones. However, she does so by comparing traditional American (i.e., Anglo-Saxon) fare—roast beef—to the unfamiliar (and what she thinks are unhealthy) foods of other nations, brought to the United States by immigrants. Such an "invasion" of the domestic space by suspect foreign entities reveals an anxiety about how the nation's changing ethnic demographic is affecting its character. In fact, by turning her story into a metaphor about morality, Ferber not only privileges American virtues over foreign ones, but she also makes the nation's moral center the dinner table—a traditionally feminine space—implying that American (white) women are the protectors of the country's morality.

Such a morality (and cautionary) tale clearly relies on a hierarchical understanding of "evolved" races (as well as on an assumption about the moral superiority of white women), and such a hierarchy becomes important in understanding Emma McChesney's story. She is, without question, a liberated, modern woman who is self-sufficient and successful. At the same time, this fable about the Roast Beef suggests that Emma's success as a white woman is based on her unwavering Anglo-Saxon moral compass that is guided by an assumption of American superiority and a distrust of foreign customs. While clearly less vitriolic than Lowell's diatribe, the Roast Beef fable is significant because it demonstrates that reactionary politics about race found their way, almost invisibly, into early twentieth-century literature that otherwise seems forward-thinking and that seemingly progressive notions about gender could not only coexist with but also depend on racist and anti-immigrant sentiment.

This same complicated blend of conservative and liberal politics is endemic to the rhetoric and literature of first-wave American feminism. The late nineteenth and early twentieth centuries saw white feminist activists beginning to draw on evolutionary ideas about racial hierarchy to "assert their own significance to civilizing missions" (Newman 58). A large part of this mission was to restore civility to American politics, which they suggested could be achieved by native-born white women gaining the vote; they would, then, be in a position to counteract the damaging effects of political participation by the "lower races." Furthermore, according to Rosalyn Terborg-Penn, during the Progressive Era, "white female suffragists did not include racial discrimination and the plight of disenfranchised Black women in their priorities for social reform. They either avoided the race question or openly opposed including Black women in the suffrage ranks" (11).

So though twentieth-century suffragists made a strategic attempt to reach out to immigrants, and especially immigrant women, hoping to convince them to join their oppositional communities, many suffragists also believed that immigrant men were to be blamed for the corruption of the political system and the immoral state of society. They also considered immigrant men, as well as African American men, to be one of the largest barriers to woman suffrage, because they believed these men were ignorant and misogynistic and would therefore vote against it. This contradictory attitude about the immigrant population, along with a consistent disrespect for African Americans, creates a powerful, vexing subtext about race in many of the late suffrage works, one that dictates to a large degree who is included in their visions of oppositional communities and who is not and that makes Jamie Harker's claim that "progressive middlebrow" writers wanted to "save the nation" seem a bit more ominous. Save us from whom?

In many ways, Marjorie Shuler's *For Rent—One Pedestal* typifies the changes the suffrage heroine and her world undergo during the transition from the nineteenth to the twentieth century. In fact, one must look no further than the book's dedication page to begin to appreciate the magnitude of this transition. Shuler, like Elizabeth Boynton Harbert in 1871, dedicates her work to her mother. However, the implications of these seemingly identical inscriptions are profoundly different. If Harbert's novel is loosely autobiographical (and there is evidence to suggest that it is), then one can suppose the author's mother, like Marjory Warner's, was supportive of her daughter and suffrage but nonetheless self-effacing, domestic, and above all, private. Shuler's mother, on the other hand, was Nettie Rogers Shuler, a prominent suffrage activist and NAWSA officer who cowrote a well-known history of the movement with Carrie Chapman Catt.[8] Shuler's mother therefore is a public figure as well as a private one, and she is both a personal and political role model for her daughter; the daughter learned not only to fight against the political injustice to which generations of women had been subjected but to follow her mother's footsteps in that fight. Thus, the author was a second- (or perhaps third-) generation suffragist who had been a member of a community of women reformers her entire life.[9]

Shuler's experience of having been surrounded by sympathetic companions all her life shapes the progression of *For Rent—One Pedestal*, whose epistolary form renders it quite different from the third-person, linear narratives of many earlier novels about feminist activism. While this formal difference is crucial to the novel's "new" vision of feminist activism, it is certainly not original or innovative in the high modernist sense. Nevertheless, such a revisioning of a classic form *is* modern in that it is one way that some early twentieth-century women writers, most notably Edna St. Vincent Millay, sought to reach their audience. As Clark observes in *Sentimental Modernism*, "Far from subverting the masculine tradition by using poetic conventions in new ways, in the very age of 'make it new,' Millay was writing sonnets. She subverts male modernism by appropriating conventional male poetics from a more classic past, speaking a colonized discourse" (71). This appropriation allows Millay to disassociate literary conventions from their conservative past, much like stories about feminist activists appropriate the heterosexual romance plot in order to revise ideas about marriage and gender. In Millay's poetry, the woman, historically the silent object of the sonneteer's adoration, expresses her own desire and sexual autonomy. Furthermore, according to Clark, allowing a new voice to speak through an old form helps Millay "negotiate the contradictory demands of a modernist art and the appeal to a powerful community of readers" because "some continuity with the middle class was for Millay as for many other women writers a prerequisite for maintaining a woman's traditions and for creating a community with women readers" (69).

For Schuler—who was perhaps even more invested in reaching a "powerful community of readers" than Millay was—the invocation of another traditional form, the epistolary novel, allows her to artistically represent the affinity for gender reform many young, college-educated, white "New Women" were discovering through their friendships at this time. The form also allows her to write a work that, by privileging female friendship over heterosexual romance, would help bring such a community into existence. In *Epistolary Responses*, Anne Bower describes the potential of the epistolary novel for conveying this individual and communal sense of agency: "While they write, letter writers are active; their encoding of a message, no matter what the message, is a form of action; they know themselves alive, they know themselves as makers of meaning, and they maintain a sense of their addressees as present. Then they send their letters off and hope for replies. Whether or not they receive return mail, they maintain the sense that response is possible—they are not, therefore, seeing themselves as completely isolated or without at least the possibility of a community of some sort" (xi). In Shuler's novel, this "possibility of community" is realized in the increasingly committed suffrage work of the protagonist, Delight Dennison, during the New York campaign of 1915, and through her letters detailing her adventures to her college friend Barbara Martin. In this way, the epistolary form suggests an oppositional community not only in its depiction of intimate relationships between suffragists but also in its representation of multiple voices in dialogue about the woman's movement.

As a heroine, Delight Dennison embodies the new face of suffrage in the twentieth century, as described by scholars such as DuBois and Margaret Finnegan.[10] DuBois argues that in the 1910s the suffrage movement shifted its emphasis from woman-as-mother to woman-as-worker, and she sees Harriot Stanton Blatch as again pivotal in the movement's re-creation of itself. According to DuBois, "Blatch's focus on self-support in the Equality League replaced the nineteenth-century emphasis on domesticity and motherhood as a basis for women's unity" ("Harriot Stanton Blatch" 165).[11] Of course, in many ways, Blatch and her contemporaries were merely responding to the changing realities of their society. The number of professional and laboring-class women increased exponentially at the beginning of the century as more women went to college and as the United States underwent rapid industrialization and urbanization.[12] At the same time, the focus on woman-as-worker tended to elide the differences between the clerical and professional work done mostly by white, educated women and the less lucrative and more physically demanding skilled and unskilled labor done by immigrant and African American women, an elision evident in Shuler's depiction of Delight as the representative new feminist activist.

Delight's first letter clearly identifies her as a skilled, educated woman-as-worker, even if she has yet to make the connection between her position and her need for suffrage:

> Barbara, My Dear:
> Behold me, Delight Dennison of Verner College and nowhere, with a manner befitting the ladies of Cranford. Fortified with a pair of tortoise-shell rimmed spectacles. They make me look heaps older. Swathed in a linen waist with choking collar. "Young ladies, young ladies," shrills the principal of this school, "teachers should never wear low collars in the school room." Perish the thought that once I broke a record at hurdle jumping. (1)

Though Delight is college educated, she now finds herself belonging "nowhere," suggesting she is solely responsible for herself. Also, the reader learns she is a teacher, an occupation considered respectable for a "lady," a designation laden with racial and class connotations. Clearly, Delight is representative of the New Woman ideal increasingly embraced by twentieth-century culture, which allowed middle- and upper-class white women to enter the public sphere and have a single lifestyle without the stigma of previous generations.[13] Within this context, the novel's title takes on greater significance. Privileged women of previous generations had been "placed on a pedestal" by their societies, from which they had a clearly superior vantage point but by which they were rendered immobile and kept separate from society. Delight, having eschewed her pedestal, is ready to live in the world in an active and engaged way. Furthermore, that Delight supports herself is relevant to her development as a suffragist, because, as Harriot Stanton Blatch observes, "The suffrage will be won by women who are economically independent. [. . .] The woman who supports herself has a claim upon the state, which legislators are coming to recognize" ("Self-Supporting Women" 29).

Although Blatch's vision of economically independent women seems egalitarian, Delight's attitude about her duties as a teacher demonstrates that the New Woman—and by extension, the new suffragist—is not only implicitly white, but is specifically Anglo-Saxon. Describing her teaching job, Delight glibly laments, "For ten days I have patiently wiped the nose of Little Italy. I have extracted yards of raffia from the blouse of thieving Young Poland. One hundred times have I demanded that Rosalie keep in line. Forty times a day I have showed Yetta which is her right foot" (1). Delight's uncritical acceptance of racial stereotypes and subsequent xenophobia is obvious, but what is perhaps less obvious is the problematic link between her xenophobia and her desire to bring about social reform. Delight invokes these stereotypes here to stress the mundane, sometimes trying, aspects of her job as a teacher, a job that places her in a position to fulfill the white woman's cultural role as "civilizer" and "moral arbiter."[14] Thus, Delight's notion of herself as a self-reliant, professional woman is inseparable from her assumption that because she is educated, white, and native-born, she is racially superior to immigrants. Thus, in her behavior toward her immigrant students we see the patronizing attitude that is writ large in suffrage fiction (and the movement itself): Delight wants to help them improve their lives by "civilizing" them.[15]

The fact that Delight is youthful and active, given to hurdle jumping, even if now she must cloak these attributes in conservative attire, is also crucial to understanding her as a new type of feminist activist heroine. Earlier feminist activist writers tried to gain the reader's sympathy by stressing the heroine's selflessness and purity and often by demonstrating her domesticity, and piety as well. However, in *Selling Suffrage*, Margaret Finnegan makes a convincing case that these qualities are superseded in the public representation of "modern" suffragists, and she relates this change to a larger transformation in American society, which "became increasingly obsessed with individual personality. Writers, physicians and advertisers encouraged men and women to develop winsome, charismatic personas that would supposedly foster intimate relationships, emotional vitality, and personal and business success" (79–80). According to Finnegan, this new obsession shaped the way that suffragists and other feminist activists presented themselves in public: "Intent on overcoming disparaging preconceptions of suffrage campaigners [. . .] suffragists used physical appearance, dress, and personality to suggest that woman suffragists (and thus potential woman voters) were attractive, stylish, charming, dignified and virtuous" (81).

Finnegan claims that these were qualities stressed in the many suffrage parades, plays, movies, and paraphernalia that were used to further the cause in the twentieth century, and they were also the ones stressed in the writings of Millay, Ferber, and others, foregrounding the charm and winsome nature of their heroines. Millay perhaps most succinctly captures this energy in the famous declaration that her "candle burns at both ends," giving off a fleeting, but nevertheless "lovely light." Heroines such as Ferber's Emma McChesney lack such a self-destructive edge; nevertheless, they share a similar engaging quality. Maureen Honey identifies this quality as "vitality" and says it is the key to the success of the "new kind of romantic heroine" in the "New Woman" fiction published in early twentieth-century American magazines ("Feminist New Woman Fiction" 91). Delight's energetic, ironic tone has real-life literary antecedents as well. Critic Bonnie Kime Scott recounts how the modernist author Rebecca West "amused [the recipients of her letters] with extended personal anecdotes and plays with rules of gender in creating her critical persona. Preparing to combat an antifeminist, she claimed a 'chivalrous reluctance, feeling that a steam engine ought not to crush a butterfly'" (*Refiguring Modernism* 44).

One need only consider Delight Dennison's moniker to realize she is cast in this mold. As a letter writer, Delight often makes puns using her name—"But I promise most solemnly," she closes in one letter, "to cram the mail bag full of Delight" (6). She also creatively addresses her friend at times, beginning another letter, "Dear Oasis in Time of Trouble" (6). Delight's skill as a lively correspondent is also apparent in the clever way she presents even unpleasant or upsetting content. Explaining her burgeoning sympathy for woman suffrage, she writes to Barbara: "It's the result of my daily promenade through the factory section of Canton toward my place of toil. There are some sights to which one may become accustomed, but I do not number among them a dead pig, a very dead pig. Each morning I have talked to myself about that pig. I have spent valuable time assuring myself that I could pass it with my head averted. But my nostrils have defied my most stern commands" (2). The squalor suggested by a dead, rotting animal in the midst of an urban area is certainly cause for moral outrage, and Delight's outrage suggests that she is genuinely concerned about the lives of the immigrants and others who live in these unsanitary conditions. However, Delight makes the topic more palatable by wittily recasting it as her internal struggle with a pair of mutinous nostrils. By extension, she makes herself seem in command of her emotions, capable of approaching situations with objective distance, qualities that would make her a "reasonable" political participant and thus "fit for self-government," like her male Anglo-Saxon counterparts.[16]

Delight's story differs from other works of New Woman fiction, however, in the explicit link it draws between women's independence and their political participation. In *One Pedestal*, Delight realizes that vitality is not enough to ensure her future success; she must have a political voice, albeit a charming one. Her slightly amused tone infuses all of her letters, shaping the way suffrage work is portrayed. It is challenging and time-consuming, but also exciting, rewarding, and spectacular. Two letters make this characterization clear. In one, Delight writes: "Dear Babs: I've been in jail. By special invitation of Big Tim. He suggested thirty days. I only stayed three hours and 5,000 people have been yelling themselves hoarse over my escape. It was more thrilling than any football game I ever saw" (33). Delight has been arrested for organizing a publicity stunt and supposedly violating a traffic law in the process. However, an arrest—a potentially dangerous and certainly indecorous circumstance for a "lady"—is rendered here as motivational, even invigorating, "more thrilling than any football game."

Another sensational stunt she relates to Barbara concerns a "Biscuit-Making Contest" at their new headquarters. The suffragists have challenged any "anti" (those women campaigning against suffrage) to make better biscuits than their representative, Delight. However, no one accepts the challenge, and Delight works alone in the window of the headquarters, "smil[ing] and mak[ing] wordless jokes with the crowd" while "each panful [of biscuits] [is] greeted with cheers" (83–84). This bit of propaganda is ostensibly designed to prove the homemaking skills of suffragists; however, in Delight's description it becomes domesticity as spectacle, not a private act but a public performance for the purpose of entertaining—and thereby gaining the sympathy of—viewers.[17]

Although much of Shuler's epistolary novel is about performance (the act of letter writing itself is a performance, a molding of language to entertain one's reader), it also provides a space for Delight's personal epiphanies about the connection between her status as a single, self-supporting New Woman and the suffrage cause. Elizabeth Campbell observes that epistolary writing often leads to self-awareness: "Once the letter is begun, the writers seem to be speaking to themselves, and though the reader is ever-present, the writer becomes immersed in a discovery of herself" (336). Delight's discovery of herself as a suffragist is chronicled through her letters to "Dear Babs." Even though she considers herself an antisuffragist, Delight takes a job canvassing for the cause because she needs an income after being dismissed from her teaching job shortly after she speaks out publicly against the town's unsanitary conditions. The woman who hires her, Mrs. Morton, suggests that "Big Tim," the local political boss, was behind her dismissal from the teaching position. In a moment of self-evaluation, Delight tells Barbara, "[Big Tim] is an avowed enemy of the suffragists. Somehow the thought of him as an ally is not wholly pleasing" (11). Through her own exploitation, Delight realizes how profoundly vulnerable women are in a society where they have no political voice.

Living amid a corrupt political system that keeps her from exercising her voice is disconcerting, to say the least, in part because it exacerbates her own feelings of vulnerability; she learns that fighting corruption can cause her to lose her job and her independence, and that she has no legal recourse to resist injustice. It is ironic, though, that both the people she wants to help and the people who thwart that effort are associated with "less civilized" races. Although the novel does not overtly portray Big Tim (the main agent of corruption in the novel) as racially "other" or a member of the lower class, part of Delight's anxiety about this corruption can be traced back to American society's nervousness about the infiltration of ethnic minorities into politics. Thus, her feelings of vulnerability and alienation stem from both her desire to help socially oppressed people and her fear that they will oppress her.

Once Delight becomes aware of the types of people who are against suffrage, such as Big Tim, she becomes increasingly uncomfortable with the idea of being associated with them, although she still is not ready to support the other side. In another moment of introspection, however, she writes to Barbara: "It is strange how combative I feel when I encounter another anti-suffragist like myself" (13). Through her letters Delight articulates the contradictory emotions she feels as she converts to a prosuffrage stance, a process that, ultimately, does not take very long. Before she has been working as a canvasser two weeks, Delight admits to her friend, "I rather think my own little bombshell will be the greatest surprise of all. Have you read it yet? If not, do so now and prepare to gloat. There it is in black and white. I am a suffragist. [. . .] One morning I woke up to the fact that I didn't need conversion" (17). The rest of the letters detail Delight's tireless and spirited work for the cause. The personal, subjective nature of the epistolary novel lets the reader experience Delight's self-discovery in a very intimate way, creating a strong bond of sympathy between the fictional heroine and those who read her letters.

The question of readers is crucial in epistolary novels in general, and *For Rent* in particular, because they signify, as Bower suggests, the "possibility of a community." For a late suffragist like Shuler, the epistolary form allows for a representation of the large, active network of suffragists across the country by mimicking on a small scale the practice of exchanging correspondence about both personal and business matters that women involved in the movement engaged in. Furthermore, the kind of community the epistolary form suggests is markedly different from that of most nineteenth-century feminist activist novels, which often portray a single woman, or a handful of women, pitted against a hostile world. By propelling the action of her novel through letter writing, Shuler places her heroine in a sympathetic environment already ripe for "revolutionary love."

When Delight tells Barbara of her first time speaking at a street meeting, she warns her friend: "Open not your arms in welcome; lift not your voice in thanksgiving. [. . .] My anti-principles are as firmly embedded as when you first began to tug at them back in our freshmen days" (2). Thus, the reader learns Barbara is already a suffragist and has been working to persuade her friend to join the cause for years. When Delight admits she is thoroughly transformed, she accuses Barbara of expediting this process with "all those deft little comments in [her] letters" (18). In this epistolary novel, Delight is always connected to other suffragists, even if she is physically alone. When she begs Barbara, "[F]or goodness sake, write! Remember one can feel the isolation of a mountain top suffrage organizing, as well as sitting in a camp" (16), the reader is also reminded that those doing battle with the status quo need the comfort and support of like-minded friends.

At the same time, *One Pedestal* demonstrates that certain kinds of like-mindedness can blunt the radical potential of community and revolutionary love as much as it can foster it. We learn in the letters that Barbara, who is also a Verner graduate and who is vacationing at her wealthy family's summer home, seems to share Delight's privileged white perspective, or at least Delight assumes she does. This assumed "like-mindedness" generates some of the most racist rhetoric associated with the suffrage movement found in the novel. For example, Delight tells Barb, "Everyone who has come into headquarters today has been chuckling over a joke I played yesterday" (58). Delight's "joke" was to go to the local library to request borrower's privileges, which are only granted to a woman if a male taxpayer signs for her. Delight initially gives the name of Mrs. McKim, the widow of one of the library's benefactors, as her reference, and she is turned down. She then tells Barb the punch line: "An hour later I returned to the library accompanied by my reference, Mrs. McKim's coachman

[. . .] A negro, with only one leg and one arm, blind, illiterate, but a man. And a taxpayer by virtue of owning a little shack on the edge of the town. The attendant was inclined to temporize, but I said, 'Here is my man taxpayer ready to make his mark.' The newspapers this morning suggested a possible change in the rules of the library" (59).

Delight's outrage at the public marginalization of white, affluent women has lead her to commit an even greater outrage on one of the most marginalized members of her society by publicly humiliating Mrs. McKim's coachman. She is, however, entirely unaware of her cruelty; she thinks it a funny joke, and, as she does when she utters racist slurs against her immigrant students, she relates the story in a confident, carefree way that suggests her reader (both internal and external) will find the anecdote equally humorous. She is perhaps right to make this assumption, given that "everyone at headquarters" has already laughed at the story. In this episode, we see the double-edged nature of Delight's relationship with Barb and the other suffragists she knows: because they are "like-minded," they share her desire for gender reform (for some women, at least) and offer her support and encouragement in her efforts to secure it, but they also share her narrow-minded racism.

In addition to Delight and her correspondent, Barbara, there is one other female who figures prominently in *For Rent*, rounding out the novel's microcosm of an oppositional community of suffragists. Mrs. Morton, the woman who recruits Delight and works closely with her, is an important topic in almost all the letters. The reader learns of Mrs. Morton after Barbara does: "I realized that the other half of my seat was in possession of Mrs. Morton, the Mrs. Morton, main topic of my last epistle to you. Babs, she's just as fascinating as I imagined" (3). From the start, Delight is taken with this interesting woman, and it is their personal affinity for each other that first draws Delight into her suffrage work (along with Mrs. Morton's offer of a place to stay and a job). Delight tells Barbara that Mrs. Morton "said she knew all the time I couldn't work for suffrage and not become a believer in it" (17). Over time, the two colleagues and roommates become very close. Responding to an apparently skeptical inquiry from Barbara about their living arrangements, Delight questions, "How can you cast asparagus on my beautiful disposition? As if I couldn't live peaceably with a hyena. And Mrs. Morton, I call her Lucia now, is anything but that. She is a reasonable individual. [. . .] We have heaps of differences, but both of us make concessions. On one thing we are agreed. We regard the apartment as a haven of refuge" (25). The widowed Mrs. Morton, although not much older than Delight, seems a replacement for the mother Delight lost as a child when she was killed doing missionary work abroad. Mrs. Morton introduces Delight to the movement and teaches her how to be a competent suffragist; she is, like Delight, a "reasonable individual," well suited for self-government. Her mother's missionary work suggests Delight's maternal legacy is fortitude and a zealous commitment to her beliefs, and the heroine's maternal replacement trains her to channel those attributes specifically for gender reform work. This shift parallels a similar one in the movement at large, in which second- and sometimes third-generation suffragists had taken charge by the 1910s and that is echoed in the different dedications to "Mother."[18]

Both Delight's former and current roommates achieve familial status in the heroine's life, and all three are bound together by affection for each other and belief in the suffrage cause. The fact that Delight has an interested and sympathetic friend to whom she can divulge the details her suffrage work and another who guides and supports her in this work suggests that the suffrage movement has come of age. The epistolary novel is the perfect vehicle for fictionalizing this world of activist women and *For Rent* anticipates some of the later twentieth-century women's novels about revolt that Campbell discusses: "While the voices in epistolary literature often seem to be angry revolutionary voices, the revolution has already occurred before the form appears in literature. The oppressed have to be free before they are able to speak, but they also have to be aware of listeners" (335). Admittedly, Delight's voice may be more amused and amusing than angry; however, that may be because she is confident of a warm reception from her listeners, both internal and external. The importance of Delight's almost allegorical name should be considered here. Rather than pushing gender reform in an angry, dogmatic way with an angry, dogmatic heroine, Shuler chooses to convert her readers to a prosuffrage stance by "delighting" them with a delightful character who composes charming letters.

The sympathetic community of modern, New Women suggested by *For Rent* distinguishes Delight's story (as well as *The Sturdy Oak* and *Banner Bearers*) from the New Woman fiction discussed by Honey. According to Honey, in most stories, especially from the 1920s and '30s, "bonding between unmarried women, a source of strength to suffragists and female professionals, is framed as a relic of the last century, unhealthy, and undesirable as an alternative to modern marriage" ("Feminist New Woman" 98). *For Rent*, written in an earlier decade, is able to preserve the importance of female friendships even as it fulfills its readers' traditional desire for a heterosexual romance.

While epistolary novels about female friendship are not unprecedented before the twentieth century, Elizabeth Campbell reminds her reader that "[t]he most common subject of epistolary novels in the past has been the love and/or seduction story" (334).[19] In confining the correspondence to letters between Delight and Barbara, Shuler's novel consigns heterosexual romance, a central feature of earlier books about feminist activists, to the sidelines and makes female friendships the most intimate relationships. Delight does develop a romantic attachment to Professor Armstrong, but Barbara and the reader are only privy to glimpses of it until the very end of the novel. When Delight first sees him while giving a suffrage speech, she recognizes him as a childhood friend. However, she tells Barbara that he is an "undesirable citizen" and that the two of them "disagreed on every conceivable point" (16). Armstrong is against suffrage, and this position makes him the butt of many of Delight's jokes, such as when she sees him talking to a very feminine teacher at his school. Delight tells Barbara, "I feel that she has the instincts of a woman in the home. Between classes they can exchange anti-suffrage treatises" (58).

Although Armstrong is a minor character, Delight refers to him often and describes the many kind services he performs for her, like seeing her home after meetings and sending her flowers after she has been stranded in a rainstorm. Both his chivalry and his name, which suggests strength and reliability, mark him as a noble, capable man, and although Delight says that he is a "disagreeable citizen," the novel makes clear that he is intelligent, thoughtful, and civilized, even if he is initially conservative in his thinking about gender. These traits distinguish him from the other men in the book (besides Mrs. Morton's love interest, Mr. Gilbert, who is also a white, affluent male), like Big Tim or Mrs. McKim's coachman, who are clearly immoral or simply ignorant and poor, thus rendering them "[un]fit for self-government." In contrast, Professor Armstrong seems the embodiment of the virtues most associated with the Anglo-Saxon race, and thus, he represents the type of "reasonable" man suffragists believe is most susceptible to conversion. He is also a socially appropriate male love interest for the heroine.

Nevertheless, Delight's account of her suffrage work takes precedence over her talk of Professor Armstrong, until the final letters, in which the two topics come together in "the greatest event of all [her] life" (121). In the penultimate letter, dated "Election Morning," Delight tells Barbara about the climactic rally of election eve: "Then happened the most wonderful thing in the world. As a type of the American man who thinks that American women should vote, I introduced Professor William Miller Armstrong" (123). Armstrong claims to have had all his antisuffrage convictions "swept away only th[at] morning" while listening to Delight's speech. In the second letter, Delight tells Barbara about the emotional reaction of the suffragists when the votes are almost counted and they realize defeat is inevitable: "Lucia was standing on a chair pledging us all to the new fight. We cheered her with tears running down our cheeks. I do not know why we cried, certainly not because we were sad" (125). Immediately thereafter, Delight sends a telegram to the state headquarters that reads, "Ready to start again tomorrow" (125).

The reader understands the prophecy of Delight's words; *For Rent* is a fictional account of the New York campaign of 1915. When the suffragists lost this election they immediately began campaigning for the 1917 referendum, which finally enfranchised the state's women. After Delight's declaration of commitment, she writes, "You heard so much about my professor when I thought we could never establish a friendly foundation for our house of love. I want you to know him for the splendid person he is" (135); Delight ends the book by asking Barbara to be her bridesmaid. In the end, the heterosexual romance emerges as a central element in a happy ending that follows on the hero's conversion to the woman's rights cause. Nevertheless, this romance is inextricably intertwined with the defiant, enthusiastic solidarity of the suffragists, and thus the "greatest thing" to have happened to Delight is not merely her marriage proposal or the culmination of her work during the campaign, but the confluence of her personal and political allegiance on this historic night.

Delight Dennison's story takes on more resonance when it is read alongside *The Sturdy Oak*, published the same year. The action in *For Rent* takes place during the 1915 New York campaign, and *The Sturdy Oak* was written to gain publicity for the 1917 one. Both books evoke the modern, spectacle-driven suffrage movement with its emphasis on personality and charm, and both employ innovative forms that give expression to the growing community of feminist activists in the real world. However, in *The Sturdy Oak*, form and content are even more closely wed, because its communal, composite structure grew out of a propaganda stunt conceived by the New York State Woman Suffrage Party (NYSWSP). Like the novel's form, its content stresses the importance of publicity in its heroines' approach to suffrage work and shows how the activist society supports them in their efforts.

In late 1915, the Publicity Council of the NYSWSP approached Elizabeth Jordan, editor of *Harper's Bazar*,[20] to organize a composite novel to be written by twenty-five of the country's leading authors sympathetic to suffrage.[21] The council saw the purpose of the project as threefold. First, it would be a lucrative fundraiser; all proceeds from the serial and book publications were to be donated to the party. Second, that these distinguished writers agreed to contribute to the book would show that the country's best, most creative minds publicly endorsed suffrage. Finally, such a literary event was sure to generate a great deal of publicity for the movement in the crucial months leading up to the vote in 1917. Although the extant correspondence among the participants shows the process was arduous at times, Jordan was able to find fourteen authors (five male, nine female) willing to contribute, including well-known contemporary authors such as Mary Austin, Samuel Merwin, and Dorothy Canfield. Ultimately, the composite novel fulfilled the suffragists' expectations; *Collier's Magazine* paid the NYSWSP three thousand dollars to serialize *The Sturdy Oak*, and Henry Holt published it in book form in November, right before the referendum vote, raising even more money for the cause. It also received national notice. It was reviewed favorably not only in the suffrage journal *Woman Citizen* but also in mainstream periodicals like the *New York Times*, which called it "irresistibly readable" ("Latest Works of Fiction" 42) and the *Dial*, which called it "a tour de force" ("Notes on New Fiction" 117). [22]

The circumstances of its publication as well as its reception clearly situate *The Sturdy Oak* in the realm of progressive middlebrow literature, much of which was published in magazines such as *Collier's*. Recently, there has been a great deal of scholarly interest in the popularity and influence of these magazines in mainstream American society of the early twentieth century.[23] According to Maureen Honey, "periodical fiction was a central component of American popular culture between the wars," and she supports this assertion with a wealth of statistics, including the fact that "as early as 1905 there was a ratio of four magazines to every household—a figure that increased dramatically over the ensuing twenty years" (Introduction 3). Harker echoes this claim and notes, as does Honey, the importance of these magazines to women in particular: "For white, middle-class women, women's magazines were an increasingly important and surprisingly substantive institution" (117). Honey and Harker agree that, while often conservative, the stories in these magazines also "contained political possibilities" (Harker 118).

The serial publication of *The Sturdy Oak* was certainly an attempt to tap into these possibilities, and studies like Harker's and Honey's provide insight into its success. Both critics mention that *Collier's* was one of the more widely circulated magazines during this time period, and Harker says that when *Everybody's Magazine*, another widely circulated magazine, paid three thousand dollars for Dorothy Canfield's *The Squirrel Cage* in 1910, it was an "unheard-of price" (117).[24] Furthermore, a number of studies of middlebrow literary culture suggest that several of the authors who wrote a chapter for *The Sturdy Oak* were among the most popular for these magazines and generated income for them. In addition to Canfield and Austin, there was Mary Heaton Vorse, Fannie Hurst, Kathleen Norris, and William Allen White. Thus, it seems safe to say that the fourteen writers who contributed to this serialized suffrage story were participating in a broader literary debate about gender roles and more importantly were sharing their vision for reform with a large, engaged audience.

Without question, this group of authors, along with Jordan, can be classified as an oppositional community, a network of people who bond together "by challenging a social order perceived to be unjust, usually by working on a shared project for social change" (Ferguson, "Feminist Communities" 372). Each is committed to suffrage and happy not only to do his or her individual part but also to work together to produce a narrative capable of generating sympathy for gender reform. Kathleen Norris's enthusiasm seems typical when she writes to Jordan that "it is an honor to be given the chance" to write a chapter of the book, and that she will "do [her] best for the sake of the Great Cause."[25] The authors, too, seem willing to suppress their writerly egos to enable the timely production of the volume. To Jordan's suggestions for revision, William Allen White responds, "Do anything you want to with my chapter of the suffrage novel. I only wrote it to help. I have no pride of authorship" and Marjorie Benton Cooke jokingly replies, "By all means make any and all necessary changes in my chapter—and god bless you for doing it and letting me off!"

The writing and editing of *The Sturdy Oak*, then, exemplifies how such a community makes the negotiations and sacrifices necessary to affect change in the status quo (or at least work together in the attempt). Of course, not everything went smoothly. Although few specific conflicts are revealed in the extant correspondence about the project, according to Elizabeth Jordan it "was *not* an easy task to get this book together."[26] She also says in the book's preface that "[the creation of this book] has not been the childish diversion it may have seemed. Splendid team work, however, has made success possible" (xvii). The novel also teaches more specific lessons about the national network of suffrage activists. As noted, one third of those involved in creating *The Sturdy Oak* were men, demonstrating the increasingly cross-gender appeal of the movement, and the authors' popularity and the book's appearance in mainstream publications prove that gender reform was a vital topic on the national cultural landscape by 1917.

The composite nature of *The Sturdy Oak* yields a text that reflects the contradictory perspectives that contribute to successful oppositional communities as well as the compromises its members must make to sustain them. In her introduction to the recent reprint of the novel, Ida H. Washington observes that "the collection of episodes by skilled writers presents a fascinating study in comparative literary styles. Realism and romanticism, descriptive, dramatic, and narrative passages rub shoulders. Only remarkably skillful editing has brought this diversity into a cohesive whole and smoothed the seams between the parts" (xv). I would add that just as each writer has a different style, so too does he or she have a unique perspective on why woman suffrage is necessary as well as his or her own ideas about the way to achieve it. In William Allen White's chapter, one male character asks why women want to be involved in the "dirty mess" of politics. His companion answers, "[T]hey think they want to clean up the mess" (139). This rhetoric resembles the expediency arguments that are grounded in the notion of woman suffrage as national housekeeping and that rely on the idea that (white) women's nurturing and domestic nature makes them radically different from men. Ethel Watts Mumford's chapter presents a more skeptical view of women's moral compass, showing that some of them, like Aunt Alys, a selfish widow, have no interest in "cleaning up the mess": "Alys lost her temper. It seemed to her she was ruthlessly being forced to shoulder responsibilities [for the well-being of her tenants] she had been taught to shirk as a sacred feminine right" (116). Henry Kitchell Webster's chapter uses E. Eliot, a self-supporting real estate agent, to speak a more egalitarian view of gender relations in the book: "It isn't that women are better than men, or that they could run the world better if they got the chance. It's that men and women have got to work together to do the things that need doing" (71).

Each of these chapters suggests diverse, sometimes contradictory, reasons for supporting woman suffrage. However, all agree that it is a crucial, pressing reform that will improve the nation. According to Ferguson, one way an oppositional community can effect change is to form "single-sex and mixed-sex alliances around issues of social justice that combine partial visions in a process of struggle without one static end point or vision" ("Feminist Communities" 376). While Ferguson cautions against giving up "utopian thinking," she acknowledges that these pragmatic partial visions constitute concrete steps toward achieving that utopia as well as a way of preventing stasis when not everyone shares the same utopian thinking. *The Sturdy Oak* signifies just such a partial vision; Elizabeth Jordan's skillful (and, as she claims in the title page, "cautious") editing preserves the authors' idiosyncratic versions of gender reform but still yields a novel that represents a unified front in its support of woman suffrage. At the same time, the chapters seem almost uniformly to reflect a white, native-born bias that undermines considerably the possibilities for expanding the oppositional community imagined by these authors.

The story is set in Whitewater, a conservative factory town in upstate New York, and it follows the career of a young, newly married, white, affluent lawyer, George Remington, who is running for district attorney in his first campaign. In the opening scenes, George issues a statement unequivocally opposing woman suffrage, an action his new wife, Genevieve, supports. Apparently, however, no one else in town supports George's decision to state his position publicly (except a pair of female relatives). The leaders of the Republican political machine, Noonan and Doolittle, think it is an imprudent campaign move (even though they too oppose suffrage), and many of the influential, affluent women in town are prosuffrage and obviously disagree with his position, although they like George personally. The plot turns on the competition between these two communities—one corrupt, one progressive—for George's allegiance and the central question becomes whether he will be complicit with the town's fraudulent politics or speak out, along with the women, for more sanitary, safe work conditions, and by extension, will support woman suffrage. Through the course of the story, first Genevieve and then George are converted to a prosuffrage stance, and the novel ends optimistically, suggesting that not only their marriage but also Whitewater will be better off for it.

Clearly, this struggle is, in many ways, a symbolic one between good and evil, between liberal-minded reform and close-minded preservation of the status quo, between concern for others and neglect of the less fortunate. This seemingly black and white battle is complicated, however, by its (often invisible) racial dimension. The women of the oppositional community of feminist activists are white, affluent, and native-born, like Mrs. Harvey Herrington, the richest woman in town and the leader of the local suffrage organization, who has "the fighting blood of five generations of patriots" coursing through her veins (158). On the other hand, the men who are in charge of the local political machine, Noonan and Doolittle, have come to America much more recently and are members of a "less civilized" race, as their Irish names attest, as are the men who work for them, Mike the Goat and Salubrious the Armenian. Thus, an equally important struggle in this story is over George as a representative Anglo-Saxon man. Will he align himself with the women of his own "race," or will he continue to cooperate in the political corruption instigated by the "lower races" of men?

As this gloss of the plot demonstrates, the process of its composition is what renders *The Sturdy Oak*'s form unusual; the novel itself reads like a linear third-person realist narrative, the form most nineteenth-century novels took, including those about feminist activists. Nevertheless, its content reflects the defining characteristics of the twentieth-century suffrage movement: its emphasis on spectacle, humor, and charm; its representation of woman-as-worker; its challenge of conventional notions about romance; its confidence as the oppositional community dramatically expanded; and the ideological contradiction between its egalitarianism and its prejudicial assumptions about race.

The Sturdy Oak's tone and plot are designed to amuse and charm readers. Almost all of the authors, their different styles notwithstanding, write with a droll, sophisticated wit. For example, Harry Leon Wilson uses pompous, formal language in his description of George to poke fun at him: "It may have been surmised that our sterling young candidate for district attorney had not yet become skilled in dalliance with the equivocal; that he was no adept at ambiguity; in short, George Remington was no trimmer" (14).[27] The knowing, amused narrative voice imbues the story with a charm not unlike Delight Dennison's. In action, too, *The Sturdy Oak* seeks to humor its audience into supporting suffrage. In one episode, George and Genevieve's single female relatives move in with the newlyweds because a friend has encouraged them to take George's statement about masculine protection literally. The complications that ensue amuse the reader and onlookers, if not the newlyweds themselves. *The Sturdy Oak* also shows how effective spectacular public demonstrations, another popular twentieth-century suffrage tactic, can be. One of the major tools employed by the feminist activists in the novel is a continuous "Voiceless Speech." The suffragists rent a building across the street from George's workplace and post placards that have "Questions for Candidate Remington" written on them such as "To conserve the threatened flower of womanhood, the grape canneries of Omega and Omicron Townships are employing children of five and six years in defiance of the Child Labor Law of this State. Are you going to proceed against them?" (77). This public exhibition garners much attention and pressures George to declare that he does intend to address these ills. The young politician is initially horrified by the exhibit, describing it as an "unwomanly" display, but Betty Sheridan, a modern, self-supporting suffragist assures him, "It's antiquated to try and run any sort of a campaign without them nowadays" (75), adding that one of the town's most respected women, Mrs. Herrington, is currently turning the placards.

Betty represents the young, independent, white "woman-as-worker" ideal of the suffrage movement at this historical moment. Like Delight, Betty is vital, active, and unattached, with arms "more used to tennis-racquets and canoe-paddles than impassioned embraces" (44). Also, like Delight, Betty is determined to support herself, although her determination is a matter of choice rather than necessity. She is the stenographer in George's law office, a position she holds even though she has a wealthy family, because she has "pinned [her] flag to the principle of economic independence" (9). The property manager, E. Eliot, on the other hand, is a different type of woman-as-worker. She is a more streetwise character, a "big-boned [. . .] intelligent, homely" (64) woman who is competent in business and who works, in contrast to Betty, to survive. When the two first meet, Betty asks E. Eliot if she believes in women's economic independence, and the latter replies: "I believe in food and clothes, and money to pay the rent, and the only way I have ever found of having those things is to go out and earn them" (67). E. Eliot goes on to say that having to work to support oneself can often keep one from doing the "real work in the world that won't earn you a living," like political activism (67).

As a businesswoman and property manager, E. Eliot has seen the terrible conditions in the factories—the ignored fire codes and the illegal work hours required of women and children—and she tells Betty of her dream of publicly challenging George to state his intention to enforce these laws were he elected, even though it could lose him the election. Betty, confident in George's ultimate morality, even if he is "old fashioned" about woman suffrage, agrees to help E. Eliot and make Whitewater "the hottest place for George Remington that he ever found himself in" (69). The alliance between these two women drives the action in the rest of the story, and what emerges is a community of politically minded, publicly active, financially independent white women bonded together in a reform network.

The "Voiceless Speech" that is Betty and E. Eliot's first coordinated effort to convert George is also a good place to begin exploring the dynamics of race and class in the novel and their relationship to gender reform and oppositional community formation. George's reasonableness and his "fundamental honesty" (105), which convince Betty that he can be converted to their cause, identify him as one of the "better element" in Whitewater, a phrase used repeatedly in the novel, suggesting the characters' moral superiority is a function of their race and class. George is an Anglo-Saxon man (like, presumably, many of the novel's readers) and so, according to the various authorial perspectives, he has a greater capacity than men from other socioeconomic and ethnic groups to be converted to a prosuffrage stance. Such a comparison is made clear by E. Eliot when she suggests that it's not just the callous owners who are threatening the safety of the women and children working in the factories but also the men in their own families. She predicts that if George were to support protective legislation, "[a] lot of laboring men would be against him. [. . .] There are a lot of these men—whatever they might say—who'd take good care not to vote for a man who would prevent their daughters from bringing in the fifteen, twenty, or twenty-five dollars a week they get for that night work" (70). E. Eliot insinuates that these men are not as civilized as someone like George because they would endanger the well being of the women in their families for financial gain.

There are other men, however, who are much more directly responsible for the long work hours, the lax fire codes, and cramped conditions that make the lives of tenement dwellers and factory workers precarious and miserable. They are members of the local Republican political machine, run behind the scenes by the perennial campaign manager Benjamin Doolittle, Wes Norton, president of the "leading merchants in town," and Patrick Noonan, "the apostle of the liquor interests" in Whitewater (120). This triumvirate representing politics, business, and the liquor interests literalizes the cultural assumption that these are the forces that conspire to make money at the expense of the factory workers. Very little is known about Norton—except that he is presumably a rich business owner—but Doolittle and Noonan are prominent players in *The Sturdy Oak*. They give voice to the arguments in favor of conservative politics and unregulated commerce in the novel. Noonan tells George,

> "There ain't no two ways of thinkin' about the prosperity of Whitewater, ye know, George. The merchants in this town is satisfied with the way things is boomin'. The factory workers is gittin' theirs, with high wages an' overtime. The stockholders is makin' no kick on the dividends—as ye know, George, being one of them.
>
> "Now, we don't want nuthin' to disturb all this. If the fact'ries is crackin' the law a bit, why, it ain't the first time such things has got by the inspector. The fact'ry managers'd like some assurance from ye that ye're goin' to keep yer hands off before they line up the fact'ry hands to vote for ye." (120–21)

Noonan's speech makes the connection between the men in the factories and the other forces of corruption even more explicit; their votes can be bought by their more powerful bosses, who are in cahoots with the liquor interests, and so on.

This web of corruption is primarily run and supported by immigrant, "lower-class" men even if affluent native-born men like Norton (and potentially, George) are involved in it. Depending on the author, Noonan's and Doolittle's dialect ranges from clear Irish "brogue" to more general stereotypical working-class speech. They are both marked as non-Anglo-Saxon and nonaffluent not only by their names, their speech, and their sentiments, but also explicitly by their awareness (and George's) of their inferior status. When George stands up to Noonan, saying that he will "do as his conscience dictates," Noonan becomes "disconcerted," because "[he] sensed with considerable irritation the social and class breach between himself and Remington, and while he did not understand it he resented it" (121). Earlier in the novel, George has an equally antipathetic reaction to Doolittle, thinking to himself that he "hated Mr. Benjamin Doolittle's colloquialisms, though once he had declared them amusing, racy, of the soil" (73). George finds himself caught between the women running the "Voiceless Speech" and those who would quell that voice, and he must choose with whom he will align himself. Improving the lives of the factory workers is clearly a commendable goal, but the novel seriously undermines its progressive message by insisting that the men of the "lower classes" and "lower races" are the very element that must be defeated if the women and children in the factories are to be saved by the morally-responsible Anglo-Saxon men and women of Whitewater. As in *For Rent* and other prosuffrage texts, *The Sturdy Oak's* view of the immigrant population is mixed. On the one hand, immigrant women in the novel are considered potential members of the oppositional community because they, like the more privileged feminist activists, are vulnerable by virtue of being women. And like the more privileged feminists activists, they also often fall into the woman-as-worker category (though as we have seen, there is a great deal of discrepancy in the lived experiences of those in this category). At the same time, however, the males in the immigrant and/or working-class population are perceived as posing the greatest threat to not only women of their own class but to the more advantaged women as well.

However, not all the "more advantaged" women of Whitewater are beyond moral reproach. "Aunt" Alys Brewster-Smith, a widow whose husband left her several tenement buildings, holds fast to an antisuffrage stance in part because she believes it is her "sacred feminine right" to "shirk" responsibility for the financial aspects of her life; consequently, her tenements are some of the worst-maintained and E. Eliot refuses to act as her leasing agent. Aunt Alys, then, is a white woman who repudiates her moral obligation to those of the "lower classes" and thus becomes just as much an enemy of the suffragists as Noonan. Genevieve, on the other hand, is portrayed more sympathetically, even though she is initially against suffrage. The difference, however, is that Genevieve, like George, is "fundamentally honest" and merely "old-fashioned" in her ideas, not selfish, and therefore, she also has the potential to become a member of the oppositional community of feminist activists and not only to change her husband's ideas about women's rights but to improve her marriage as well.

At the beginning, Genevieve is a sheltered young wife who believes it is improper to interfere with her husband's business or political practices. As she tells one friend, "I would no more think of intruding in George's business affairs than he would think of intruding in my household duties" (4). Genevieve has complete faith in the traditional ideology of separate spheres; consequently, unlike Delight or Betty Sheridan, she is happy to remain isolated on the pedestal on which George has placed her. However, Betty and E. Eliot help to awaken Genevieve not only to the deplorable conditions stemming from poverty and unfair labor practices but also to her potential role in remedying them. Genevieve begins internalizing this lesson when E. Eliot speaks at her club, the Woman's Forum, about the connection between woman suffrage and the unsanitary, unsafe lives of the factory workers. Genevieve's interest is piqued by this lecture, and upon returning home, she looks at George, "not in limpid adoration, not in perfect acceptance of all his views, unheard, unweighed; but with a question in [the] blue depths" of her eyes (82). Genevieve has learned about the unenforced protective laws and the proposed new ones, and she wants to be sure her husband will support and enforce them if elected. George's reaction to this questioning look, exaggerated for effect, underscores the significance of her awakening: "George felt his universe reel about him. [. . .] Genevieve was thinking on her own account" (82).

Genevieve's interest in the factory conditions grows and so does her independence of mind. The Woman's Forum decides to suspend its commitment to "discussion only" and take action by organizing an investigative task force called "Seeing Whitewater Sweat" (93). Here, we see the women's club making the crucial step from thinking of factory workers and their families as objects of private charity to bringing their pressure to bear in the public sphere to improve the lives of the laboring class. Genevieve has a corresponding transformation; as she delves deeper into this issue, she declares her intention "hereafter to be a live woman and not a parasite" (117).

Like many white women who become involved in politics, Genevieve is empowered when she "assert[s] [herself] as the rightful, natural protector of uncivilized races" (Newman 57), and this empowerment produces an "existential moment," a "reflexive moment of subjectivity, when [. . .] [a] person evaluates and critiques who she is and what she takes as her interests" and during which she "can reject, expand and reformulate the prudential and moral codes and norms [. . .] [she] has hitherto been taught to interpret as part of herself" (Ferguson, "Moral Responsibility" 127). During this moment, Genevieve becomes aware of herself as a human being capable of thoughts and emotions independent of her husband's, as a human being who has social and moral obligations to individuals outside the home. Consequently, she becomes increasingly active in the feminist community with which she is in sympathy. In this pivotal moment, Genevieve shifts from acquiescing unquestioningly to her husband's opinions to thinking critically for herself. George, nervous about the political fallout that could result from the Woman's Forum undertaking an investigation of the factories, asks Genevieve to help postpone it; she replies, "But this is the only moment when we can find out whether or not you are a candidate who will do what we want" (102). George then asks: "*We*, Genevieve! Who do you mean by 'we'?" (102). Her answer to this crucial question reveals that she has been completely converted: "'Oh, George,' she gasped finally, 'I think I meant *women* when I said 'we.' George, I'm afraid I'm a *suffragist*. And oh,' she added, with a sort of wail, 'I don't want to be, I don't want to be!'" (102). George wants to blame Betty for this change in his wife, but Genevieve assures him that he is the reason for her transformation: "'You made me see why women want to vote for themselves. How can you represent me, when we disagree fundamentally?'" (102). Genevieve has taken her first step into the modern world, becoming aware of the pitfalls and shortcomings of the nineteenth-century concept of middle-class marital relationships and finding her own voice as a twentieth-century suffragist.

Genevieve's transformation is typical of the experience of affluent club-women who get their first taste of community activism through the benevolent interest of their organizations. In the nineteenth century, countless women found a socially acceptable entrance into the world of politics by crossing the space between the domestic sphere and the public domain through charitable club work. Many of these women became suffragists as well because they accepted Frances Willard's idea of the vote as "home protection" against societal evils and as a way to help the less fortunate. According to DuBois, this "Lady Bountiful" approach to feminist activism was the dominant mode as late as the turn into the twentieth century. Many affluent activists, she explains, "saw their reform efforts as public expressions of their place in the family," which translated into the first generation of progressives believing "poor women were as dependent as children on the loving protection of reformer-mothers" ("Harriot Stanton Blatch" 163). The irony, of course, is that a movement devoted to gender equality and independence for women replicates both the hierarchy and forced dependence of (some) women found in a traditional patriarchal society.

In her book, *Tales of the Working Girl*, Laura Hapke illuminates how the Lady Bountiful mentality can turn insidious. Hapke reports that undercover work by affluent women hoping to expose the injustices of the factory system was "all the rage" in early twentieth-century America. Citing numerous examples of heiresses like Marie Van Vorst who infiltrated factories and mills posing as "working girls" and then publishing their findings, Hapke claims, "Very soon magazine and book publishers were catering to the widespread curiosity about these reverse Cinderellas" (48). Hapke acknowledges that these investigations led to positive material changes, but she also notes that these amateur reporters whose work "pointed sympathetically to the chasm between their lives [...] and the women who remained behind" at the same revealed contempt for the woman worker (50). These privileged women reporters judged working and/or immigrant women by their own standards of sexual and social propriety and harbored the belief that these women aspired to lives that emulated those of the privileged classes.

These stories of working women, which were part of the middlebrow literary milieu, are clearly alluded to in *The Sturdy Oak*; by placing Genevieve in the role of a "reverse Cinderella," it points out the naïveté, as well as the elitism, latent bring about gender reform. Genevieve's observation to George that "this is the only moment when we can find out whether or not you are a candidate who will do what we want" shows she has begun to see herself a part of a community of women, but her speech to the women in the tenements shows that she needs to think more critically about her use of the word "we." She does not yet see the ways economic hardship and/or racial oppression can complicate the ideal of commonality among women. The "we" of her oppositional community at this moment is a romanticized vision of white, middle- and upper-class women working harmoniously with grateful immigrant and native-born working women who have the same vision. E. Eliot, on the other hand, represents the more worldly understanding of the diversity among women. It is significant that Genevieve assumes the identity of Marya Slavonsky, a factory woman whose work I.D. Genevieve found when she was inspecting the tenements and whose name indicates an Eastern European background. It never occurs to Genevieve that she cannot "pass" for Marya, but the other women in the factory of course immediately recognize that Genevieve is not who she says she is. Her naïveté emphasizes just how wide the gap is between the rich, Anglo-Saxon woman and her impoverished, immigrant counterpart. This scene demonstrates not only Genevieve's lack of insight, but more broadly, the idea that "women" are not a monolithic entity. It challenges the notion of an inherent femininity, a notion endorsed elsewhere in *The Sturdy Oak* and in other novels about feminist activists. Genevieve's revelation about the terrible conditions in Whitewater is applauded in the novel, and her desire to reform them is likewise depicted sympathetically. However, the book shows that this step can only be the first of many if Genevieve is to rise above, in E. Eliot's words, the class of "misguided, well-meaning enthusiasts" and become an effective feminist activist.[28]

The heroines in two stories written around this time period by popular middlebrow writers who were *not* suffragists serve as interesting contrasts to *The Sturdy Oak's* version of a Lady Bountiful character and shed further light on the novel's critique of affluent women's activism. Edna Ferber's story "Sisters Under Their Skin" from the collection *Emma McChesney & Co* (1915) is, in many ways, the fictional embodiment of Harriot Stanton Blatch's aspirations for the Equality League, a community of employed women who, regardless of their income, would be bound together by sympathy and understanding. The story begins, "Women who know the joys and sorrows of a pay envelope do not speak of girls who work as Working Girls. Neither do they use the term Laboring Class, as one would speak of a distinct and separate race, like the Ethiopian" (178). Like E. Eliot, Emma McChesney, the former saleswoman and now company president, is a woman from the middle class who nevertheless feels a kinship writer. She does not realize that her fellow immigrants in the tenements make interesting subject matter until she witnesses their humiliation at the hands of a "'friendly visitor' of the charities" (195). This Lady Bountiful is a malevolent, irredeemable character whose "indignation seethed in her voice" (196) when she entered the apartment unannounced and found the occupants enjoying themselves and consuming a cake and other treats mailed to them by a friend. The "friendly visitor" storms out, and when Sophie asks why she had come in the first place, the others tell her, "To see that we don't over-eat ourselves!" (196). Yezierska's tragic story ends with the oldest man in the group, the recipient of the gift, being jailed and charged with "intent to deceive and obtain assistance by dishonest means" because he has not disclosed the gift to the "betterment society" (197).

Sophie realizes that she must speak out against this distortion of charity, and she takes her pen in hand at the end of the story: "'Ach! At last it writes itself in me! [. . .] It's not me—it's their cries—my own people—crying in me! [. . .] [T]hey will not be stilled in me, til all America stops to listen'" (200). While the "friendly visitor" is not necessarily a suffragist, she obviously represents the affluent white women involved in the reform movements of the Progressive Era. The vilification of such a woman by an immigrant writer who was also most likely a recipient of such charitable efforts provides a richer context in which we can situate Genevieve's initial efforts at activism, as does Edna Ferber's critique from the perspective of an affluent woman who has chosen not to become an activist. Each story demonstrates the perverse forms activism can take when the affluent woman practicing it does not appreciate the humanity and respect the autonomy of those she would like to help. Ferber's and Yezierska's stories help us understand the skepticism of the factory women in *The Sturdy Oak* and also demonstrate why it is just as dangerous for Genevieve to continue idealizing herself as a "St. Agatha spreading alms and wisdom" to the poor as it would be for her to continue idealizing her role as George's wife (125).

The Sturdy Oak, however, is much more concerned with increasing the size and effectiveness of the feminist reform community than with criticizing it, and thus the novel imagines a way for Genevieve to become a more effective suffragist as well as a more enlightened wife. Like most fictional accounts of feminist activism, this novel privileges marriage; however, like other twentieth-century texts, it revises the narrative form of the heterosexual romance plot. The love story in *For Rent—One Pedestal* follows the more common courtship-as-conversion trajectory but it plays a less prominent role than in feminist activist novels from the nineteenth century. And *The Sturdy Oak* picks up where most nineteenth-century feminist activist novels leave off: the "happily ever after" ending. When *The Sturdy Oak* opens, George and Genevieve are still in an idyllic state of newlywed bliss; they share romantic sentiments about chivalry and the "oneness" of a married couple as well as certain ideas about how those things relate to woman suffrage. When George speaks out publicly against suffrage, it is because he imagines "his own Genevieve, fine, flawless, tenderly nourished flower that she was, being dragged from her high place with the most distressing results" (15). Genevieve, too, idealizes the protective role her husband will play in her life, thinking that she "had given herself irrevocably into the hands of this man. [. . .] His strong, trained mind would be her guide, his sturdy courage her strength. He would build for both of them, for the twain that were one" (2). In some ways, the stakes are higher in a novel about the evolving romance of a married couple; they have already committed to a life together, and in a society in which divorce is rare, they must learn to accommodate each others' changes.

In this more complex rendering of a heterosexual romance, there are not only two, but three, important figures. The third is the exterior community of feminist activists whose actions are catalysts to George's and Genevieve's recognizing each other as autonomous human beings who are prone, like all human beings, to making mistakes. It seems to George that once Genevieve becomes interested in politics, it is like he has "married a stranger," and when Genevieve tells him she will always love him, even if she does not agree with him, he is nonplussed, looking at "this strange, new Genevieve, who, promising to love, reserved the right to judge" (84). The community that is responsible for Genevieve's growing moral and intellectual independence from George also affects George, both indirectly, through Genevieve's transformation and also directly, through the effect they have on his campaign. The feminist activists in *The Sturdy Oak* are motivated at least in part by the frustration they feel because they have no political or legal recourse for cleaning up Whitewater's corrupt government, a duty they feel is theirs as affluent, white, native-born women. Thus, their feminism, while bolstered by their sense of privilege, is also of a piece with their feelings of social responsibility.

It is, not surprisingly, this oppositional community of feminist activists that ultimately wins George's support, because he too feels a sense of social responsibility. Over the course of the novel, George is forced to admit that he shares their moral indignation over the factory conditions, and this admission leads him to support woman suffrage as a potentially positive influence on politics. George's anger is heightened even further when Noonan and Doolittle assign two of their "cronies," Mike the Goat and Salubrious the Armenian, to kidnap E. Eliot and silence her during the campaign. Genevieve is taken as well, and though the two are returned unharmed, George is forced to admit he is working with unconscionable men who have gotten involved in politics for purely selfish reasons and who are not above endangering lives for political gain. Once George realizes that the women are right about Whitewater's politics, he must by extension acknowledge that they are competent, rational beings who should have equal legal rights. George's change of attitude is evident in his newfound respect for his wife's abilities: "He marveled especially at Genevieve because he had never thought of Genevieve as doing such things [as campaigning and organizing parades]. But she had done them—he felt that somehow she was a different Genevieve [. . . .] [H]e had an undefined sense of *aliveness*, of a spirited, joyous initiative in her" (171). By the end of the novel, both he and Genevieve have learned valuable lessons about the other's humanity and their more enlightened perspectives promise to make their marriage happier and more substantial. Upon returning to their home after the campaign, George tells Genevieve, "it's a better home than when we first came to it, for now I've got more sense. Now it is a home in which each of us has the right to think and be what we please" (173).

Of course, the suffragists' "victory" in securing George's allegiance is troubling in many ways since the novel is as much about quelling the power of the immigrant and working-class population as it is about supporting woman suffrage. The ending of the novel especially demonstrates this dual purpose. The fact that the "henchmen" who commit the most reprehensible act in the novel— the kidnapping of innocent women—are immigrants literalizes the fear that white women are especially vulnerable in a world where the "lower races" have too much agency, and the fact that they are identified by racist nicknames (one of which identifies the henchman's country of origin) underscores the prejudice against immigrants in the book. George articulates his choice to his best friend and law partner, Pennington Evans, in a way that encapsulates the novel's clear-cut dichotomy between white women—source of morality, civilization, and positive transformation—and immigrant men— source of corruption, savagery, and decline: "It's no use, Penny. *Our* women have seen the light and beaten us to it; we've got to go with them or with Noonan and his—Mike the Goat!" (emphasis added, 146).

George's "our" is as telling here as Genevieve's earlier "we." The women of his own Anglo-Saxon "race" and from his own wealthy background are the ones with whom he and Penny will align themselves because they represent morality and civility. The novel's vision of an oppositional community becomes more expansive by its inclusion of white Anglo-Saxon men at the same time that it becomes more emphatically exclusive by its rejection of men of other races. To complicate matters further, while the oppositional community embraces immigrant and/or working-class women, this welcome is fraught with potential pitfalls. Therefore, *The Sturdy Oak* models for its readers a powerful, growing oppositional community capable of bringing about positive reform, a community in which women have more independence and social agency, making their personal lives more satisfying and egalitarian. The "other side of the coin" in this equation, however, is that activists justify themselves in large part by appealing to the idea that their reform work will solidify a different kind of community, a community committed to maintaining its native-born upper-class Anglo-Saxon privilege in the face of the threat posed by the growing independence and social agency of immigrants and other marginalized groups.

It is, in fact, the strength and pervasive influence of this oppositional community of suffragists that differentiates *The Sturdy Oak* from most other feminist activist fiction. Most of the other novels I have been considering end with a happy marital union that liberates the domestic sphere, intimating that one day this private liberation will lead to wider reform. In *The Sturdy Oak*, however, authors write beyond this ending, imagining an oppositional community of feminist activists whose work brings about tangible change in the public sphere, beginning with their success in convincing George to expose the corrupt political machine and declare his own liberal convictions. This climactic scene begins with George's description of the coordinated suffragist effort, which also ominously foreshadows the backlash to it: "Now and again [George] paused at his window and looked down into Main Street. Below him was a crowd that was growing in size and disorder; the last afternoon of any campaign in Whitewater was exciting enough; much more so were the final hours of this campaign that marked the first entrance of women into politics in Whitewater on a scale and with an organized energy that might affect the outcome of the morrow's voting" (158). As part of this organized energy, the suffragists have reinstated the Voiceless Speech, "their last chance to assert the demands of good citizenship," and this demonstration "attract[s] hundreds of curious men, vote-owners, belonging to what, in such periods of political struggle, are referred to on platforms as 'our better element'" (159). By affecting the vote of the "better" men like George, Pennington, and others who believe in "good citizenship," the suffragists play an indispensable role in "cleaning up" the town's political corruption and redressing its social injustice.

However, this demonstration also calls forth those who would oppose this "national housekeeping": "Also drifting into Main Street were groups of voters of less prepossessing aspect—Noonan's men, George recognized them to be. These jeered and jostled the marching women and hooted the remarks of the Voiceless Speech—but the women, disregarding insults and attacks, went on with their silent campaigning. The feeling was high—and George could see, as Noonan's men kept drifting into Main Street, that feeling was growing higher" (159). As the story moves toward resolution, this feeling grows higher still, until a riot seems to erupt on the streets of Whitewater. The scene intimates the violence that is just below the surface in a selfish, corrupt community that has strayed from its democratic and humanitarian principles and that silences the voices of women, in the home, in the factory, and at the polls. At the same time, it makes a connection between immigrant groups and this kind of undemocratic violence. Undoubtedly, how one votes on suffrage becomes, in this book, a litmus test of one's class, race, and civility. Those who support it are of the "better element," affluent, native-born, enlightened men like George and Pennington, and those who would oppose it are "less prepossessing," less rich, of immigrant descent, and dangerous. In fact, this scene is reminiscent of one in American history, the New York City draft riots, which were led by Irish men angered by the Conscription Act of 1863. They did not believe that they should be forced into service for the benefit of African Americans and so thought they were asserting their white privilege by objecting, but according to Jacobson, "many non-Irish onlookers and commentators [. . .] registered their own Republican claims by questioning the rioters' full status as 'white persons,' [. . .] decry[ing] the 'barbarism' of the riots and [characterizing] the rioters themselves as 'brute,' 'brutish,' and 'animal' " (54). *The Sturdy Oak*, then, seems to rely on this cultural memory to make its middlebrow audience—primarily Protestant, white, Anglo-Saxon—fearful of what might happen in the United States if women are *not* given the vote.

Ultimately, George restores order to this chaotic environment. Through the fray, he makes his way to a window near the Voiceless Speech, from which he sends "forth a speech which had a voice" (166). He first breaks with the Republican Party and announces himself an Independent, and then continues with his "Voiceful Speech":

> "I want to tell you that I shall enforce all the factory laws. [. . .]
>
> "I want to tell you that I shall enforce the laws governing child labor and the laws governing the labor of women.
>
> "I want to tell you that I shall enforce every other law, and shall try to secure the passage of further laws, which will make Whitewater a clean, forward-looking city, whose first consideration shall be the welfare of all.
>
> "And, ladies and gentlemen[,] [. . .] I wish I could address you all as fellow-voters! I want to tell you that I take back that foolish statement I made at the opening of the campaign.

"I want to tell you that I stand for, and shall fight for, equal suffrage!
"And I want to tell you that what has brought this change is what some of the women of Whitewater have shown me—and also some of the things our men politicians have done—our Doolittles, our Noonans." (167)

This powerful speech is the culmination of George's conversion; it also gives voice to the most progressive and most reactionary impulses in the book. The young politician has been profoundly affected by the efforts of his wife and "some of the women in Whitewater," the feminist oppositional community, to improve "the welfare of all"; these efforts have changed his political stance. He also breaks the hold that the business and liquor interests have on Whitewater, thus symbolically restoring independence and moral conscience to the city's politics.

The reader thus sees how the women are capable of bringing about a change in Whitewater's society at large by imagining what the public sphere (and not just the private) could be like if women had the vote. For the rest of that eventful day, George places his campaign in the hands of his new manager, Mrs. Herrington, and she and the other women spread the news of his eleventh-hour conversion so successfully that George ousts the incumbent. By first drawing attention to the campaign and then by disseminating the news of George's declaration, the suffragists foster a desire for change in their townspeople (and in particular, the men of the "better element" who can vote) and provide them with the opportunity to bring about that change by electing George. Genevieve, Betty, E. Eliot, Mrs. Herrington, and others have helped usher in a new, more honest government that will be especially responsive to the needs of its working-class citizens. At the end of *The Sturdy Oak*, the strength, competence, and power of the suffrage movement are embodied in the transformation of Whitewater's political scene. Women are now a political force with which to be reckoned, whether they have the vote yet or not.

Nevertheless, as we have seen, this powerful force derives much of its legitimacy in the novel by relying on racist stereotypes to describe who is responsible for the problems in the first place. It is not just, as George says, "what some of the women of Whitewater have shown [him]" that brings about his political conversion, but also "some of the things our men politicians have done—our Doolittles, our Noonans" (167). The second half of this equation draws a distinction between those of the most evolved "white race," who are not—except for a few greedy businessmen and selfish women—implicated in this corruption, and the "lower white races"—represented by Doolittle and Noonan—who are identified as the source of all the trouble. It also encapsulates, once again, how the progressive gender politics promoted in *The Sturdy Oak* are of a piece with the bigoted stereotypes about ethnic and immigrant minorities the book simultaneously disseminates. In this context, the name of the town and the name of the novel take on added resonance. "Whitewater," beyond what seems a literal allusion to a river, also foregrounds the need for white, i.e., "clean," drinking water, and thus sanitary, healthy living conditions, which should be a right of every citizen. At the same time, one cannot ignore the prominence of "white" in the town's name, perhaps suggesting that it is the "white," native-born male and female citizens who must be in charge to insure these conditions. "The sturdy oak" is also an allusion-laden phrase. As many reviewers and scholars have pointed out, the novel lampoons the popular contemporary cliché that a man should be "the sturdy oak" in a relationship while the woman should be the "clinging vine" by showing Genevieve's developing strength and George's moments of weakness. However, it is possible that a more obscure reference is also being made here. In an *Atlantic Monthly* article from 1896, Francis Walker writes that newer immigrants "have none of the ideas and aptitudes which fit men to take up readily and easily the problem of self-care and self-government, such as belong to those who are descended from the tribes that met under *the oak trees* of old Germany to make laws and choose chieftains" (emphasis added, 828). This association between oak trees and the origins of the Anglo-Saxon race suggests a less ironic, more conservative interpretation of the title. Granting women suffrage would return power to native-born, white American citizens, and, perhaps, in the readers' minds, reinstate Anglo-Saxon dominion over national politics.

The Sturdy Oak was one of the last fictional works to be written about the suffrage movement before it was dissolved by the successful fulfillment of its goal—the passage of the Nineteenth Amendment and its ratification in 1920. However, one could argue that Oreola Williams Haskell's book, *Banner Bearers: Tales from the Suffrage Campaigns*, written on the heels of ratification, is the culmination of the twentieth-century suffrage fiction's effort to "make it new" as well as the most fully realized picture of the achievements, shortcomings, and complexities of the mature suffrage movement. Haskell gives a sense of this ambitious project in her foreword:

> The little world of the suffrage worker was one of hard application and intense living. It had its saints and its sinners, its clear-visioned leaders and its devoted disciples, its silver-tongued orators, its poets and its artists. It had its humor, its pathos and its passion. [. . .]
> I who have been of this world, who love, understand and admire it, here aim

to give some sketches, however inadequate, of those who have waged its battles and won its victories [. . . .] To the many who have given themselves to the work of suffrage may these pages seem like the diary they have never had time to write, or like the portfolio of old photographs that, though faded, make the once vivid past live again. (3–4)

Although Haskell claims for her book a certain historical authenticity, her professed "love and admiration" for the suffrage movement infuse her work. Haskell may not need to convert readers to a cause already won, but like *For Rent* and *The Sturdy Oak*, *Banner Bearers* has an air of propaganda about it. Nevertheless, the flexible form that Haskell chooses, as well as the volume and breadth of her work, produces an insightful, revealing portrait of the twentieth-century movement, sometimes in spite of itself.[30] The text's twenty-two discrete yet interrelated stories allow the author to expand on and complicate previous depictions of feminist activist heroines, oppositional communities, and heterosexual love.

Several recent critical studies have enhanced our understanding of what a short story cycle is and what it does. In his work *The Contemporary Short Story Cycle*, James Nagel defines the genre as "the collection of a group of independent stories that contain continuing elements of character, setting, action, imagery, or theme that enrich each other in intertextual context" (15). *Banner Bearers* without question falls within these parameters. All the stories are set in a very specific time and place, New York in 1915 and 1917 during the campaigns, and often even more specifically, at the national suffrage headquarters. There are recurring characters in the stories, including Mrs. Leeds, a borough leader, Anna Storr (a thinly veiled allusion to Anna Howard Shaw), and Mary Genston Hale and Charlotte Chester Cleeves (both of whom seem to be based on Carrie Chapman Catt in her different roles as New York State president and then the national president of NAWSA).[31] The theme, of course, is the tireless work done for, and the inherent rightness of, the woman suffrage movement in America. Given *Banner Bearers*'s focus on the feminist activist community, J. Gerald Kennedy's observation about the short story cycle's communal element is suggestive: "Perhaps insofar as story sequences present collective or composite narratives, they may all be said to construct tenuous fictive communities" (xiv).[32] *Banner Bearers*'s form mimics the connections and disruptions that define any community, especially an oppositional one comprising a diverse group of people working for political change. Kennedy also provides a useful critical term for understanding short story cycles—the "collective protagonist," which is "either a group that functions as a central character (a couple, an extended family, a special-interest group) or an implied central character who functions as a metaphor (an aggregate figure who cumulatively may be 'typical' or 'archetypal' or 'the essence of' or 'the developing presence of' or 'the soul of' and so on" (59). The suffrage community is the fictive one constructed in *Banner Bearers*, and the term "collective protagonist" applies in two ways. The community itself is really the central character, but along the way, there are several diverse characters whose actions are "typical" nonetheless of the devotion and reform-mindedness that embodies Haskell's archetypal feminist activist heroine.

Unlike *For Rent* and *The Sturdy Oak*, with their small but representative collection of heroines—Delight Dennison and her friends Barbara and Lucia, and Genevieve, Betty, and E. Eliot—and certainly unlike nineteenth-century fiction about feminist activism with its clearly-identifiable central heroine, *Banner Bearers* has well over twenty feminist activist heroines who all have a moment on "center stage" in their stories; none, however, achieves prominence over the rest. This technique allows *Banner Bearers* to diversify the concept of fictional feminists in the twentieth century by depicting women of varying ages, marital status, and ethnic backgrounds in different socioeconomic situations.

In the first story, "The Invader," the heroine is very similar to the young, witty, college-educated women found in *For Rent* and *The Sturdy Oak*. Leslie Draycote is a field organizer for the New York Woman Suffrage Party, and she "invades" a small town outside the city. She is described as "very pretty," "unmistakably a lady," and behaving "with a blending of girlish appeal and of dignified deference" (8–10), and when she relates her background, she sounds very much like Delight Dennison or Betty Sheridan: "I was born, as the novelist says, of liberal-minded parents, educated in co-educational institutions and for a while earned my own living—teaching" (18). Leslie organizes a town meeting during which many people are convinced to support suffrage, including Pembroke Clarke, an affluent young man. The story ends with a budding romance between them. This story, then, seems like a miniature of many feminist activist narratives, and Leslie Draycote is typical of the popular, New Woman heroine in twentieth-century suffrage fiction.

This story is typical, too, in the way that it constructs the archetypal suffragist as implicitly white and native-born. She is "unmistakably a lady," and has had a "co-educational" college experience, which makes clear her racial and social status. And Leslie's speech (like some other stories in this collection) relies quite heavily on eugenics, a theory many intellectuals at the time accepted. For example, Leslie seems to be covertly employing eugenicist rhetoric when she tells her audience that suffragists encourage each woman to escape the confines of the home where she is "heedless of all the world forces outside that are at work threatening the purity, the well being, the safety of everything she holds dear. We are urging her to heed the call that comes from her to help with the great problems that concern the race [. . . .] We want to make her strong and wise, a fit mother for the race" (27). She appeals here to what in many ways, is clearly the relatively conservative strain of expediency arguments in favor of woman's rights, but her arguments are tied specifically to improving a particular "race" of people through better parenting. While this race could be simply the human race, it is more likely that Leslie is invoking the language of "variegated whiteness," voicing her concern first, for the Anglo-Saxon race, and then, perhaps, her desire to uplift the "lower races" of the immigrant and African American population.

This uplifting through purity and mothering is a hallmark of eugenics, a theory closely tied to scientific racialism and social Darwinism. Eugenicists claim that "races" can be improved by creating optimal conditions for their evolution. Methods of achieving these conditions range from the benign— healthy diets and living environments—to the sinister—forced sterilization of those people considered genetically undesirable. Furthermore, they claim that all of humanity can be improved by avoiding interbreeding, through which the "higher" races are "diluted" by the "lower races." A popular phrase during this era was "race suicide," which had been invoked earlier in the century by leaders such as Theodore Roosevelt to warn native-born, white Americans that intermingling with immigrant races would result in their being outpopulated and ultimately in their disappearance. While today eugenics is almost universally discredited as primarily a pseudoscientific justification for racism, it had considerable credibility in the early twentieth century. It certainly influenced the ideas of those who believed child-rearing was critical to bringing about progressive reform because, as Jacobson observes, many of those who were interested in eugenics "saw the immigrant [. . .] [primarily as] a parent of future-born American citizens" (69) and so thought that improving the lives of the mothers and children of these more marginal white "races" would protect American society. Leslie Draycote's desire, then, to make "more fit mothers for the race" suggests that giving white women the vote would be a positive eugenicist move because it would help the race improve and thus evolve.

Leslie Draycote is the white, educated, native-born woman-as-worker suffrage heroine familiar to readers of twentieth-century feminist activist fiction. However, "Sizing Up A Boss," the second selection in *Banner Bearers*, describes a considerably different kind of a feminist activist in the figure of "The Big Boss." This story is told from the perspective of reporter Meta Martin, who is writing a character sketch of the state suffrage organization's president, Mary

Genston Hale. Miss Hale is an older woman with "snow white hair, faultless complexion and dark blue eyes" who is known as "the busiest woman in New York" (40). As Miss Martin investigates, she hears diverse as well as contradictory reports about the Boss from people who know her well. She is described as the "slickest politician extant," "easy going—always ready with a joke and smile," "[d]angerous," and "a clear thinker, methodical and business like" (33–34). Miss Hale is also said to be domestic and she treats her friends warmly and the Irish woman who works for her kindly. All these descriptors, however, reveal her power and her almost celebrity status; "The Boss" is as influential as any male politician in New York. Miss Hale is not, like Leslie Draycote, the woman-as-worker but rather the suffragist-as-executive. Nevertheless, perhaps not surprisingly, Mary Genston Hale shares with Leslie Draycote a penchant for xenophobic rhetoric, telling Meta Martin, "We have to win out in the face of the Old World idea of woman's inferiority brought to us by our foreign born" (44). Though both heroines do indeed share assumptions about their own racial superiority, they are considerably different otherwise. In fact, in *Banner Bearers*, there are a plethora of suffrage heroines whose stories, while still implicitly maintaining a white, native-born bias, differ considerably from their fellow activists' stories in other respects. These feminist activist heroines comprise mothers who have lost daughters, young girls who have just moved to the city from the farm, rich widows, young wives on their death beds, nurturing grandmothers, and wealthy debutantes, just to name a few.

Banner Bearers also depicts a number of women who do *not* fit comfortably into the affluent, Anglo-Saxon suffragist mold. For example, "Rea, the Orator" is a factory worker who begins her lecturing career as a spokeswoman for the trade unions. Other socially marginalized characters—such as Josephine Cassidy, another trade-union speaker, and Mirra Volshen, an immigrant suffragist who canvasses in the tenements—are actually the principal heroines in their respective stories. Perhaps because of its sheer volume and its fragmented form, the text is able to give center stage at times to these factory workers, trade-union representatives, and immigrant women, thereby problematizing the privileged perspective from which most of the stories are told. It should be noted, however, that while *Banner Bearers* includes heroines from the "lower white races," it does maintain its monolithic whiteness by not including any African American females. Finally, there are many male suffrage heroes in this book (males who do not need converting), further diversifying the list of characters who can be called protagonists in this work.

So many different types of feminist activists, each devoted to the cause, produce the collective protagonist described by Kennedy, making the oppositional community of feminist activists the central heroine of the book. I do not, however, employ the term "collective protagonist" in a simplistic way. To be sure, these women and men work collectively to achieve woman suffrage, and the representation of so many characters united by a communal desire to see women enfranchised impresses on the reader the strength, solidarity, and widespread influence of the woman suffrage movement at this historical moment. Nevertheless, they do not all pursue this work in a homogenous, "collective" fashion; rather, what motivates them to seek gender reform through woman suffrage varies as do their methods for securing women's enfranchisement. This diversity is underscored by the formal properties of *Banner Bearers*; although there are recurring characters who link many of the stories, most of the characters only appear in one story, creating the sense that they are functioning in their own, smaller worlds as well as in the larger one of suffrage. Since these worlds never intersect in the text, one can imagine that many of the characters have never met and never will. Haskell's "collective protagonist" is therefore capable of depicting the connections among members of an oppositional community without erasing the differences that could potentially undermine that community.

This juxtaposition of heroines is not the only way *Banner Bearers* foregrounds communal activism; several stories in the collection vividly depict the countless daily activities that strengthen the bonds among suffragists. "Tenements and Teacups," for example, is about a committee of suffragists taking a break from their hard work and telling stories. It begins, "Pale and weary, the Squad came, one by one, into Headquarters. It was not only the last canvassing day before the Weekly Meeting, a day of heroic efforts to round out the week's record, but it was also the day for making up reports" (47). Like the book's title, "the Squad," the group's nickname, invokes military terminology (common in suffrage rhetoric) to denote both a sense of purpose and the mutual dependence of its members.[33] The women's tireless effort is signified by the sense of urgency accompanying their work, by their exhaustion, and by the mundane tasks they set about doing once inside headquarters, such as sorting "intention cards" and typing the results. The setting and action at the start of the story, then, paints a picture of an intimate oppositional community. And as the women finish their reports and take a break, they share stories about their week's campaigning, and through the act of storytelling, the sense of community is expanded considerably, in both number and richness of experience.

The first woman, Laura Steff, ironically titles her story, "The Fit and the Unfit." She has, she tells her squadmates, underestimated a new recruit, a wealthy, well-traveled novice. Mrs. Loring, the new recruit, surprises Laura by simply talking to many of the immigrants about their home countries, which she has visited, instead of making the typical suffrage appeals. By establishing a common ground of experience and appealing to their love of and pride in their native countries, Mrs. Loring creates sympathy for the cause. Another member of the Squad, Margaret Main, tells Laura, "Your story about someone who took a priceless thing into the tenements, reminds me by contrast of someone who took something out" (54). In her tale, "The Cure of the Tenements," Margaret relates how she visited the home of a rich, bitter widow living alone, convincing the older woman to canvass with her. Once in the tenements, the widow realizes how selfish she has been in her misery and that many in the tenements experience the same grief and loss she does. The widow is cured of both her solipsism and bitterness when she determines to help a "little seamstress" who has had no company but the suffragists, either; the widow embraces her and says, "Why, my dear, we're just alike" (58).

The final story is told by Mary Bradley, who has discovered a talented orator, Rea, among the female factory workers organizing a trade union. Rea, initially opposed to woman suffrage, learns more and agrees to speak for them because most speakers "don't see the bigness of the thing" (64). Rea's gift is quickly discovered and she is "snatched up to the pinnacle of suffrage oratory where the Cleeves, the Hales, and the Storrses speech and spout" (65). After this story, the Squad members, refreshed by their food and discussion, return to work. In Haskell's idealized vision, the bonds of affection and political commitment generated by the late suffrage movement extend beyond the Squad and into the homes of the richest and poorest in the city, uniting a diverse body of characters through a revolutionary love that recognizes a common humanity and shares a belief in gender reform. Also, with its communal shape and its independent—though interrelated—stories, "Tenements and Teacups" echoes the form of *Banner Bearers* as a whole. As Kennedy suggests, in its structure the short story cycle "curiously resembles the gathering of a group to exchange the stories that express its collective identity" (194). In fact, one could argue that the story's significance reaches beyond the textual border of *Banner Bearers*, serving as a microcosm of most of the books in this study, which likewise rely on storytelling to increase the number of real and imagined members of the nation's feminist oppositional community.

Other stories that make the reader aware, in unique ways, of the infinite variety of suffrage work and its far-reaching community of supporters are "A Musical Martyr" and "Switchboard Suffrage." The first is a short, funny story about Esther Marr, a "small town girl who had come to the city to wrest a living from a typewriter" (158) and who becomes enraptured with the suffrage movement. Esther develops a longing to "do something distinctive and special for the cause" (159); she sees a sign advertising "something new in suffrage"—"The Girl Bugler"—and decides she will also learn to play the bugle for outdoor meetings. Esther goes to headquarters on the weekend to practice (after being thrown out of her apartment) and she unwittingly helps the cause in three different ways. Her terrible playing scares away a talentless young woman auditioning to be a street speaker, thereby saving Mrs. Sylvester, the woman interviewing her, from having to turn her down. It also makes the high-strung leader of the French Committee (also meeting at headquarters) resign her position and go in search of peace and quiet, leaving an opening for a more competent person to take over. Finally, the Board of Directors, trying to avoid the media, is also secretly meeting at headquarters, and Esther's playing interrupts them in the middle of a heated debate, unintentionally averting them from passing a resolution that would have proven detrimental.

In the end, Esther is asked to stop playing the bugle at headquarters, but the narrator says, "it might have consoled Esther Marr somewhat if she had known that already her musical efforts had done three things for the Cause she loved" (171). This story introduces the reader to the many levels of suffrage work that are occurring all at once, which impresses on the reader the diverse activities happening across the city simultaneously as suffragists work unceasingly toward their goal. In a comical way, the story also suggests the inevitability of women's enfranchisement, because even a person's mundane, daily behavior inadvertently brings them closer to the vote.

The other story, "Switchboard Suffrage," is a short, first-person vignette spoken by the switchboard operator at headquarters. She frantically fields requests for pamphlets, street speakers, official comments, schedules, and other needs. In between these calls, she issues asides to a listener who has stopped by her desk. The plethora of calls she answers, as well as her running commentary on a typical suffragist's harried life, gives the reader the impression of a large, well-organized, professional community whose influence reaches across the city. The story is also interesting, however, because of what it reveals about the limitations of community. When a caller asks for "Mrs. Bullmount," the operator tersely informs her, "This isn't her organization. You want the Pickets, the National Woman's Party. No, we don't picket. It takes all our time to soothe the feelings of those who are offended by such antics, I mean tactics" (294–95). "Mrs. Bullmount" is clearly a derogatory reference to Alice Paul and her more militant brand of activism, and *Banner Bearers* insists on distancing NAWSA from the NWP.[34] While this disapproval of Paul and her tactics is to be expected, the fictional operator's condescension toward more recently converted suffragists is surprising. She tells her friend, "[T]hey're rolling in like Jordan's tide. Coming in at last so's they'll get some of the credit if we win. Most of 'em like to be on the bandwagon, but isn't it sickening to think they'll go about blowing how WE WON, and here's the real workers worn to a frazzle and won't have enough strength left to brag" (293). Resentment about the influx of new members is rarely expressed by suffragists, fictional or not, and its appearance in this story reveals a chink in an ostensibly harmonious community. Perhaps those members sincerely devoted to gender reform see in these "bandwagon suffragists" the vulnerability of their oppositional community to being "mainstreamed." Furthermore, this derogatory reference to new members, as well as the dismissive one to Mrs. Bullmount, are frank reminders of the divisions and conflicts inevitable within such a diverse oppositional community, even if its members are united by a common goal.

Radicals and late-comers notwithstanding, *Banner Bearers*'s overarching contention is that the feminist activist community is held together by a transcendent sympathy among women, suggested by the permeable boundaries of the tenement in "Tenements and Teacups" and described explicitly in a story that appears much later in the cycle, "The Heart of a Chief." The "chief" in this case is Charlotte Chester Cleeves, a character clearly modeled on Carrie Chapman Catt, the internationally known president of NAWSA at the time of ratification, In this story, Cleeves tells a woman who is seeking her help: "[T]he one feeling of which I am the most conscious as I travel up and down the highways and the byways of the world is my love for women. [. . .] With that love in one's heart, one can go to any woman, Turkish, Chinese, Armenian, Arabian, Russian, the highest and the lowest alike, and there will come a sympathy and an understanding that overcomes the barriers of strange languages and the iron bounds of old customs, a feeling that makes one meet another on the common ground of sex, sweeping away all the artificial things that society builds up" (316). In this description, we see another way that the short story cycle can present diverse or even contradictory perspectives. Whereas elsewhere, the idea of "race" seems integral to the prosuffrage rhetoric, here, Cleeves seems to suggest that scientific racialism—at least in so far as it creates a hierarchy among races—is simply one of the "artificial things that society builds up," dismissing its importance in the face of shared gender oppression.

According to Cleeves, the suffrage movement welcomes all women into its folds equally since they are already inherently bound together through their shared experience as females. Thus, regardless of ethnicity or class, all are accepted unequivocally into the oppositional community of feminist reformers. At first glance, such undifferentiated solidarity seems a worthy goal for this oppositional community; however, it becomes more problematic when one considers the way this essentializing representation ignores the racism and classism endorsed elsewhere in this book and in other twentieth-century suffrage fiction, and more importantly, the way that the description excludes difference even as it seems to embrace it. First, Africans and African Americans are conspicuously absent from Cleeves's list, and second, in this story and elsewhere, the social customs and the other material conditions that make the lived experiences of women radically different are not acknowledged as central to the identity of those women; rather, they are "[swept] away" as insignificant or "artificial" (316).

Juxtaposing these stories from *Banner Bearers* with another story published by Yezierska in the same year underscores the ways that privileged women can maintain—at the same time that they seem to reject—a hierarchy among women. In "Soap and Water," Yezierska's narrator is initially denied her teaching diploma from the college's dean, the aptly named Miss Whiteside. The narrator tells us that Miss Whiteside "said that she could not recommend [her] as a teacher because of [her] personal appearance" (132). According to the narrator, "She told me that my skin looked oily, my hair unkempt, and my finger-nails sadly neglected. She told me that I was utterly unmindful of the little niceties of the well-groomed lady. [. . .] And she ended with: 'Soap and water are cheap. Any one can be clean'" (132). Here, Miss Whiteside seems to acknowledge the narrator's economic disadvantage but nonetheless dismisses it as insignificant, promoting the ersatz democratic idea that all women can achieve the "niceties of the well-groomed lady" regardless of their socioeconomic position. By assuming that the difference between the narrator and her classmates is confined to the surface and can be eradicated by a little "soap and water," Miss Whiteside misses how deep-seated the difference is and how much American social structure—and her own progressive endeavors—is organized around it.

Such a fundamental understanding is not lost on the narrator, however, who is a laundress putting herself through school with little time, energy, or opportunity to worry about the "niceties of a well-groomed lady." She admits, "Often as I stood at my board at the laundry, I thought of Miss Whiteside, and her clean world, clothed in the snowy shirt-waists I had ironed. I was thinking—I, soaking in the foul vapors of the steaming laundry, I, with my dirty, tired hands, I am ironing the clean, immaculate shirt-waists of clean, immaculate society. I, the unclean one, am actually fashioning the pedestal of their cleanliness, from which they reach down, hoping to lift me to the height that I have created for them" (135). Miss Whiteside's belief that all women can be "ladies" is very much like Mrs. Cleeves's belief that differences in ethnicity are "artificial barriers" that are, like dirt, only surface details "covering" each female's essential womanhood.

From her less privileged perspective, Yezierska's narrator is able to see not only how false an assumed commonality among women is but also how belief in an essential womanhood undermines any possibility of a genuine community and revolutionary love among women that acknowledges the radical differences in their lives. Given this perspective, one must wonder, when the rich widow says to the seamstress in "Tenements and Teacups," "Why, my dear, we're just alike" (58), does the seamstress agree?

If *Banner Bearers* often overly idealizes the harmony achieved by such a diverse, diffuse oppositional community as the New York suffrage society, the book's cyclical form does accommodate at least one story that registers the discord that is to be expected to accompany such diversity. "Stallfed," for example, depicts the hostility between two suffragists from different socioeconomic and ethnic backgrounds. Mrs. Anson Beverly is one of the "bandwagon suffragists," a woman who, like her limousine, "fairly reeked of luxury" (99). The story pits this selfish, condescending woman against Josephine Cassidy, a suffragist and labor organizer, whom Mrs. Beverly sponsors on the latter's trip to New York to deliver a speech at a trade-union meeting. While the tension in this story clearly derives from the women's dissimilar class backgrounds, it seems likely that there is also a racial element involved; Mrs. Beverly's surname is of Old English origin, while Josephine Cassidy's name identifies her as being of Irish ancestry. Josephine is the rare working-class, immigrant heroine in suffrage fiction who actually speaks for herself, and her impassioned lecture is likewise unique in the way it directly appeals to her peers and acknowledges the peculiar bond between male and female workers: "I am one of you [. . . .] I come to you out of the circle of your working sisters, the women with rough hands and tired faces who help you do the rude work of the world. [. . .] Thank God I don't have to answer the old argument—woman's place is in the home—when I speak to you. You know why the sister and the daughter of the workingman have to go out into the stores and factories" (104).

After delivering the speech, Josephine returns with Mrs. Beverly to her mansion, where tension between the two women grows. Josephine overhears Mrs. Beverly declare that although she is a suffragist because "she is as up-to-date as anyone," she is "not accustomed to associating with the lower classes." And then comes another rare moment in suffrage fiction, a working-class woman reprimanding a wealthy one: "You are stallfed, soft in mind, body and soul, stuffed to repletion with luxuries, dying slowly because the canker of idleness and silliness is eating at your heart. How dare you take a great cause for a fad, to dally with it as you would with a poodle? [. . .] How dare you cast a shadow over the rocky path along which the workingwomen of the world are stumbling toward the goal of emancipation? Stallfed—a pampered, worthless animal. [. . .] I am one of the lower orders you despise, and you despise me because you are stupid. [. . .] No one can be a suffragist who is not first a democrat" (111).

As in *The Sturdy Oak*, the reader sees a woman worker's frustration with an affluent counterpart who ostensibly wants to help her. However, Mrs. Beverly's insincerity is the culprit here rather than the sort of naive, misguided enthusiasm that hindered Genevieve. Being prosuffrage has become "fashionable," and as a member of the "fashionable set," Mrs. Beverly does not want to be left behind. Josephine (and Haskell) is careful to clarify that Mrs. Beverly's shortcoming is not her wealth per se. Rather it's her particularly selfish, self-indulgent attitude, a conceitedness that makes her toy with a cause believed in so passionately by many women, poor and rich. Josephine's censure exemplifies how internal criticism and frank dialogue are necessary to improving an oppositional community, and the story's ending demonstrates the benefits of this self-critique. Mrs. Beverly learns how arrogant she has been, and when Josephine returns to visit this local organization months later, Mrs. Beverly is a changed woman who insists on doing the most menial jobs on the committee. Nevertheless, in a book that often idealizes cross-class relationships, this story intimates that there are vexed class issues rumbling under the surface in the woman suffrage movement. But unlike the Yezierska story, it does not go far enough in exposing the way that upper-class women depend on the more oppressed situation of working-class women to empower them; instead, "Stallfed" rather problematically suggests that a sincere commitment to suffrage reform can render this hierarchy irrelevant.

As much as *Banner Bearers* is about a diverse oppositional community of women united by their attempts to escape gender oppression in its various forms, its stories also reveal a great deal about the males who are included in that community as well as about those who are excluded. For example, in "Sissies," Marcus McCann, a small, poor, ignorant young man heckles other men marching in a suffrage parade, calling them "sissies." He is then "set straight" by a "big man" who forcibly leads him to his luxurious hotel room and tells him, "It's the big, virile men, the descendents of those who conquered the vast stretches of the western plains, descendants of those who had the hardy pioneer spirit that are most in favor of giving women a chance. It's the men with red blood in their veins and the spark of adventure in their souls, the men who left the East to its old set ways, that are the most generous and progressive" (287–89). This description, on the literal level, pays homage to the western states, like Wyoming, which gave women the vote well before the rest of the nation. More generally, though, it suggests that the more "masculine" a man is, the more he will be in favor of woman suffrage, and the allusion to the settling of the American West once again associates this masculinity (and heterosexuality and wealth) with native-born white men.

Men who are not Anglo-Saxon but still "white" stand in a considerably more vexed, though not irredeemable, relationship to the suffrage community. Like *The Sturdy Oak*, the story "Winds and Weathervanes" portrays immigrant men as agents of political corruption and reactionary gender politics. In Haskell's story, Patrick Quinn, an Irish man, is a leader of the local Democratic Party. Quinn is, predictably, against woman suffrage, as he tells the suffragist Mrs. Parker in rather colorful language: " 'I'd like to save them poor ladies from themselves. I know that voting is going to demoralize them sumpin fierce. it's [*sic*] going to break up their homes and keep 'em from getting married. Men aint [*sic*] going to marry women and support them in idleness and have them shoving against them in the polls' " (145). Like Doolittle and Noonan, Quinn is a caricature, speaking simplistic, easily refuted arguments against suffrage, though unlike Doolittle and Noonan, Quinn seems more like a buffoon than a villain. But what primarily distinguishes *Banner Bearers*'s depiction of this immigrant politician from its literary precursors is his redemption at the end of the story. His wife Maggie "laid down the law," telling him that "its [*sic*] time the mothers got their innings" (155). Here, we see the fruition of twentieth-century suffrage tactics to reach the immigrant population, especially the women, who will then potentially influence the men in their lives.

Quinn's conversion has an historical precursor. The Tammany Hall machine, which ran New York politics during the Progressive Era, was largely responsible for defeating woman suffrage in 1915, but in the 1917 campaign its members decided at the last minute not to oppose the state's suffrage referendum, thus insuring its passage. Most historians agree that they in part ended up deciding to support suffrage because many of the members had wives and daughters who worked for, and sometimes lead, the various state suffrage organizations. In reality (and in other stories in *Banner Bearers*), the leaders of Tammany Hall were primarily native-born and affluent, although they had wide support among the immigrant population, especially the Irish, because they had a tacit agreement with newly arrived men whereby they would help them find jobs and housing and in return the immigrants would vote for them and overlook their often corrupt political practices. While *Banner Bearers* gives voice to the idea that immigrants were largely responsible for the political corruption in early twentieth-century America, it is still significant that the short story cycle opens up the possibility of Irish and other immigrant men joining the oppositional community of feminist activists. In so doing, it deemphasizes native-born Americans' xenophobic anxiety about the "older European races," even though the book still depicts Quinn and other immigrant men in a condescending, stereotypical way.

It is worth noting that Mr. Larew, the leader of the local Republican Party in "Winds and Weathervanes," who is a native-born, American man from the South, occupies an analogous role to Patrick Quinn. While he is not, like Quinn, caricatured as ill-spoken or simplistic, he is depicted as being extremely reactionary, believing "women should be taken care of by men" (147). Mr. Larew, then, represents another mainstay in suffrage rhetoric; the white southern man is also considered a barrier to women's enfranchisement, because of his "old fashioned" ideas about gender, ideas that distinguish him from the more liberal, native-born white men from other regions of the country. Like Mr. Quinn, however, Mr. Larew is "converted" by a member of his family; when his daughter Virginia is born, he wants her to have "every privilege, advantage and right the world can give her" (156). While Mr. Larew's racial attitudes are not at issue in this story, white southerners were also typically identified as a racist element that had to be appeased by suffragists; for example, Anna Howard Shaw, the president of NAWSA from 1904 to 1915, refused to pursue fully a federal amendment for woman suffrage, because she argued the organization would lose the support of the southern suffragists, who wanted a state-by-state referendum, ostensibly so they could have more control over which women actually got the vote. There is certainly historical proof of southern suffragists' racism, but scholars Rosalyn Terborg-Penn and Marjorie Spruill Wheeler contest the clear-cut dichotomy between regions, arguing that "northern suffragists made the southern suffragists the scapegoats for their own racism" (Terborg-Penn 6). Thus, Mr. Larew's presence in *Banner Bearers* is perhaps an attempt to deflect racist charges against the northern suffrage community by reminding readers of the seemingly more prejudicial attitude of white southerners with regard to race and gender.

To the twenty-first-century reader of late feminist activist fiction, however, northern suffragists' prejudice against African Americans is evident. For the most part, *Banner Bearers* is void of African American characters, as are *The Sturdy Oak* and *One Pedestal—For Rent* (with the exception of Mrs. McKim's coachman), and such an absent presence signifies a corresponding absence in the mainstream American suffrage movement.[35] One story in Haskell's collection, however, demonstrates the way that African American men are completely marginalized in the book's model of oppositional community formation. "The Yellow Button" stresses the suffragists' patriotism during World War I, and during a train ride, Mrs. Slaight, the main character, encounters many people with whom she discusses the war effort. During this ride, she is approached by an African American man who addresses her in a comic, minstrel way: "'Scuse me lady, but if dey is anythin' I kin do to make you more restfulsome ah'd be mos' gladfully obligated to do dat'" (199). The porter has seen her "yaller button" (a suffrage pin) and wants to express his thanks to the "suffragette ladies [who] give money for a Y hut for cullud soldiers at de [war] camp" where his son is stationed (200).

At the end of the trip, she is greeted by a very public display of not only this porter's gratitude but also that of others on the train. According to the porter who has been attending her throughout her trip, "The [other] pohters want to show dere feelins, ma'am" (204). Mrs. Slaight, therefore, walks through "two rows of uniformed and blackfaced men standing at rigid attention," whose "black hands flew to wooly heads in snappy salutes" as she passed and whose "humble but adoring eyes" watched her walk through. "The Yellow Button" demonstrates the way Haskell fantasizes the gratitude of African Americans who have been helped by white feminist activists. This fantasy is clearly fueled by white women's self-perception as the "empowered sanctified uplifters" of African Americans, a role that, according to Louise Michele Newman, white female activists had claimed in relation to African Americans since they first entered the abolitionist movement (62). Further, this minstrelesque portrayal of African American men precludes any possibility of their being members of the oppositional community; they are simple, childlike creatures who display no concern for larger social questions. As such, they are radically different from all the other characters in this book, including those who are initially antisuffrage, like Quinn and Larew. This difference underscores the subtle racism that informs not only the perspective of suffragists but others at this time period. Those of the "lower white races," such as the Irish, at least have the potential to assimilate into mainstream society; African Americans, however, are designated as fundamentally "other." As such, they are not considered worthy of recruitment by white suffragists, at least according to this fictional portrayal, which attributes to the porters an infantile acquiescence in reform sentiment but denies them any political agency.

Banner Bearers, then, is perhaps the most intriguing fictional portrayal of the twentieth-century American feminist community. Its form inclines it to revealing the ambiguities, complications, and contradictions inherent in forming such a community; in spite of its investment in portraying the harmony and inclusivity of the community, its diverse subject matter allows the reader to glimpse the discord and exclusivity that a more seamless narrative might conceal. *Banner Bearers*'s fragmented form also lets it alter the idea of "romance" more radically than any other work of feminist activist fiction in this study. In her introduction, Ida Husted Harper describes *Banner Bearers* as having "twenty-two [...] sketches, each embodying one special feature of the many sided effort to win the vote and all expressed in narrative style, a number of them with a love story interwoven" (5–6). In fact, the number of stories with the traditional heterosexual romance plot of courtship is five, and there are three other stories in which heterosexual couples figure prominently. This distribution means that less than half the stories are concerned with romance as conventionally understood; the rest depict women (and sometimes men) working together as friends and colleagues, involved in a wide variety of activities, concerns, and plots that have nothing to do with courtship or marriage. This shift in focus decenters the heterosexual romance plot completely, making it only one of many narratives in the text instead of a central thread as in the earlier novels about feminist activist heroines.

Furthermore, the various permutations of the romance plot in the cycle reiterate the cross-class and cross-cultural appeal of gender reform, even if they rely on stereotypical characters to do so. In "The Invader," the hero and heroine seem to be of the prosperous, predominantly white, native-born middle class, like the book's middlebrow readership. "Silent Forces" and "When Hester Hikes" take place among the very affluent "society set" in New York. The first is a story of negotiation in which Elinor, a suffrage sympathizer although not an active worker, shows Richard, who is pursuing her, that she believes in gender equality and is not like the other debutantes in their circle. Richard reveals to her at the end that he, too, is a member of the "Silent Forces" of sympathizers because he has seen firsthand the corrupting influence of the narrow sphere in which society women are inscribed. "When Hester Hikes" is the traditional story of a suffragist whose love interest must convert to supporting suffrage before she will accept him. There is a twist, however. While Hester is away on a suffrage hike, it is a male family friend who enlightens her future husband about gender roles by loaning him a book by Lester Ward, a prominent intellectual who writes about evolution from a feminist perspective.[36] In "The Nail," Mirra Volshen, a Jewish immigrant, encounters a young man, Mr. Mendel, also Jewish, who is against woman suffrage. Mirra is an intelligent, dedicated suffragist who can speak five languages and who is as sympathetically portrayed as any other woman in the book; however, like Patrick Quinn in "Winds and Weathervanes," Mendel is caricatured, both because of his "race" and his "Old World" ideas about suffrage. Nevertheless, despite his passionate, temperamental nature and his insistence that women are only suited to be wives and mothers, Mendel, who is liberal in many other ways, is converted to suffrage by his love for Mirra as well as by his firsthand knowledge of the dangers of factory work. Thus, like Patrick Quinn, Mendel is also seen as capable of conversion and consequently, good citizenship. Among other things, the juxtaposition of these various stories with a "love interest intertwined" represents the exponentially growing ranks of men who would eventually vote to give their counterparts the same right.

More provocative than these multiple heterosexual romance narratives, however, is *Banner Bearers*'s overt attempt to expand the definition of romance as it applies to women. Haskell begins questioning the word's narrow connotation of sexual love for a man in her foreword where she describes the cultural changes wrought by the suffrage movement: "It developed a new loyalty—that of woman to woman; a new romance—the love of woman for the woman leader; a new faith—that of the woman in the greatness of her sex and the possibilities of her womanhood" (3). Using the word "romance" to describe a woman-to-woman relationship is certainly radical; the passion and ardor normally reserved for a woman's spouse is, Haskell suggests, apparent in a woman's love for her leader. This new romance is evident in the adulation of many suffragists in the book. The reporter in "Sizing Up A Boss" experiences it when she finally interviews Mary Genston Hale: "Meta Martin, feeling that she was looking straight into the mind and heart of the woman before her, felt a sense of awe that struggled with a boundless admiration. For a few moments she tried to express it" (45).

Esther in "A Musical Martyr" has a similar reaction upon meeting Mrs. Tilney, the borough chairman: "Esther, beholding a woman handsome with a wholesome, outdoor beauty, brimming with vitality, full of scintillating ideas, with breezy, democratic manners and a spontaneous and brilliant smile, fell at once under the spell of her charms, as had hundreds before her. Henceforth Esther put herself out to play vassal to this queenly leader" (158). Alair Dumain is equally overcome by Charlotte Chester Cleeves in "The Heart of a Chief." Alair, a talented public speaker, had been encouraged to solicit Cleeves for help by her recently deceased husband, who had a familial connection to the great leader. However, Alair is too nervous to approach her and so studies her from afar for several months, becoming so consumed that she has dreams "of the wonder woman, leading, leading, on and on across the world" (301). Gradually, "her spirit became enkindled, until at length she caught from Charlotte Chester Cleeves some of the passionate devotion, the steady determination [. . .] that made her all at once one with the army of workers in the city and akin to their leader in a deep and vital sense" (303). These striking encounters show these women experiencing stirring physical feelings and subsequently becoming enchanted with not only the cause but also the person. Admittedly, there is a potentially disturbing element in this adulation; after all, any relationship in which one member is so clearly under the influence of the other is problematic. However, Haskell seems to be depicting the almost religious reverence suffragists have for the movement and extending it to its leaders. Thus, the author liberates the term "romance" from its heterosexual moorings, applying it to this intense revolutionary love that instills unwavering devotion in suffragists for those who lead them.

In her essay "Femininity Slashed: Suffragette Militancy, Modernism and Gender," Caroline Howlett makes some observations about how the British suffrage movement disrupted the connection between femininity and heterosexual romance that prove useful for reading *Banner Bearers* as well. In order to blur the "bald distinction between 'life' and 'art'" that keeps us from reading "a set of cultural practices" employed by the suffragists as "modernist" (73), Howlett analyzes how activists' attention to feminine dress and their interest in looking attractive "disrupted femininity by displaying it in the context of militancy"(73). For example, "[t]here is much evidence that the 'beauty' and femininity of the suffragettes with whom [potential activists] came into contact were of vital importance in attracting women to join the movement" (75). The stories in *Banner Bearers* about suffragists who are captivated by their female leaders certainly adds to this evidence and connects the idea that looking good was a militant act to the American suffrage movement. Howlett argues that when women's goal in dressing well is to attract other women (instead of men), the heterosexual order is radically subverted. Howlett goes so far as to argue that through such a "woman-oriented feminine performance," suffragists "succeeded in disrupting the meaning of femininity in general [. . .]" and thus "femininity lost its stability as a signifier in the heterosexual economy" (77). In a similar way, Haskell's story of "a new romance—the love of woman for the woman leader" radically disrupts the stability of the heterosexual romance narrative and reinterprets femininity, displacing the patriarchal economy altogether.

Haskell's aptly titled "A Touch of Romance" liberates the term "romance" even further. The narrative follows a traveling suffragist, Mary Norris, whose work is thwarted by both well-meaning friends and her domineering uncle, all of whom believe she would be happier giving up her political work and finding a husband. What is most revolutionary about this story, however, is not the action but the rhetoric. The centerpiece of the story is a lengthy speech in which Mary addresses what she regards as her friends' and family's misguided intentions. She tells the crowd, "Then, too, there are those who lament over what they choose to call the absence of romance in my life. They say this of one who is in daily touch with the romance of a great cause" (217). Mary begins her redefinition of romance by claiming that passion and fulfillment can come from work and belief in an ideal as much as it can come from a relationship with another human being. She continues by comparing the contradictory ways "romance" is applied to the lives of women and men:

> No one says to boys and young men that there is but one romance in the world for them, the romance of a personal love. Our books are full of men's romances of adventure and high enterprise. We have had the knight, the crusader, the explorer, the inventor, the martyr and the Seeker for the Holy Grail. To-day, woman may enter this larger life of mingled thought, fancy and fact. She may have her pretty hearthfire love just as women did of old, but she may have also the romance of adventure and of big enterprise to fire her imagination, stir her pulses, spur her on to the heroic effort and to touch the spiritual forces of her soul. (217–18)

Mary's speech presages in many ways Northrop Frye's analysis of romance in *The Secular Scripture*. According to Frye, romance in its broadest sense is intimately associated with imagination, as opposed to realism, which is grounded in the material world of experience. Frye also argues that romantic fiction "brings us closer than any other aspect of literature to [. . .] man's vision of his own life as a quest" (15). Frye, however, is primarily referring here to the masculine tradition of Sir Walter Scott and others. Mary's redefinition opens this tradition to women, claiming for them both a creative and a literary prerogative that once exclusively belonged to men. The suffrage movement has made a metaphorical space in which they can imagine a world in which prescribed gender roles have vanished, a future with more opportunities and more choices. It has also allowed for a radical rethinking of the concept of romance in feminist activist fiction. The heroine is no longer confined to the heterosexual romance plot; "she may also have the romance of adventure and of big enterprise." Her life can be written as a quest that is not necessarily destined to end at the altar, and an infinite number of stories are now possible that do not have to include "personal love" with a hero as the central component.

In some ways, *Banner Bearers* is a watershed text in the tradition of feminist activist fiction. Works that come before are primarily concerned with influencing what readers think about woman's rights, and woman suffrage in particular, and the works that come after are written from a more distanced perspective, providing a retrospective analysis. *Banner Bearers*, however, is positioned at the historical moment when suffragists are celebrating their victory and anticipating their future with excitement. As such, it provides a unique opportunity to ponder what the movement gained and lost during its seventy-two-year existence. Three stories at the end of the collection are especially fruitful in this respect. The first, "Methods," shows the way perceptions about feminist activists have shifted over time. In it, a family has scheduled a conference to decide how to spend a recent inheritance. The three female members, Mrs. Arbuckle, her daughter, Eloise, and an Aunt Essie, use this family conference as an opportunity to test the "methods" of their various affiliations, NAWSA, the NWP, and an antisuffrage organization, respectively. The males in the family discern the plan from the way each woman is dressed. Stephen Arbuckle, the son, observes, "It's as plain as a drop of ink in a pan of snow. [. . .] It's the colors. Mother, yellow, white and blue, the conservative wing; siss, yellow, white and purple, the militants; Aunt, pink with roses, the antis" (272).

The story distinguishes among the women not only by their clothing but also by the charities they recommend and the tactics they use. Aunt Essie, in a "cooing voice," suggests using the money to build a homeless dogs' shelter, and she ends her appeal by "bursting into tears" (278). On the other end of the spectrum, Eloise, "with youthful disdain," demands that the money be used to subsidize the work of female artists, because they have "mighty little" chance of success otherwise (277). In fact, Eloise feels so impassioned, she threatens to "organize these struggling geniuses and have them besiege the guardians of this fund night and day to apply it to their needs" (277). Mrs. Arbuckle, meanwhile, is calm and reasonable in demeanor, telling the group, "Most people [. . .] are influenced by reason and common sense, and can be brought to a conclusion by the patient insistence on good points, presented calmly[,] pleasantly and continuously" (276). With this method, Mrs. Arbuckle argues for her proposed charity, eugenics, which she calls "the science that will teach the race how to bring into the world children that are well born, fitted to cope with disease, adversity and world conditions" (274).

Although the story makes very plain with whom the reader should sympathize, the grandmother's commentary at the end makes the point overtly: "Not only is suffrage to be decided, but also the methods that must obtain between men and women. Will they decide for reason, and the pleasantness of equality, or for threats and force, or for the tears and the foolish sentimentality?" (280). This triptych of women, and by extension, methods, is significant for feminist activist fiction. A certain type of heroine, the lady-like, respectable white suffragist, had by this time become mainstream, and those opposed to woman suffrage like Aunt Essie were pushed to the side because they were seen as holding with outmoded views. At the same time, more militant activists like Eloise remained on the fringe of society. However, the acceptance of a "certain type of suffragist" did not come without a price. Much of the woman's rights movement's sweeping vision for gender reform, stated in the Declaration of Sentiments in 1848, had been watered down to narrow, expedient goals like woman suffrage. Without question, the "conservative" branch of feminist activists had achieved important advancements for women, but the fundamental challenge to gender oppression that was the legacy passed down from Stanton and her magazine, *The Revolution*, survived in the more militant feminists, who would continue to lobby for equal rights legislation after ratification of the Nineteenth Amendment. What had not been lost, however, was the assumption of white privilege that had informed the work of most feminist activists ever since the abolitionist movement. Mrs. Arbuckle promotes eugenics, a detail that reminds the twenty-first-century reader that for all its accomplishments, the liberal gender politics of the woman suffrage movement has always been inextricably dependent on reactionary racial politics, a disturbing symbiosis about which Anna Cooper complained thirty years before.

The final two stories in *Banner Bearers* complement each other nicely, because each, in very different ways, remembers the past and points to the future with optimism. "Four Generations" is about the last days of a suffrage pioneer, Phoebe Caldwell, who was a feminist activist "when it took real courage, real strength of character to fight for suffrage" (320). She lives with her daughter and granddaughter, second- and third-generation suffragists who are driven (especially Ina, the granddaughter) by a fervent desire for Phoebe to live to see the suffrage amendment pass. Phoebe, unbeknownst to her daughter and granddaughter, makes plans to attend the great "Pageant of Protest," a spectacular suffrage show to be staged at the largest opera house in New York. Once there, Phoebe is pressed into service to represent the pioneers on stage, and the adulation and gratitude she receives from the other suffragists is a highlight of her life. However, Phoebe is injured after the show and dies a few days later. Before she does, she tells her granddaughter, "I have my reward already. [. . .] Do not feel sorry, Ina, that the pioneers cannot stay to the end. We blazed the trail. We did a glorious thing. To make possible the rest. That is our reward. The victory—I'll—I'll know it wherever I am" (333). While this story portrays the new, spectacle-driven suffrage movement of the twentieth century, it is also a poignant reminder of the legacy of feminist activism in the United States. In its portrayal of three generations, the story depicts an oppositional community that spans time as well as space and that is bound by a revolutionary love not only for each other but for those not yet born. The title, "Four Generations," underscores this continuity and points to the next generation that will reap the benefits of the suffrage movement.

"The Great Shortcut" depicts a very different intergenerational relationship. The title refers to the passage and ratification of the federal amendment, a more direct route to gaining the vote than state-by-state referendums, and the story takes place after passage but before ratification. Parker Flint is an important politician in the New York Democratic Party, and in his cynical political ideas and his corrupt methods of achieving power, he typifies the white leaders of Tammany Hall. Flint, however, can feel his control of the party slipping. Already, he is being challenged by younger, more progressive men who are now also advising the governor, a job that heretofore belonged to Flint exclusively. These younger men urge the governor to facilitate ratification, but Flint opposes it. Flint's opposition, however, is worn away, first, by a visit from the daughter of his first love, a devoted suffragist like her mother, and then by his own daughter, Alice, who is a recent, enthusiastic convert. She appeals to her father to support "The Great Shortcut" and the age to which it leads, "a wonderful age when Woman the Passive Spectator will be no more and Woman the Creator will come, to be a powerful lever to control mighty forces. [. . .] It will not be your age, Dad, but mine. Yes, mine. A age when men will not sorrow that their daughters are not sons, since both sexes will have equal opportunities, equal rights, equal incentives, equal hopes, ambitions and rewards" (346).

The "Old Boss," as Flint is known, is finally persuaded, "in the two strongest ways, through his love of Alice, through his love for power" (348). Only by embracing the progressive future can Flint remain influential, at least for the time being. When ratification happens, he tells Alice, "It has been a great fight, as great a one as the world has ever seen. It will be a fine thing to look back upon" (350). Alice replies to this concession, "I will leave the looking back to you, Dad. As for me, I am content to look ahead" (350). *Banner Bearers* ends with this exchange, suggesting a utopian changing-of-the-guard in the political world, the historical precedent of which was Tammany Hall's reversal on the suffrage question between the 1915 and 1917 campaigns. It depicts the dissolution of the old, corrupt order and the beginning of a new age when women will have the voice in government for which they have fought for over seventy years. There may, however, be more to this utopian prediction than Flint's daughter admits. While women's political participation is seen as a harbinger of social reform and gender equality, Parker Flint's conversion might also be read symbolically as a hopeful sign that woman suffrage will help quell some of the political corruption associated with the immigrant population and restore control of American life to the Anglo-Saxon race, much as Flint's conversion reinstates him in the governor's office.

By focusing on both the formal and ideological aspects of *Banner Bearers*, as well as those of *For Rent* and *The Sturdy Oak*, I have attempted to follow the lead of the many feminist critics who have problematized the distinction between "high" and "low" culture in the early twentieth century, situating these works in the murky center of middlebrow American literary culture, in which, as Botshon and Goldsmith argue, writers "successfully married [artistic and popular success]" (11). Given their overt political agendas for bringing about a utopian changing-of-the-guard in the political world, it is tempting to foreground the content of these works to the exclusion of their form, treating them as pure polemic rather than as conscious literary constructs. I would argue, however, that the authors of *For Rent—One Pedestal, The Sturdy Oak,* and *Banner Bearers* are aware of the importance of their form and use the structure of their books to enhance their readers' emotional response and make their arguments more persuasive. They hope thereby to create even more sympathy for the increasingly popular movement and they connect their attempt at being "literary" to their desire for popularity and gender reform. The authors adapt literary conventions, both traditional and modern—the epistolary form, the composite novel, the short story cycle, and the heterosexual romance narrative—to their liberal agenda. These works also "share a common concern with women's autonomy as free agents" (Honey, "Feminist New Woman" 87) that is characteristic of American New Woman stories, but again, they modify this popular contemporary genre to make explicit the causal relationship between feminist activism and women's autonomy; women can gain greater independence not only by possessing the vote but also by joining an oppositional community that is agitating for it.

At the same time, I have attempted to show that these books are also middlebrow in that they rely, paradoxically, on some of the more conservative assumptions of their mainstream audience in order to promote their progressive ideas about gender reform. As I have noted, Rubin identifies the audience for middlebrow fiction as "white Anglo-Saxon Protestant readers," and I contend that the race and social privilege this designation implies extends to twentieth-century feminist activist communities, both real and fictional. Not only are most of the heroines in these works implicitly and explicitly constructed as white and native-born, but their ability to persuade their intended white, native-born audience often depends on their easing the xenophobic and racist anxieties of that readership regarding the increasing power and influence of ethnic minorities, specifically those of the "lower white" and African American races. In order to exploit these anxieties, the texts often cast immigrant men as the antagonists, depicting them as politically corrupt and opposed to woman suffrage, and when they depict African American men at all, they do so in an infantilizing, demeaning way meant to make clear the contrast with the maturity and intelligence of the white suffragists, underscoring the latter's ostensibly greater capacity for self-government.

Immigrant and/or working-class women occupy a rather ambiguous place in the fictional gap between these enlightened white, middle-class suffragists and these corrupt or ineffectual ethnic male antagonists. All three books stress the essential womanhood that unites white suffrage leaders with their more socially and financially disadvantaged female counterparts, and in fact, following Harriot Stanton Blatch's lead, they seem to construct a vision of a feminist oppositional community comprised primarily of "the woman worker, both wage-earning and professional" (DuBois, "HSB" 163) that, at least rhetorically, ignores the class and ethnic distinctions among women of all the "white races," though, historically and fictionally, the community was never entirely open to African American women, even though they, too, belonged to organizations that supported suffrage.[37] What is clear, however, is that by and large, these works about twentieth-century feminist activists romanticize the solidarity of the feminist activist community by dismissing the diversity of its members as "artificial," as Haskell does in *Banner Bearers*. By attempting to ignore the organic, fundamental importance of race and class in women's lives and pretending that these things do not create a hierarchy among women, these books perpetuate that hierarchy in their depictions.

As we have seen, however, even this romanticized vision of a reform community is not seamless; the discontent of immigrant and/or factory women rises to the surface in some fictional episodes and reading these examples of feminist activist literature alongside the stories of Edna Ferber and Anzia Yezierska helps further reveal the tensions and fissures in the community of American feminist activists. Thus, I would suggest that fictionally depicting the mature suffrage movement presented these authors with a uniquely "modern" task. T. S. Eliot's famous line from *The Waste Land* (a "high" modernist text if ever there was one), "These fragments I have shored against my ruins," is often quoted as emblematic of the modernist challenge to make connections among disparate things while still accommodating the fractures. The formal nature of the three texts in this chapter allow them to engage in a similar balancing act between unity and disparity, which, perhaps, diffuses the importance of the disparity in a way that is counterproductive. Nevertheless, in each case, the work foregrounds communal solidarity while it simultaneously problematizes it through its unwillingness—or more often, its inability—to conceal the dramatic contradictions and fissures just below the surface of the twentieth-century suffrage movement.

In her book *The History of the Woman's Party*, Inez Irwin presents the historical correlative to this literary balancing act: "It was an all woman movement. Indeed, often women who on every other possible opinion were as far apart as the two poles, worked together for the furtherance of the Federal Amendment. [. . .] It was as though, among an archipelago of differing intellectual interests and social convictions, they had found one little island on which they could stand in an absolute unanimity" (468). Just as the literary texts invoke an essentialist notion of womanhood to overcome differences among women, the movement itself relied on a shared sense of the injustice they had experienced as women to forge bonds among its feminist activists. On that island of shared injustice, though, members of the National Association of Colored Women stood alongside women like Belle Kearney who argued that giving women the vote would ensure white supremacy. Wealthy native-born suffragists who wanted to "protect" their way of life from the influx of immigrants and the encroachment of rapid urbanization had very different motives for standing on this suffrage island than the female immigrants and factory workers who wanted the vote to protect their lives and livelihoods from the insensitivity and greediness of capitalist moguls.

Unfortunately, the American feminist movement that was founded in the nineteenth century and flourished in the first two decades of the twentieth was not nearly as successful at shoring up its fragments as its fictional counterparts. Eventually, it became evident that an oppositional community whose rhetoric was based on an idealized (and exclusionary) construction of womanhood that ignored the differences of race, class, and ethnicity among its female members was bound to fail. After ratification, NAWSA declined into the much smaller, politically toothless League of Women Voters, and although Alice Paul kept the members of the National Woman's Party politically active, theirs were small, ineffectual voices. Most white women voted along the same party lines as their husbands, fathers, and brothers; African American women were consistently disenfranchised through Jim Crow laws, just like their male counterparts. The end result was that women's political participation actually declined between the 1920s and the 1950s, until the civil rights movement of the 1960s created a renewed political fervor that eventually launched the second wave of feminism in America.

CHAPTER FOUR

The Political Is Personal

What Henry James's *The Bostonians* Can Teach Feminist Activists

Any study about American fiction devoted to feminist activism in the nineteenth and early twentieth centuries must necessarily consider Henry James's 1886 novel, *The Bostonians*. It is, after all, the only canonical text from the nineteenth century whose central heroines are woman's rights activists. For that reason, it has for years seemed anomalous not only in James's oeuvre, but in American literature in general.[1] Nevertheless, at the time James wrote to his editor, J. R. Osgood, to describe his plans for the novel, the author thought his topic exemplary rather than unique:

> The subject is good and strong, with a large rich interest. The relation of the two girls should be a study of those friendships between women which are so common in New England. [. . .] At any rate, the subject is very national, very typical. I wished to write a very *American* tale, a tale very characteristic of our social conditions, and I asked myself what was the most salient and peculiar point in our social life. The answer was: the situation of women, the decline of the sentiment of sex, the agitation on their behalf. (*Complete Notebooks* 19–20)

James's assertion that the debate over gender reform was the "most salient" point in American life was made at a time when the woman's movement was taking its first tentative steps into the national limelight, making it clear that it was not a "fad" that would soon die out. For example, in 1882 (during which time James was visiting the United States) both houses of Congress established standing committees to hear reports on woman suffrage. To twenty-first-century readers, his related contention that the subject of woman's rights was a "very national, very typical" one for fiction might seem less plausible, given the critical invisibility of most novels written about feminist activism. However, as I have shown, there were in fact several authors writing fiction about the "agitation on [women's] behalf" throughout the second half of the nineteenth century. Because I am interested in the dialogic relationship between these literary texts and the actual woman's rights movement, as well as what real-world feminist activists can learn from such a relationship, my focus up until now has been novels expressly written to promote women's rights. It might be difficult to see the possibility of either dialogue or instruction in *The Bostonians*'s relationship to real-world feminist reformers, but I would maintain that the potential for both exists in James's novel.

Unfortunately, many woman's rights activists contemporary with James did not see this potential. In a review published on March 13, 1886, in the *Woman's Journal*, the official organ of the American Woman Suffrage Association (AWSA), Lucia T. Ames offers a critique of *The Bostonians* that is representative of the way most of them received his novel.[2] Although Ames claims that "[I]t seems hardly worth while to take the trouble to issue a protest against this caricature," she issues a rather lengthy one. She calls *The Bostonians* "inartistic," claims the two female protagonists, Olive and Verena, "belong neither to Boston nor any other city," and assures her reader that this fictional "world of abnormal women" will "elicit a universal protest." She ends by suggesting a new name for the novel— "The Cranks." There is no evidence of a massive outpouring of disapproval from feminists—like Ames predicted—but any number of woman's rights activists likely kept quiet not because they tacitly approved of the novel but because they were indifferent to it. In her article "Feminist Sources in *The Bostonians*," Sara Davis deSaussure writes, "the feminists who might have raised objections to the novel were busy writing their own history and were uninterested in the unflattering picture of women's rights in *The Bostonians*" (586).

Ames's disavowal of the suggestion that there was any resemblance between James's depiction of the woman's rights activists and the real-world woman's movement, on the one hand, and the apathetic silence of many other feminist activists, on the other, set a critical precedent for disassociating *The Bostonians* from the actual woman's rights movement and by extension, from novels that depict feminist activism sympathetically.[3] On the rare occasion that it has been compared to other fictional portrayals of gender reform societies, James's novel is most often yoked together with books like Sarah Josepha Hale's *The Lecturess* (1839) or Bayard Taylor's *Hannah Thurston* (1863), which oppose woman's rights ideology by depicting feminist activism in a derogatory way.[4] However, the complexity and volume of critical essays about James's woman's rights novel, many of which argue persuasively for an underlying feminist intent, suggest that *The Bostonians*'s relationship to the other books in this study is more complicated than mere opposition.[5] Indeed, many recent critics (and some earlier ones as well) stress the indeterminacy of the novel's political position. Jean

Gooder, for example, concludes that at the end of the novel "we are still left with glaringly unreconstructed oppositions" that enact "the 'bewildering modernity' of James's subject" (114). Gooder's contention articulates the impossibility of claiming for *The Bostonians* any definitive political purpose, feminist, antifeminist, or otherwise. Therefore, my concern is not with James's agenda, but with his insights.

It is, after all, *The Bostonians*'s insightful portrait of feminist activist heroines that connects it to the other novels in the tradition I have developed thus far. The most telling characteristic of a work in this tradition is its impact on its real-world counterpart, the ways it contributes to the formation and continuing viability of actual feminist oppositional communities. A work overtly sympathetic to the woman's movement models a vision of reform for its readers to emulate and also analyzes that vision. An ambiguous novel like James's, however, is not so easily categorized. Still, although the author's intentions are impossible to elucidate, I think it safe to assert that he was not, like the other authors I study, consciously writing to either convince his readership to support the "agitation on [women's] behalf" or to help feminist activists improve the way they conduct their political work. Nevertheless, I believe the key to opening a productive dialogue, albeit perhaps a speculative one, between *The Bostonians* and the nineteenth-century woman's rights movement lies in Lucia T. Ames's scathing commentary.

Ames begins her review by admitting that one often wishes to "see himself [...] in the light of other people's opinions [...] because there is a certain satisfaction in seeing what is familiar through the eyes of another, if that other be a man of insight" (82). And she had anticipated, she continues, that James's novel would provide her with an "opportunity to obey the injunction 'Know thyself.'"[6] Ames's subsequent remarks make clear, however, that the Jamesian portrait of the woman's movement did not in fact give her that chance, and we can assume that therefore she does not consider James to be a "man of insight." Ames's dissatisfaction stems from two things. First, she charges (fairly, I would argue) that *The Bostonians*'s representation of the tenets of feminist reform is vague: "We nowhere find any bill of particulars as to the causes of martyrdom and tyranny under which women are at present suffering, and we do not recollect that any specific demands are made whereby this terrible condition of things shall be ameliorated" (82). Her other accusation is, as we've seen, that the novel is full of "abnormal women" who bear no resemblance to actual feminist reformers; unfortunately, this complete disassociation between the actual and fictional activists prematurely shuts down a potentially useful reading experience.

If James's novel is weak on the particulars of the woman's rights movement, it is nonetheless an exhaustive, accomplished study of the psychology of reform movements in general and the woman's rights movement in particular. James is, contra Ames, unquestionably a "man of insight," and his perceptive depiction of these particular Bostonians could have been a useful tool for helping a nineteenth-century feminist activist "[k]now [her]self." Ames is right to criticize the novel for representing the woman's rights movement as a monolithic entity and for suggesting that the movement was plagued across the board by the shortcomings it identifies. But by being so quick to discredit James's vision, Ames and other real-world activists missed an opportunity to improve their oppositional community. Had they given it a chance, they might have gleaned some lessons relevant to all groups working together to bring about social change and in particular those working to eradicate the power imbalance created by sexism and other types of oppression. Unlike the reviewer in the *Una* who is able to find an instructive model of feminism in Dickens's Mrs. Jellyby, even though she believes the character has been "caricatured to an extent which greatly injures the force of the delineation" (4), Lucia Ames is incapable of the resisting reading that makes it possible for real-world activists to discern ways to improve their work and their oppositional communities from sources that may not be entirely sympathetic or flattering to their movements. However, at least one member of the woman's rights community, Celia B. Whitehead, was; she wrote a fictional account of what happens "beyond the ending" of James's novel that helps to illuminate what *The Bostonians* can teach feminist activists.

The importance of Whitehead's new ending, however, can only be appreciated after one has considered the often astute portrayal of activism in James's novel. When one reads *The Bostonians* with Ann Ferguson's model of an ideal oppositional community in mind, it becomes clear that the novel warns its readers of the inherent instability and ineffectualness of a feminist reform community that does not originate from two essential elements, revolutionary love and existential communitarianism. Most of the other works in this study arguably rely on the feminist notion expressed in the slogan "the personal is political"—the characters' activism grows out of their individual experiences and affective relationships. However, in *The Bostonians*, both Olive and Verena must learn that their political ideals must have relevance to their personal lives and by extension that their ideology must be suffused with sincere passion. Because they do not understand this connection at the outset, their attempt at forming a feminist oppositional community is doomed to fail, and one could argue that the tragedy of *The Bostonians* lies in this wasted opportunity.

The genesis of this failure is presented in the early pages of *The Bostonians*, which depict the initially flawed nature of Olive's and Verena's activist work. Each heroine's flaw is different, but its origin is the same: a belief in the impersonal nature of feminist ideals. The reader first becomes aware of Olive's desire to be free of personal entanglements when she says of her sister, Mrs. Luna, that she could hate her "if she had not forbidden herself this emotion as directed to individuals" (41). Soon thereafter, Olive has a similar thought upon considering how handsome Basil—her politically conservative cousin who is visiting from Mississippi—is and how much he probably dislikes feminist reform: "[I]t had already been a comfort to her, on occasions of acute feeling, that she hated men, as a class, anyway" (51). In both instances, Olive suppresses her emotional responses to people by reducing them to abstractions, by stereotyping them. Clearly, Olive's feminist zeal is of a piece with this reliance on abstraction. She "regulated her conduct by lofty principles" and she has "a theory she devotedly nursed" about the way she should interact with poorer people (52). There is nothing wrong with "lofty principles" or a "theory" of correct behavior, but Olive's attachment to them suggests, as does her thinking of people as a "class," that her feminist work is grounded in rigid ideas instead of springing from unmitigated interaction with the actual world. The narrator makes the reader privy to the insidious dark side of Olive's abstract activist impulse, an elitist desire to distance herself from the types of people she finds vulgar or distasteful: "Miss Chancellor would have been much happier if the movements she was interested in could have been carried on only by the people she liked [. . . .] A common end, unfortunately, however fine as regards a special result, does not make community impersonal" (129). What Olive intuits is that the effort to effect a fundamental shift in a society's ideology must begin materially, with diverse individuals becoming "personal" with each other, and it is this breaking down of barriers between "types" (at least, barriers between herself and types she dislikes) that Olive disdains. As Nina Auerbach has noted, for Olive, "feminism's main drawback is the intrusion of other women" (127). While I would argue that Olive changes her mind about other women over the course of the novel, her preference at first for reform ideals over individual reformers is her downfall.

Like Olive's initial vision of reform work, Verena's activist endeavors as a public speaker are described as "impersonal." Before Verena's first speech, her father, Selah Tarrant, intimates to his audience that "any success that he and his daughter might have had was [. . .] thoroughly impersonal" (79). Selah repeats the term after the performance, reminding his audience that "the affair was so impersonal" (87). Of course, Selah Tarrant's actions and words are often presented by the narrator as suspect or insincere. However, Verena echoes his sentiments when she repeatedly responds to her admirers, "It isn't *me*." While her protestation might also be taken as judicious self-effacement, the narrator implies that Verena is not in charge of her talent: "She proceeded slowly, cautiously, as if she were listening for the prompter [. . . .] Then memory, or inspiration, returned to her, and presently she was in possession of her part" (84). In this context, "impersonal" means something quite different from what Olive means when she uses the word. Ostensibly, it means that Verena has no interest in achieving personal fame or in being aggrandized for her "gift." The underlying suggestion, however, is that Verena is not in control of her words or actions; she is only responding to a "prompter." The narrator provides some insight into Verena's "impersonal" interest in her work when he confides to the reader that "Verena took life, as yet, very simply; she was not conscious of so many differences of social complexion" (97), by which he means that Verena is ignorant of the class hierarchy in Boston; it can be inferred, however, that she has done little critical thinking on her own about societal inequalities, financial, gendered, or otherwise. Verena has not come to her reform work through personal reflection, and that is her shortcoming. Like Olive's belief in principles and theories, her inability to reflect critically is not morally reprehensible; after all, Verena is a young girl who lacks experience. However, like Olive she fails in her attempt to become a feminist activist because of her shortcoming; her lack of self-reflection makes her vulnerable to pressure from the status quo.

At this stage in her life, Verena has committed herself to gender reform prematurely; she is not yet able to be a successful activist because she has not experienced Ferguson's "existential moment," the moment of critical self-awareness necessary to achieving that success. Verena's situation seems peculiar because it is a reversal of the majority's maturation experience; instead of being raised in an environment where status quo interests are unquestioningly accepted as natural, Verena has grown up in a world equally complacent about the "naturalness" of defying those normative interests. What Lucia T. Ames calls Verena's "weakness" and Sallie Hall calls her "anemia of selfhood" (214) is only a youthful lack of reflection. However, her subsequent experiences remind the reader that a successful feminist activist must independently commit herself to defying society's expectations, because it is almost impossible to maintain an oppositional stance unless it is freely chosen.

Although I would argue the nature of Olive and Verena's relationship changes dramatically over the course of the story, the seeds of its dissolution are already present at its inception. Olive's distaste for the vulgarity and shabbiness of the reform world, which underlies her desire for an "impersonal community," is made clear by the narrator when he confides that Olive "mortally disliked" Miss

Birdseye's home and wondered "whether an absence of nice arrangements were a necessary part of the enthusiasm of humanity" (57). For Olive, the reality of reform life is much less appealing than her theories, and this fact about her makes one suspicious of her "preoccup[ation] with the romance of the people" and her express desire to "know some *very* poor girl" (62). The word "romance" implies the way Olive idealizes poverty and the "masses" and so it is not difficult to understand her immediate attraction to Verena: "With her bright, vulgar clothes, her salient appearance, she might have been a rope-dancer or a fortune-teller, and this had the immense merit, for Olive, that it appeared to make her belong to the 'people', threw her into the social dusk of that mysterious democracy which Miss Chancellor held that the fortunate classes know so little about, and with which (in a future possibly very near) they will have to count" (101). The reader has also learned, however, that Verena is "very young and slim and fair" and speaks with "extraordinary simplicity and grace" (76, 84). Olive is drawn to Verena in part because in the younger, poorer woman she has the opportunity to pursue her "romance of the people" without having to subject herself to the reality of their situation. In Olive's eyes, Verena's beauty, eloquence, and charm makes her unlike the people, even if she belongs to them. As Olive believes, "Miss Tarrant might wear gilt buttons from head to foot, her soul could not be vulgar" (101).

At this moment, Olive feels Verena could be "a friend of her own sex with whom she might have a union of soul" (101). She grandly states that the realization of such a friendship between them will depend on a "double consent," an ostensibly equal exchange, but she actually plans to "[take] possession" of Verena, which can only result in an inherently unequal relationship (101, 100). Olive believes that "if she could only rescue the girl from the danger of vulgar exploitation, could only constitute herself as protectress and devotee, the two, between them, might achieve the great result" (104). Clearly, Olive feels overwhelming sympathy for Verena and what she perceives as the younger woman's vulnerable situation, and it is this sympathy that Olive hopes will bond them together in working for the "great result" (104). However, sympathy can erase difference; as Kristin Boudreau explains, "Although sympathy presents itself as a mode of resemblance—often understood as synonymous with agreement—in fact it more often operates across spaces of unbridgeable difference. [. . .] [S]ympathy must begin with difference, which it can transcend only by transforming one side of the exchange into a version of the other" (23). Olive thinks of Verena romantically as a "flower of the great Democracy" for whom it was "impossible to have an origin less distinguished" (128); Verena is thus profoundly different from Olive, who "belonged to the *bourgeoisie*—the oldest and best" (61).

Verena's difference is what first attracts Olive; at the same time, however, Olive wants to bridge that difference by "train[ing]" Verena to be as refined as herself, by "polish[ing]" her (132).

Sympathy, then, is an inferior motivation for forming an oppositional community. Ferguson's ideal model of a reform community revolves around a different kind of emotion, "revolutionary love":

> The best possibility for developing a viable [oppositional community] arises when individuals involved [. . .] act out of revolutionary love rather than ego needs, guilt, or *obligations to principles of justice held only as abstract beliefs*. Revolutionary love involves a commitment to a set of ideals connected to social justice, such as the rights of all humans to material and social equality, to be heard, and to democratic participatory decision-making and autonomous self-development. It also involves emotional bonding with, and care and concern for, others who are denied these rights, a feeling of social kinship and imagined community with them, and a desire to renounce one's own social and material privileges in order to challenge such existing inequalities. ("Feminist Communities" 382, emphasis added)

Both revolutionary love and sympathy are concerned with bridging difference; however, revolutionary love is distinguished by both its egalitarian nature and the fact that it addresses itself to reality instead of dwelling in the realm of abstraction. It stems from "autonomous self-development," and ideally produces a community among reformers in which the more privileged members voluntarily renounce their advantages. At the beginning of her friendship with Verena, however, Olive is motivated primarily by "abstract beliefs," which make her sympathize with, instead of love, her new friend. She theoretically wants to renounce her wealth in order to help less fortunate women, but in fact, she initially uses her money to distance Verena from her parents and their unrefined lifestyle. She also tries to remake the young woman in her more privileged image, thus creating a dynamic in which she controls Verena, a dynamic that she cannot later undo.

Although Verena is perhaps less accountable for her actions, given her relative naïveté, she does not in her friendship with Olive meet Ferguson's criteria for successful participation in an oppositional community. Verena has not experienced the transformative "existential moment" in which a would-be reformer realizes her personal investment in reconstituting the status quo, nor has she entered the oppositional community because she *chose* to do so, which would amount to taking up Ferguson's existential communitarianism. Rather, Verena simply finds herself a part of an oppositional community. Her earliest reform ideas evolve out of the circumstances of her birth, as Olive recognizes during the younger woman's first visit to the elegant home on Charles Street: "[Verena] had been nursed in darkened rooms, and suckled in the midst of manifestations; she had begun to 'attend lectures,' as she said, when she was quite an infant, because her mother had no one to leave her with at home. She had sat on the knee of somnambulists, and had been passed from hand to hand by trance-speakers; she was familiar with every kind of 'cure,' and had grown up among lady-editors of newspapers advocating new religions, and people who disapproved of the marriage-tie" (105). Olive thinks some of the doctrines Verena has internalized from this childhood are rather outlandish, such as her casual preference for "free unions" (105). Regardless of their propriety (or ostensible lack thereof), the text makes it clear that Verena's opinions at this point are really those of her parents. In moving from their home to Olive's, then, Verena is given the opportunity to begin thinking critically about these doctrines and perhaps arrive at her own reasons and methods for resisting gender inequality.

This first intimate meeting between the two heroines, however, does not open the space in which she (or Verena) might come to adopt existential communitarianism. Rather, it draws attention to Verena's tendency to embrace political (and personal) allegiances without much forethought. Olive asks Verena "where she had got her 'intense realization' of the suffering of women," and Verena responds rather enigmatically but "always smiling" by questioning "where Joan of Arc had got her idea of the suffering of France" (105). While Olive thinks this answer "prettily said," she "remember[s] afterward it had not literally answered the question" (105–06). Verena is unable to answer Olive's question because she has never answered it for herself; Olive is wrong to believe that Verena has ever had such an "intense realization." Olive continues to press, asking Verena "to assure her of this—that it was the only thing in all the world she cared for, the redemption of women, the thing she hoped under Providence to give her life to" (106). The juxtaposition between Verena's instant, short reply and Olive's earnest appeal is interesting: "Oh yes—I want to give my life! [. . .] I want to do something great!" (106). Revealed in this exclamation is not only Verena's enthusiasm, but also the vagueness of what she hopes to accomplish ("something great") as well as the suggestion that her work is perhaps partially motivated by a desire for success and recognition. Olive ends their interview by asking Verena if she knows what it means to "give her life," to "renounce, refrain, abstain," for the cause of woman's rights: "'Oh, well, I guess I can abstain!' Verena exclaimed, with a laugh" (107). The reader, more so than Verena, realizes with what intense seriousness Olive asks this question, and Verena's flippant, good-natured response seems discordant. Olive, however, takes Verena's commitment seriously and soon thereafter decides "to take a more complete possession of the girl" (145).

Anthony Scott makes an interesting observation about the progression of this friendship that begins so inauspiciously: "[O]nce Olive possesses [Verena] as an object, she begins to desire her as a person, who will belong to her not by contractual fiat but by choice" (61). Olive begins to think of Verena less as a "gifted being" and a "flower of the great Democracy" and instead sees her more as an intimate friend. This change, along with Verena's responsive enthusiasm to Olive's feminist ideas, creates a stronger, more admirable bond between the two women. The ensuing months are the happiest and most promising in the women's friendship, a time described as "the most momentous period of Miss Chancellor's life" (170). Olive, seeing that Verena has "expanded, developed on a most liberal scale[,] [. . .] had never known a greater pleasure" (178). Furthermore, the narrator says (although it is unclear whether this is his perspective or Olive's) that Verena "was disinterestedly attached to the previous things they were to do together; she cared about them for themselves, believed in them ardently, had them constantly in mind" (178). Olive finds happiness in Verena's maturation and, if the narrative perspective is correct, Verena has become more thoughtful about and more engaged with their plans for feminist reform, developing a "disinterested attach[ment]" to them. The growing intimacy and interdependence of the two women is clear in the description of how they spend their evenings: "Olive often sat at the window with her companion before it was time for the lamp. They admired the sunsets, they rejoiced in the ruddy spots projected upon the parlour-wall [. . . .] They watched the stellar points come out at last in a colder heaven, and then, shuddering a little, arm in arm, they turned away, with a sense that the winter night was even more cruel than the tyranny of men—turned back to drawn curtains and a brighter fire and a glittering tea-tray and more and more talk about the long martyrdom of women, a subject as to which Olive was inexhaustible and really most interesting" (185). This glimpse of domestic harmony reveals not only their genuine, reciprocal affection but also their mutual interest in the subject of woman's rights. While Olive is still the one more focused on the "long martyrdom of women" in this passage—she seems to be the one doing the talking—the implication is that Verena also, to a certain extent, finds the subject "really most interesting."

As the two women's commitment to each other and their reform work develops, so too does the reader's awareness of their surrounding oppositional community: "This little society was rather suburban and miscellaneous; it was prolific in women who trotted about, early and late, with books from the Athenaeum nursed behind their muff, or little nosegays of exquisite flowers that they were carrying as presents to each other" (187). However, the dissension among and condescension of certain members in this community suggests that it is a problematic society. Olive and the well-known woman's rights leader Mrs. Farrinder, toward whom "Olive passed, in three months, from the stage of veneration to that of competition," tacitly battle over who will publicly lead the movement (174). This clash between the two activists supports Auerbach's contention that "the larger community of women in *The Bostonians*" contains no "lovingly personal solicitude" (126). Auerbach goes too far here; there are moments of personal solicitude in the community, especially regarding Miss Birdseye "of whom Olive saw more this winter than she had ever seen before" (188). As Miss Birdseye becomes integral to this inner circle, however, the reader sees that it is still a community founded more on sympathetic bonds than egalitarian, loving ones: "In her own person she appeared to Olive and Verena a representative of suffering humanity; the pity they felt for her was part of their pity for all who were weakest and most hardly used" (189). Miss Birdseye (like Verena previously) represents a class of people, instead of a human being in her own right, and the pity that Verena and Olive feel for her seems almost identical to the sympathy Olive feels for Verena at the beginning of the novel. Even though the power of sympathy to unite these women cannot be completely discounted, the tone here once again suggests an underlying condescension that prevents true revolutionary love.

The tensions within the larger community intimate that the feminist reformers, including Olive and Verena, have still not achieved a balance between their political ideals of equality and their personal affinities for each other. Even though Olive now sees Verena as an individual, Scott's use of the words "belongs" and "possess" to describe their relationship reminds the reader of the flaws at its center. The choice to which Scott refers is not Verena's resolution to be a committed feminist activist per se, but it does allude to what Olive sees as a precondition for undertaking reform work, namely, a decision never to marry. In a moment of violent emotion, Olive asks of Verena, "Promise me not to marry!" although the following day, in a calmer mood, she amends this demand: "I don't want your signature; I only want your confidence—only what springs from that. [. . .] You know what I think—that there is something noble done when one makes a sacrifice for a great good. [. . .] It seems to me very poor, when friendship and faith and charity and the most interesting occupation in the world—when such a combination as this doesn't seem, by itself, enough to live for" (151). Olive wants Verena to feel as she does, that it is best to renounce men and the marriage institution and be content with their work and friendship. Olive's apparent motivation is to save Verena so that she may continue her feminist work. However, the reader recognizes Olive's personal motivation as well. She wants to insure that no other attachments will take Verena away from her; Olive wants to continue "possessing" Verena. While the reader knows that Olive desperately wants this renunciation, she does not know what Verena thinks, other than "the girl was now completely [under] Olive's influence" and that "she wished to please her if only because she had such a dread of displeasing her" (153). Therefore, when Verena "declare[s] she should like to promise" (153), it is not because she independently rejects heterosexual love, but because she hopes to make her friend happy by embracing her ideals.

The preference for a lifestyle outside the heterosexual norm that this exchange suggests has been given much attention by critics interested in *The Bostonians*'s portrayal of homoerotic (or homosocial) relationships; as with most aspects of James's novel, however, there is no consensus about the nature of this portrayal. Lucia T. Ames's review of James's "abnormal women" anticipates critics such as F. W. Dupee, who finds Olive a case of "perverse sexuality" (131), or Irving Howe, who says Olive's "unnatural" behavior is antithetical to "the rhythms of life" (165, 168). Of course, more recent critics have argued for a sympathetic reading of this female relationship. Terry Castle says Olive is "American literature's first lesbian tragic heroine" (171), and Kathleen McColley argues that "James focuses on female relationships and their implied homoeroticism, suggesting liberating possibilities inherent in female friendships" (151). Despite these varying opinions, the scholars all agree that Olive and Verena's friendship stands in contrast or represents an alternative to heterosexuality. My reading, however, is closer to Anthony Scott's. He argues that what is "morally questionable about the bond between Olive and Verena is [...] not the sexuality of the tie as such but its structural resemblance to conventional (married) heterosexuality—that is, its asymmetry of power, its possessiveness, its use of coercion disguised as consent—that subjects it to critique" (60). Olive and Verena's relationship is destined to fail not because it is so different from the heterosexual norm, but because in its imbalance of power it is too much like it.

It is this dynamic—Olive's domination on one side and Verena's lack of agency on the other—that makes their oppositional community vulnerable to normative pressure from the outside, a pressure embodied in the character of Basil Ransom. In *The Bostonians*, Basil is the only male character who disapproves of woman's rights, and as such, he seems an anomaly. However, as Alfred Habegger observes, Basil might be in the minority in the novel but historically it was the other way around: "Basil's solitary opposition to the women's movement reverses the actual power relations of nineteenth-century men and women" (225). While Basil's southern background and his reactionary politics would have marked him as unusual in a cosmopolitan place like Boston or New York, his virulent, condescending disapproval of the "roaring radicals" (37) working toward gender reform would have been more common in late 1870s America than the sympathetic approval of the elite Henry Burrage. Basil believes that there is "no place in public" for women and that "what is most agreeable to women is to be agreeable to men" (329). Although the narrator observes here and there that the reader will think Basil's ideas are ridiculous, they are in fact only mildly exaggerated versions of the typical arguments men and women opposed to woman's rights made. Understanding, then, that the majority of men and women in the real world would have agreed with Basil that women belong in the home and ought to occupy a subordinate marital role (even if Basil is marginal to the reform world depicted in the novel) provides insight into Verena's eventual capitulation to his advances. One could make the case that "as a representative of his sex," Basil is the "most important personage in [this] narrative" (37) because he embodies the strength and seductiveness of conventional thought, showing its ability to undermine oppositional communities when they are not built on a solid foundation.

During one of Verena's first interviews with Basil, the reader is reminded that one reason Olive and Verena's oppositional community rests on a shaky foundation is because Verena has not made a fully informed, mature decision in rejecting the status quo. Verena tells Olive that she wants to spend time with Basil because she is "curious" about the "other side" of the argument for gender reform. When Olive dismissively replies, "'Oh, heaven,'" Verena tells her, "'You must remember I have never heard it'" (293). When she does hear it, she is captivated in spite of herself. Although she finds his ideas "crudely profane," she nevertheless is "impressed by his manner and the novelty of a man taking that sort of religious tone about such a cause" (328). Until this point, Verena has only heard prowoman's rights ideas talked about with such reverence. A few moments later, Basil tells Verena, "You think you care about [woman's rights], but you don't at all. They were imposed upon you by circumstances, by unfortunate associations, and you accepted them as you would have accepted any other burden, on account of the sweetness of your nature" (330). Without addressing the relative merits of woman's rights ideology, Basil has spoken the truth to Verena about the origin of her activist work; in fact, he even echoes her words from the beginning: "It isn't *you* [. . .] but an inflated little figure" (328). Verena's reaction to his version of her development is chaotic and emotional, consistent with the confusion of one forced to question what she has always believed: "The description of herself as something different from what she was trying to be, the charge of want of reality, made her heart beat with pain; she was sure, at any rate, it was her real self that was there with him now, where she oughtn't to be" (331).

This conversation is one of many during which Basil continues to "press, press, always to press" (377) his ideas and his passion on Verena until she is convinced she shares them. While one might want to argue that Verena's transformation is a conservative version of the "existential moment," that her epiphany is that traditional notions about heterosexuality and the roles of the sexes are the "truth," I would maintain that ample evidence in the text suggests otherwise. Habegger has argued that James's depiction of Verena is implausible because "it is all wrong that she should completely renounce thought for sentiment" (223). He claims this renunciation would be out of character, since "Verena has enjoyed an unusually unconstrained girlhood, [...] possesses a lively assertive spirit [...] and loves excitement and activity" (223). However, I do not see that any of those qualities would make Verena an especially contemplative young woman, and as we have seen, her commitment to feminism has not been fortified by sustained self-analysis or by a sincere, personal investment in it. To date, she has pursued it primarily to please first her parents and then Olive, all of whom dominate the young woman at different times. I would argue, therefore, that since Verena is not particularly thoughtful in the first place, it is misleading to describe her as renouncing thought for sentiment. She is unable to resist a passionate appeal that does move her both emotionally and physically. Certainly, one should not underestimate the persuasive power of physical attraction and passion in Basil and Verena's relationship. As Jean Gooder remarks, for Verena, her outing with Basil "is the beginning of a growing equation of her 'real self' with her sexual self" (110). Verena has neither the strength of her personal convictions nor a truly supportive oppositional community to help her resist such a forceful heterosexual passion or the status quo so seductively attired.

The narrator explains that when Verena finally admits to herself that she has succumbed to Basil's insistent pressing, "it was simply that the truth had changed sides; that radiant image began to look at her from Basil Ransom's expressive eyes" (374). David Van Leer has argued that in this equation, Verena "admits that there is no qualitative difference between her two allegiances" (101). She has no more chosen a belief in traditional gender roles than she chose her feminist activism; rather, she has traded one dominating companion for another. What makes this "choice" particularly tragic is that it is made at the same time that Olive has an epiphany—her own "existential moment"—that opens up a space for a truly alternative relationship between the two women. After Olive has violently resisted and finally resigned herself to Verena's preference for

Basil, she goes for a long walk near the water during which she thinks critically about her soon-to-end friendship: "Verena had submitted, she had responded, she had lent herself to Olive's incitement and exhortation [. . .] but it had been a kind of hothouse loyalty, the mere contagion of an example, and a sentiment springing up from within had easily breathed a chill upon it" (397). Olive sees clearly that she has been the driving force behind Verena's activism. The younger woman has not personally chosen her work, and Olive sees for the first time the fragile nature of this kind of feminism, as well as her own role in Verena's defection from the movement. Nevertheless, when a few moments later, Olive fears that Verena has drowned in a boating accident, she realizes how personal her affection for Verena has become: "Her heart failed her [. . .] and she gave a cry [. . .] which expressed only a wild personal passion, a desire to take her friend in her arms again on any terms, even the most cruel to herself" (399).

The reader's first thought is that the terms "most cruel" to Olive would be Verena's marriage to Basil. However, the text has admitted that many of the terms of Verena's life have been "most cruel" to Olive. When Olive visits Verena's familial home at the beginning of the story, almost every aspect of it disgusts her. After seeing Mrs. Tarrant in her domestic space, Olive concludes "there was no manner of doubt left as to her being vulgar" (129). Olive is likewise horrified by their home, thinking there "was nothing in the house to speak of; nothing to Olive's sense, but a smell of kerosene" (132). This is the moment in which Olive definitively resolves to separate Verena from her past and her family, her reasoning being that she does not see why "when parents were so trashy this natural law [of filial affection] should not be suspended" (132). Olive's dislike of the Tarrants is not completely unjustified, at the least from the narrative perspective; still, her refusal to accept anything about Verena's life heretofore is of a piece with her general impulse to dominate the young woman through a sympathetic, but not loving, bond. However, at the end, the reader sees how much Olive has grown through her relationship with Verena. She is willing to embrace her friend on any terms, not just her own. She no longer romanticizes Verena but accepts her as a fully autonomous, complete being; Olive's recognition of Verena's personhood enables her to register a purely unselfish affection that opens her to the very personal nature of feminist reform work. The lesson for real-world feminist activists here is similar to one that Martha Nussbaum identifies in another novel James wrote during this time period, *The Princess Casamassima*: "the sort of thought [and emotion] we usually call personal promises a politics richer in humanity" than abstract ideology (210).[7] By extension, an oppositional community based on revolutionary love is better than one founded on sympathy alone. Olive's transformation, however, has come too late to save her relationship with Verena. When she returns to the cottage, she finds the younger woman alive but "crushed and humbled" by Basil's insistence. Olive, however, has given up her selfish desire to possess Verena by coercion, and simply "[takes] her hand with an irresistible impulse of compassion and reassurance" (399).

There is a gap in the action of *The Bostonians* after this pivotal scene, leading the reader to believe momentarily that their friendship will survive after all. But this narrative lapse only creates the conditions necessary for one of the most sensational endings in American literature. As Verena is about to give her first great speech in Boston's Music Hall, Basil determines to "[wrest] her from the mighty multitude" (413) and make her his wife. With an increasingly disgruntled crowd chanting in the background, Basil goes to Verena backstage. He eventually silences all objections and pleadings from Mrs. Tarrant, Olive, and Verena to let the show continue and takes Verena out of the Hall and presumably to the altar. Like most novels about feminist activists, then, *The Bostonians* ends in the imminent marriage of the heroine. In this case, though, there is no happy feminist conversion narrative in which the male becomes an enlightened supporter of gender reform. Instead, the promised marriage brings with it the silence of the heroine and the end of her reform work, which seems at first glance a patently antifeminist activist plot, as in *Hannah Thurston*.[8] However, no one who pays attention to the violent, sinister language with which James describes this scene can argue the novel unequivocally advocates the conservative ending. To Verena's entreaty that she be allowed to speak for a moment to the crowd because she could "soothe them with a word," Basil tells her, "Keep your soothing words for me—you will have need of them all, in our coming time" (430). The ominous nature of this rejoinder presages the final scene in the novel, in which Basil "by muscular force, wrench[s] her away" (432) from Olive, her parents, and the waiting audience, while Verena shrieks Olive's name. Once they are outside, Verena claims she is glad now that it is over, but the narrator reveals, "[T]hough she was glad, [Basil] presently discovered that, beneath her hood, she was in tears. It is to be feared that with the union, so far from brilliant, into which she was about to enter, these were not the last she was destined to shed" (433).

It is commonplace in Jamesian scholarship to see Olive as the tragic figure in this scene, perhaps because of the final description of her "offering herself to be trampled to death and torn to pieces" by the crowd as she ascends the platform (432).[9] However, I would argue that Verena's is the more tragic story. It is she who is sacrificed in what is "perhaps the most subversive ending to a heterosexual romance plot" ever (Kahane 78) because neither Olive nor she had managed to grasp the very personal nature of gender reform in time to save her. Basil's subjugation of her, however, puts her in the unenviable position of a woman who will learn firsthand why women are working for more legal and social equality, because there seems to be little hope for any independence in this marriage. In contrast, there is hope for Olive. Although she has insisted throughout the book that she cannot publicly speak, it is she who "with a sudden inspiration [. . .] rushed to the approach to the platform" (431). And although she says she is "going to be hissed and hooted and insulted," she is greeted by a "hush [that] was respectful" as "the great public waited" to hear what she had to say (432–33). Sara Blair interprets this moment as one in which "Olive Chancellor becomes a newly heroic figure of feminist passion," pointing out the "possibilities Olive's performance opens up, for some genuinely democratic but regulated kind of cultural exchange" (165–66). Olive's encyclopedic knowledge of women's history, along with her thoughtful understanding of the tenets of feminist reform—which the novel reiterates several times are her strong points—makes her a potentially brilliant, persuasive orator. By the close of the novel, Olive's relationship with Verena has clearly changed her; it has helped make her feminist thinking less abstract, and she is now able to complement her knowledge with the capacity for feeling a consistent, genuine revolutionary love for individuals. Thus, one way in which Olive's "feminist passion" is "newly heroic" is that her recent experiences may undercut her preference for an "impersonal community" of feminist activists. If so, she very well may become a truly committed member of a successful oppositional community.

In her essay "The Other Bostonians: Gender and Literary Study," Elaine Showalter envisions the feminist potential for James's heroines. She takes the title from a letter James wrote to his brother after he completed the novel, in which the novelist laments, "I shall have to write another. 'The Other Bostonians'" (qtd. in Showalter 179). Showalter uses this declaration to imagine a "feminist *Other Bostonians*": "In this novel, perhaps, Verena would not leave Olive and would not be silenced; she would give her great speech, 'A Woman's Reason,' to cheering crowds at the Boston Music Hall, and Basil would go back to his pathetic dreams of avenging the fallen South" (180). Although, as my argument suggests, the flawed nature of Olive's and Verena's feminist activism throughout most of the book would prevent this outcome even in an alternative ending, Showalter's impulse to imagine a happy, feminist life for them suggests that this possibility is latent in the text, that the characters' shortcomings could be overcome in the future beyond it. This potential should not be underestimated when considering *The Bostonians*'s relevance to its contemporary feminist activist readers. For although the majority of those readers chose to ignore the lessons of revolutionary love and existential communitarianism James's novel could have taught them, the possibility that a better oppositional community could emerge from the flawed one in James's novel was not lost on at least one woman's rights activist, Celia B. Whitehead.

In 1887, Celia B. Whitehead, using the pseudonym Henrietta James, published a small twenty-seven-page pamphlet entitled "Another Chapter of 'The Bostonians.'" While this text is clearly intended as a parody of James's novel, the way Whitehead develops the characters and plot demonstrates she is a keen reader of the original story. In her brief introduction, Whitehead says she felt compelled to write another chapter because "Mr. James left the hero and heroines of his remarkable story at the most interesting period of their existence" (1). James's characters, Whitehead intimates, were on the cusp of a transition, a "most interesting" moment, rather than about to resign themselves to unhappy fates, and she carries them through this transition. She picks up where the novel leaves off, with Olive approaching the podium. In this moment, Olive becomes an eloquent speaker in her own right, giving the speech "A Woman's Reason," which she knew by heart: "Then she went on, with a growing fervor, a new sense of power and responsibility, and a passionate enthusiasm, telling them what Verena would have told them" (4). In this tale of the other Bostonians, Olive has gained a "new sense of power and responsibility" from the ordeal through which she has passed. Whitehead imagines how Olive changes after embracing revolutionary love and recognizing how personal reform work should be:

> In the silence of her chamber that night Olive looked back over the past and saw that in trying to prepare Verena for this work she had been preparing herself. Perhaps it could not have been done in any other way. From that night she was a changed woman. If before she had been consecrated to the enfranchisement of woman, how much more now. The memory of the friend who had been so much to her and was now gone out of her life filled her with a pitying sweetness before the unknown. Now there was no more hesitation, no more pushing and urging others forward. She went forward herself, and those who had known her before marveled at the change, and all who listened to her thrilled with the words she spoke. (5)

Whitehead recasts Olive's future path. Instead of seeing, as Basil had, Olive "offering herself to be trampled to death and torn to pieces" (James 432), the revisionist author imagines her emerging from this horrific experience with a new purpose and commitment. The affection for her friend lingers as "a pitying sweetness" whose revolutionary quality motivates Olive to treat others in an egalitarian way. Instead of "pushing and urging others forward," she now pushes herself to feminist agitation, and the result is that she has a significant impact on those to whom she appeals.

In Whitehead's addition the reader sees the fruitful aftermath of Olive's existential moment, and she also sees the painful yet necessary experience Verena must endure before she will be ready to join a feminist oppositional community. Verena's trial is, not surprisingly, the reality of her marriage to Basil. Whitehead shows how their marriage, rather than being founded on shared interests and a free exchange of ideas, is purely physical. Once "[Basil] had taken legal possession of her," Whitehead's narrator wonders, "what more was to be said or done?" (7). Their marriage is based on a "dreadful nothingness": "They had no mutual acquaintances, their literary tastes were as divergent as can well be imagined" (7). Basil, bored with his wife now that she is conquered and still longing for material comfort, once again spends a great deal of time with Mrs. Luna, who rehires him as Newton's tutor. During these lonely, empty months, Verena begins to question her decision, although in a parodic jab at James's narrator, Whitehead's refuses to confirm exactly the nature of these questions:

> Did Verena reflect that as soon as he really "got hold" of her she had ceased to "please him very much"? And as she thought of Olive did she feel that the world was all a great trap or trick of which women were ever the punctual dupes, so that it was the worst of the curse that rested upon them, that they must most humiliate those who had most their cause at heart? [. . .] Did she ask herself if women must forever be the sport of men's selfishness and avidity? Did she ask why she had consented to be bound to please one individual and failed even to please him thus, when, free, she could be "charming to all the world"?
>
> These are mysteries into which I shall not attempt to enter, speculations with which I have no concern; it is sufficient for us to know that all human effort never seemed to her so barren and thankless.(18)[10]

This litany of questions shows Verena, at the depth of her despair, questioning her previous suppositions and coming to grips for the first time with the reality of a traditional heterosexual union and the concomitant vulnerability of women. These questions prepare her for her "existential moment," her conversion through personal experience to a belief in the necessity of gender reform. In this passage, Whitehead's mimicry of James is significant; in its form and tone it recalls to the reader the barrage of self-inquiry Olive subjects herself to before her own existential moment.

Basil leaves Verena for Mrs. Luna soon thereafter, and Verena, along with her baby daughter, returns to Olive, after whom she renames the baby. Olive reiterates her desire to "take her friend in her arms again on any terms," adding "the baby too" to this union (19). At this point, the reader learns that Olive has "taken up active work" and that "her compassion had sweetened and mellowed into an exquisite tenderness" (19). Verena senses the change in her friend and finds in their reconciliation the true alternative to an unequal, coercive relationship, a friendship founded on revolutionary love: "She felt that all the old intensity and constraint were gone and a sense of freedom, security, and repose, that she had felt the want of ever since the fateful night at Miss Birdseye's when she first met Olive Chancellor and Basil Ransom, came to her" (19). It is important that Whitehead implicate Olive as well as Basil in Verena's former unhappiness; it is not only the shortcomings of her male partner that have made her miserable but also the misguided sympathy of her friend. Their new friendship, however, is a source of strength for the recently abused wife. Once Verena heals from the shock of her abandonment, she also returns to her activist work, "all the time with a look of one who sees in reality something dreamed of before" (22). Verena has experienced firsthand the painful reality of gender oppression, and with the supportive, respectful love of her also-changed friend, she determines to oppose it with renewed vigor.

Whitehead imagines how Olive's and Verena's transformative experiences improve their activist community: "There were two to carry on the work instead of one—two, better prepared than either could have been without the help of Basil Ransom and Adeline Luna" (25). After this initial recommitment, their oppositional community is fortified—as are those of so many fictional feminist activists—by an equal, loving heterosexual relationship. Verena is revisited by Henry Burrage, who also has changed over the years. His "fondness for music had grown to a passion" (26) and he has become a music teacher. He still loves Verena and offers her a relationship based on mutual respect and autonomy: "He could live without her and should never urge her to live with him. The man who wants a woman to marry him who has to be urged into it, he could not comprehend. Her work should be held sacred. She should not be *his*, [she] should belong to herself and be free, without command or solicitation from him, to live her own life" (26). Olive, who hated Basil's proposal, is happy about this offer because she now realizes "a man *could* be found possessing the other generally recognized and essential qualifications who would not interpret marriage to mean ownership" (26–27). Olive and Verena have learned their lessons about the true nature of an oppositional community and thus Whitehead concludes her revisionist ending to James's novel with a promise of happiness: "[T]his time we leave [them] in smiles and not in tears" (27).

Whitehead's response to James's work is atypical of nineteenth-century woman's rights activists like Lucia T. Ames in that it engages the book on its own terms. Nevertheless, Whitehead's other chapter speaks volumes about the impact *The Bostonians* could have had on real-world feminist activists. Whitehead sees clearly that James's heroines are not irredeemable dupes of the latest fad; rather, they are flawed human beings who have the capacity for making great changes in society. However, each must first learn that before she can change the world, she must change herself. In this "other chapter" of *The Bostonians*, the novel's implied message for feminist activists becomes explicit: the political must always be personal.

Coda

In considering the role that fiction played in creating and sustaining the first wave of feminist activism in America, it seems appropriate to return to Oreola Williams Haskell's short story, "Tenements and Teacups," because in many ways, it encapsulates the optimism of feminist activist fiction written between the years 1870 and 1920. The members of the "Squad" exhibit an unequivocal belief in the rightness of their cause and its potential for changing the world, and they gain strength from belonging to a community of like-minded reformers. It is also clear that the author firmly believes that storytelling plays a pivotal role in bringing about these changes and contributing to such a community; telling stories both attracts new members and nourishes those already involved in the movement.

It is appropriate, too, that this story was written in 1920, the year the Nineteenth Amendment was ratified and suffragists were still feeling heady from their success and confident about their future. However, what feminist activists could not know at that moment was that most of their revolutionary work was behind them instead of in front of them. It was the activist process throughout the nineteenth and early twentieth centuries, not the end result of the vote, that actually brought about the most advances for women. By entering the public sphere *en masse* and chipping away over the decades at educational and professional barriers, woman's rights activists had exponentially increased opportunities for many American women, although many inequalities still existed, especially because of race and class bias. Unfortunately, once they achieved their ultimate goal, the enfranchisement of women, most political communities of feminist reformers disbanded, and after a honeymoon period in which both Republicans and Democrats courted new women voters, their voices were relatively negligible in actually determining U.S. legal policy (although that is no longer the case as "women's issues" have become pivotal ones in campaigns).

In some ways, female suffrage came at a particularly inauspicious moment: two years after the end of World War I. American society, rattled by the tumultuous violence and cultural upheaval it had just endured, attempted a forced return to "normalcy" and as part of that effort tried to reinstate traditional middle-class gender roles. This conservative backlash is clear in an essay from the June 1919 issue of *Scribner's Magazine* entitled "The Limits of Feminine Independence." The author claims that the recent world war had "served to set once more in high light an old truth [. . .] [of] the fundamental differences between the sexes which quasi-feministic propaganda had begun to discredit and confuse" (Grant 733–34). The result, according to the article, is that America has returned "automatically to primitive instincts and the habits of the tribe" (Grant 733). The author's use of "primitive instincts" is telling in that it could describe a visceral, fearful reaction to something considered dangerous, although he probably did not mean the phrase to convey that sense. In postwar America, anything perceived as a challenge to patriotism or to the nuclear family—both conservative mainstays of the culture—was considered threatening. According to historian Sarah Jane Deutsch, American society's "primitive instincts" thus led it particularly to fear the spread of communism, aptly named the Red Scare, which was ostensibly working to overthrow democracy and capitalism. Additionally, it expressed fear of homosexuality (especially of homosexual women), which was perceived as a corrupting influence on conventional family life.

The unorthodox feminist activity of white middle-class women, especially collectively agitating for reform, was also perceived as threatening and according to Deutsch, conservatives quelled it by connecting it to these two sources of anxiety: "In an era in which any organizing at all was suspect, women in the 1920s could either organize together for equality and rights and be labeled 'red' and fired, or they could try to go it alone" (424). Furthermore, during the 1920s and '30s, "Women did not cease [. . .] to rely on other women for support and intimacy. As with politics, however, the range of tolerated behavior shrank, and what had been acceptable before the war was now questionable" (439). Just as women became reluctant to protest together because they could lose their jobs, America's pervasive homophobia discouraged them from creating large single-sex reform communities. Thus, the threat of association with communism and homosexuality played a large role in the demise of widespread, "acceptable" feminist activism like we see in suffrage novels from the 1910s, such as *For Rent—One Pedestal*, *The Sturdy Oak*, and later, Haskell's short story cycle, *Banner Bearers*.

Nevertheless, the feminist activist heroine did not fade from the literary scene; rather, the disillusionment and conservative political backlash she experienced in the wake of women's enfranchisement were incorporated into her story. A brief look at two novels from the 1930s, Sinclair Lewis's *Ann Vickers* (1933) and Janet Ayer Fairbank's *Rich Man, Poor Man* (1936), demonstrates this development. Both Lewis and Fairbank supported woman suffrage in the 1910s; Lewis's wife, Dorothy Thompson (to whom his book is dedicated), was an ardent suffragist, and Fairbank likewise was quite involved in the movement. However, the authors' ambivalent portrayals of their heroines' feminism a little more than a decade after ratification reveal that the writers had become disenchanted with the promise of a better world through woman suffrage and, in some ways, had to share mainstream America's increasingly reactionary attitude about gender. In each case, the heroine's suffrage work serves as a gateway activity into further social reform work. However, while Lewis's Ann Vickers ends up a happy, married woman who defines her feminism very differently at the end of the story from the way she does at the beginning, Fairbank's Barbara Smith ends up completely on the fringe of American culture, poor, divorced from her husband and child, but still clinging to the feminist idealism with which she starts out.

The key to each woman's development is the way in which she adjusts to the more conservative social realities in America after suffrage. As the heroine who negotiates these new realities as mainstream society would prefer, it is appropriate that Ann Vickers becomes disillusioned with organized feminist activism even before women get the vote. She believes she has "stopped being an individual" and has become a "cog" instead; therefore, she decides to quit "and find out what Ann Vickers is now and whether she's become anything besides 'one of those young women at Suffrage Headquarters'" (132–33). While she still believes women should be enfranchised, Ann rejects communal feminist activism because she perceives it as a threat to her individuality, a sentiment that is in line with young professional women's attitudes in the 1920s and '30s. According to Deutsch, women "who wanted to succeed in the public world [. . .] believed the most important thing to leave behind was 'sex-consciousness,' their sense of themselves as women who shared interests with other women. They abandoned any organized quest for general social reform and opted instead for individualism" (424). Nevertheless, Ann's experiences as a suffragist, and specifically, a brief stint she spends in jail, lead to her future vocation: prison reform. She does not abandon her goal of improving society, but she loses interest in gender reform and gives up communal activity, charting a more individual, less inflammatory path that proves successful for her.

It is perhaps not surprising that Ann's "successful negotiation" of an increasingly conservative America includes her wholesale rejection of both lesbianism and communism. In an introduction to the novel's reprint, Nan Bauer Maglin notes that "[d]uring the 1920s, Ann becomes more moderate, gradually replacing her earlier radical views with liberal ones" (xvi). However, Lewis makes it clear that his heroine's early "radicalism" never included an acceptance of homosexuality. Ann is repulsed by what she calls the "cloying hypnotism of involuted sex" during her college days, and she dreads the "treacherous sweetness" of the attention she receives from her roommate, Eula (69). The novel endorses Ann's homophobia, as it does her individualism, as an attitude that saves her from what postwar America perceived as the excesses of feminist activism. In fact, part of Ann's project as a prison superintendent later in the novel is to eradicate homosexual relationships among the inmates to "protect" many of the young women who are incarcerated. Just as the author insists on Ann's heterosexuality, he leaves no doubt that his heroine is patriotic. While she is not completely unsympathetic to socialist and communist views early in the novel, she rejects them later on, and the novel demonstrates how much more effective she is when she works within the system. Ann writes moderate articles about prison reform and publishes them in a mainstream liberal magazine, the *Statesman*. These articles elicit the outrage of the *Proletarian Pep*, "the chief Communist journal of America." This journal's editorialist calls the *Statesman* the "wishy-washiest of all milk and water liberal sheets" and says that Ann is a "Social Fascist [. . .] [who] under a disguise of so-called Liberalism [is] secretly helping the Capitalists to bring about war with the U. S. S. R." (384–85). By parodying communist rhetoric, Lewis distances his heroine from any potentially threatening connection to radical social movements, just as he distances her from lesbianism through her obvious disgust. In this way, Lewis panders to the reactionary fears of his readers and presents a "milk and water" version of reform that his readers will find palatable.

I do not mean to suggest, however, that Ann Vickers is a completely conservative, antifeminist heroine. In fact, much of her story is incredibly unconventional. She has an affair and an abortion, goes through a divorce, and finally marries a man who is not purely respectable. The novel does not judge Ann for these actions, but depicts her sympathetically as a complex, fully realized character. Furthermore, Ann achieves great personal success; she is known nationally as a leading expert on the penal system and is even given an honorary doctorate for her progressive leadership in this system. In this way, we see the progressive legacy of earlier feminist activist heroines. It is now possible to imagine such a liberated personal and professional life for a woman—at least a white, middle-class one—who is happily accepted by mainstream society. However, the price for such acceptance in the 1930s was a rejection of the very movement that made women's success possible. In a 1927 *Harper's* article, "Feminist—New Style," Dorothy Dunbar Bromley writes, "The pioneer feminists were hard-hitting individuals, and the modern young woman admires them for their courage, even while she judges them for their zealotry and their inartistic methods. [. . .] They fought her battle, but *she* does not want to wear their mantle" (552).

In such a conservative climate, part of this rejection stems from the affirmation of those "primitive instincts" about the differences between the sexes noted above. Ann Vickers articulates such instinctual thoughts when she says, "How simple we were when we used to talk about something called 'Feminism'! We were going to be just like men, in every field. We can't. Either we're stronger (say, as rulers, like Queen Elizabeth) or we're weaker, in our subservience to children. For all we said in 1916, we're still women, not embryonic men—thank God!" (409). Thus, the meaning of the word "feminism" for Ann has changed and Lewis's narrator uses the term, without irony, when he describes Ann as "the Captive Woman, the Free Woman, the Great Woman, the Feminist Woman, the Domestic Woman, the Passionate Woman, the Cosmopolitan Woman, the Village Woman—the Woman" (562). This litany of contradictory adjectives seems an attempt to fill out Ann Vickers's more "mature" individualistic definition of feminism. In many ways, though, the list seems more like a veneer for the novel's conservative ending since these words are used to describe Ann as she speaks to her new husband in "meek ecstasy," telling him he has saved her from "the prison of ambition, the prison of desire for praise, the prison of [her]self" (562). Here, the revolutionary potential of the feminist activist heroine has been attenuated severely by her retreat to the role of self-effacing wife, even if she has a lucrative career and is allowed to vote.

Written three years later, Barbara Smith's story in *Rich Man, Poor Man* is the reverse image of Ann Vickers's. Instead of the story of a feminist activist who has "successfully" negotiated the reactionary climate of postwar America, Barbara's story seems a cautionary tale about the activist who remains committed to her radical ideas. Like Hamlin Garland's feminist heroine, Ida Wilbur, Barbara begins her political career in the Midwest, campaigning to improve farmers' economic conditions through the Progressive Party. Barbara is also an ardent suffragist, and when she marries Hendricks, a wealthy young man she meets through the Progressive Party, she returns to Chicago with him and continues agitating for both causes. The first indication that Barbara's story will not turn out like Ann's is the fact that she remains immersed in the suffrage movement. Instead of becoming disillusioned with its communal nature and focus on gender equality, Barbara grows increasingly militant in her commitment. She joins the Congressional Union, the historical precursor of Alice Paul's National Woman's Party. Hendricks disapproves of this decision because he thinks it indecorous for a society wife to be affiliated with such an infamous group as well as imprudent for her to attack the president by picketing him (a tactic of the Congressional Union) when he supports much of the Progressive platform. However, Barbara insists that there is "only one plank that [she is] interested in, and that is woman suffrage" (268). While Fairbank, like Lewis, portrays suffrage activity somewhat sympathetically, the novel nevertheless shows how Barbara's militancy alienates her from her husband and friends. Hendricks finds her zealotry "unnatural" in a woman and believes that her emotional capacity is limited by her political fervor: "It was strange, considering ardor was what she brought to her crusades, that it should be lacking in her private life, but he was quite certain that when a cause which seemed to her important intervened, softer considerations of a personal nature would fall into second place" (289). The implicit criticism here is that she puts her activist work before her primary roles as wife and mother.

Once World War I is over and woman suffrage is won, Barbara does not, like most feminist activists, retreat from organized political activism; rather, she alienates herself further from both her family and her community by becoming intimate with the radical Bohemian subculture. She and Hendricks are estranged because he was unfaithful during the war, and while everyone believes she should forgive him, she welcomes the freedom she feels justified in claiming. Thus, she moves to New York to be near Della Masters, a woman she met during the suffrage campaigns. Once there, Della introduces her to Luke McCarthy, a writer for the *Liberator*, and other Bolshevik sympathizers. Hendricks visits her in New York, and is "amazed to see that she had apparently accepted without question a miscellaneous group of Greenwich Villagers [. . .] and that she excitedly accepted their dictum as a new gospel of freedom" (595). In his opinion, "She was much more combative than she had been before, and she now considered herself an authority on matters about which her husband suspected she knew very little about" (595–96). It should be noted that Hendricks's life has progressed very differently from Barbara's. He has entered the family's banking business and tempered his earlier liberal views considerably, which causes an even deeper rift between himself and his wife. Therefore, it is not unreasonable to assume his more conservative opinions color this depiction of Barbara's political activity. Regardless of the accuracy of Hendricks's assessment, however, he is right in seeing that Barbara has moved out of mainstream culture. The text does not spend much time with her while she is a part of this subculture; instead, she is increasingly marginalized while her husband's story becomes central. The reader loses sight of her completely shortly after Hendricks's visit when she sails to Russia with Della, where they hope to "have an interview with Trotsky" (603).

Near the end of novel, Luke McCarthy comes to Hendricks's office to ask him to divorce Barbara so that she and Luke can be married. The confrontation between these two men reveals a great deal about the cost of Barbara's unrepentant radicalism. Aside from his one act of indiscretion, Hendricks has been portrayed as a loving, well-meaning husband throughout the novel, and he has been especially devoted to his and Barbara's daughter, Ann. Hendricks agrees to the divorce but insists on giving Barbara a financial settlement in exchange for custody of Ann. Luke does not think Barbara will agree to these terms, but Hendricks has clearly been the more responsible and responsive parent, and there seems little doubt he will end up with the child. Luke, however, promises to be a very different kind of husband. He claims he is better able to handle Barbara because he understands "[t]here are times when a woman needs clubbing" (611). The exchange of a loving husband and daughter for a union with a radical, violent communist does not bode well for Barbara, intimating that one must pay a price for transgressing the boundaries of acceptable feminist activism in postwar America, especially if one joins an even more marginalized reform movement: communism. By depicting Barbara's activism as degenerative, the novel suggests that a woman's commitment to political ideas in the current society is not only futile, but also potentially dangerous. It also links communism with barbarism and gratuitous violence, undermining even further the legitimacy of its agenda. Ultimately, Barbara's story seems a dubious fulfillment of Ida Wilbur's prediction that "One radicalism open[s] the way to the other. Being a radical is like opening the door to the witches" (Garland 42). While Hamlin Garland meant for his heroine's prophetic words to describe a world of broader sympathies and greater understanding among reformers, in Fairbank's book, they take on a more ominous meaning. Barbara's devotion to feminism has certainly opened her to associations with what the novel implies are wrong-headed, destructive causes, and as the reader learns, in postwar America, it is best for the feminist activist to keep the door closed.

However, her pending marriage is not the end of Barbara's story. It is a testament to the conflicted nature of Fairbank's book that its most sympathetic portrayal of Barbara comes in the final pages, in an epilogue of sorts. It has been several years since she and Hendricks have seen each other, and he is now a wealthy, complacent man, remarried to a doting wife. Driving past Union Square in his limousine, he sees Barbara giving a speech, and his driver reminds him that it is "the nuts' big day" in the Square (625). He gets out to see her more clearly, and although she "looked worn" and her figure had "thickened somewhat" (625), Hendricks thinks she seems happy. He, like everyone else, is overcome by the power of her voice, and she is warmly applauded by the other "nuts" who listen to her. As Hendricks walks away, he realizes he is glad that he has seen her, because he has been reminded why he loved her: "That wholehearted commitment seemed to him a wonderful thing, and as he made his way through the dwindling crowd he found himself envying, as he always had, her power of consecration. It seemed to him a long time since he had known the supreme contentment of unquestioning faith—since he, too, had been free" (626). While Barbara is apparently at peace in this scene, Hendricks is not. Writ large, his nostalgia for the "unquestioning faith" that Barbara represents recalls the disillusionment of American society in the 1920s and '30s. Having seen their world destroyed by war, most people found it difficult to maintain an "unquestioning faith" in anything, so they reacted by rebuilding their world along predictable, conservative lines. In this new America, feminist activists—fictional and real—were either reintegrated in a nonthreatening way or marginalized and rendered powerless.

Perhaps it is fitting that the tradition of American fiction about feminist activism I trace in this study begins and ends with cautionary tales: Sarah Josepha Hale's *The Lecturess* (1839) and Janet Ayer Fairbank's *Rich Man, Poor Man* (1936). Like Hale's much earlier heroine, Fairbank's Barbara loses her husband and child because of her political commitment, but unlike Hale's character, Barbara is allowed to live and be "free," albeit at a safe distance from mainstream society. While clearly this latter ending is a happier one for the feminist activist heroine, in many ways it is only marginally so. If we compare these two novels as "symbolic acts," we see that the first wave of feminism in America at best achieved a partial victory over historical and literary expectations for women. These narratives make clear that feminist activism (and the representation of it in fiction) has not been able to eradicate completely the stigma of women's political participation nor has it managed to overcome society's heterosexist insistence that heroines be punished for not privileging their domestic roles above their public ones, even though, as I have argued, they made significant inroads on both fronts.

The question, then, becomes, why not? In part, as Ida Wilbur, Garland's heroine, sagely warned her reform community, it "must include more or fail" (151). Like Marian Farrinder, Hale's tragic lecturess, Ann Vickers and Barbara Smith are representative feminist activist heroines, but they only represent a certain kind of American woman—educated, relatively affluent, white, native-born. As an oppositional community, the nineteenth- and early twentieth-century woman's movement never did overcome the tunnel vision of its privileged white leadership, although as I have argued, there are feminist activists—fictional and real and white, African American, and immigrant—who challenge this myopia in various ways. Therefore, the movement does not completely achieve Ann Ferguson's ideal of a community bound together by the choice—and not merely the social identity—of its members and by an egalitarian revolutionary love that could sustain it in the face of pressure from the status quo. By shrinking from a more radical, inclusive vision of feminist reform in novels and elsewhere, those promoting first-wave feminism insured that the activist heroine (and real-world activists) would eventually be held back by her own fear of other marginalized groups—the communist, the homosexual—instead of being strengthened by working alongside them. And, if she was not, then she was neutralized by being branded a "nut."

While this seems a rather gloomy ending to the tradition of nineteenth- and early twentieth-century feminist activist fiction, I would suggest that the conclusion of Fairbank's novel is a hopeful one for those who would continue advocating, not only for women, but for all marginalized groups. Like the reviewer for the *Una* whose resisting reader finds a heroine worth emulating in Dickens's Mrs. Jellyby, I find hope in Hendricks's final impression of Barbara. In showing that her feminist activist heroine experiences the liberation and "supreme contentment of unquestioning faith" in her convictions, Fairbank seems to suggest that those few who continue to pursue their reform work in spite of mainstream society's disapprobation, who maintain an allegiance to a genuine oppositional community, and who recognize the larger structures of oppression that are pervasive in our society, achieve a freedom the rest of the country has lost, or perhaps, has never found.

INTRODUCTION

1. Although the singular noun "woman" in "woman's rights" and "woman suffrage" might seem awkward to modern readers, I employ these terms because of their historical accuracy. I also employ them because the choice of the singular noun by nineteenth-century feminists was strategic, intended to unify women across boundaries of class and race and region by stressing their commonality. Of course, as later historians have noted, the conception of their commonality was narrowed considerably by the white, middle-class perspective of the leaders of reform, and I think this limitation is also important to keep in mind. Nevertheless, while middle-class values were dominant in the movement, they were often internally contested. See Nancy Cott's *The Grounding of Modern Feminism* for further discussion of this issue.

2. Sarah Josepha Hale (1788–1879) was an incredibly influential woman in nineteenth-century America. Although she promoted the idea that women should stay in their domestic sphere, she worked outside the home as the editor of *Godey's Lady's Journal*. In this capacity, she controlled the content of the nation's most popular women's magazine, disseminating her views about women's proper roles. Maria W. Miller Stewart (1803–79) was born to African parents and "bound out" to a clergyman's family at the age of five. As an adult, she was an abolitionist and essayist, and in 1832 she became the first American woman to address publicly a mixed-gender audience. Sarah Grimké (1792–1873) and Angelina Grimké Weld (1805–79) were born to a slaveholder in South Carolina, but as adults they moved to the North, joined the abolitionist movement, and delivered speeches in New York and Massachusetts during the late 1830s. Karlyn Kohrs Campbell observes, "Their lectures were the beginning of major efforts to break the barriers against women speaking in public" (*A Critical Study of Early Feminist Rhetoric*).

3. Barbara Bardes and Suzanne Gossett's *Declarations of Independence: Women and Political Power in Nineteenth-Century American Fiction* is one of the first and most comprehensive of the critical studies about feminist activism's relationship to American literature. They look at several ways that women's political participation influenced American literature, but they dismiss what they call "pro-woman's rights novels" as "little more than fictionalized didactic tracts" (180) and reduce them summarily to a single thesis: "All agree that the vote, and only the vote, can ensure protection for women" (180).

In her book, *Passions of the Voice: Hysteria, Narrative, and the Figure of the Speaking Woman, 1850–1915*, Clare Kahane specifically explores the nineteenth-century phenomena of women entering the public arena as speaking subjects. However, *The Bostonians* is the lone example of novels representing feminist activists in her book. Thus, her picture of the fictional incarnation of the speaking woman is incomplete because she omits novels less ambivalent about the value of reform and the positive potential of women's political intervention.

In contrast to Kahane's book, which offers a psychoanalytic reading, Caroline Levander's *Voices of the Nation: Women and Public Speech in Nineteenth-Century American Literature and Culture* looks at the social work accomplished by novels that pay attention to women's voices and how they helped construct and solidify the emerging middle-class culture of the nineteenth century. Levander ultimately argues that depictions of women speaking in public serve a conservative function by devaluing such public performance, a contention that is problematized considerably by the tradition of feminist activist fiction discussed in this book.

4. Davidson and Hatcher are the editors of *No More Separate Spheres* (2002), a collection of essays that includes many articles from the *American Literature* issue of the same name and whose goal is to begin this dismantling. Another collection of essays, *Separate Spheres No More: Gender Convergence in American Literature, 1830–1930*, edited by Monika M. Elbert, was published two years earlier, attesting to the current scholarly determination to deconstruct this pervasive binary.

5. In her influential *Dimity Convictions: The American Woman in the Nineteenth Century*, Barbara Welter defines this cultural ideal as having four characteristics: purity, piety, submissiveness, and domesticity (21).

6. In *The Grounding of Modern Feminism*, Nancy Cott notes that the word "feminism" was not widely used until 1910 and was not listed in the *Oxford English Dictionary* until 1933 (3–4).

CHAPTER ONE. "True Christian Philanthropy"; or,
a Release from the "Prison-House" of Marriage

1. Elizabeth Cady Stanton, along with Lucretia Mott, is credited with getting the woman's rights movement underway in America by organizing the Seneca Falls Convention in 1848. She met Susan B. Anthony (who began her activist career working for the temperance movement) a few years later. The two became lifelong friends and activist partners. In 1869 they founded the National Woman Suffrage Association (NWSA) and began publishing *The Revolution*, which was the official journal of the organization. William D'Arcy Wentworth Thompson (1829–1902) was a classics scholar and became chair of the Greek department at Queen's College Galway (in Ireland) in 1864. He was quite progressive in both his politics and his pedagogy. The passage quoted in *The Revolution* comes from his book, *Wayside Thoughts* (1868), and the poet laureate he refers to here is Alfred Lord Tennyson whose poem "The Day-Dream" was published in his 1842 *Poems*.

2. The simultaneous founding of two national suffrage organizations happened, in part, because of a dispute over the passage of the Fourteenth and Fifteenth Amendments.

INTRODUCTION

1. Although the singular noun "woman" in "woman's rights" and "woman suffrage" might seem awkward to modern readers, I employ these terms because of their historical accuracy. I also employ them because the choice of the singular noun by nineteenth-century feminists was strategic, intended to unify women across boundaries of class and race and region by stressing their commonality. Of course, as later historians have noted, the conception of their commonality was narrowed considerably by the white, middle-class perspective of the leaders of reform, and I think this limitation is also important to keep in mind. Nevertheless, while middle-class values were dominant in the movement, they were often internally contested. See Nancy Cott's *The Grounding of Modern Feminism* for further discussion of this issue.

2. Sarah Josepha Hale (1788–1879) was an incredibly influential woman in nineteenth-century America. Although she promoted the idea that women should stay in their domestic sphere, she worked outside the home as the editor of *Godey's Lady's Journal*. In this capacity, she controlled the content of the nation's most popular women's magazine, disseminating her views about women's proper roles. Maria W. Miller Stewart (1803–79) was born to African parents and "bound out" to a clergyman's family at the age of five. As an adult, she was an abolitionist and essayist, and in 1832 she became the first American woman to address publicly a mixed-gender audience. Sarah Grimké (1792–1873) and Angelina Grimké Weld (1805–79) were born to a slaveholder in South Carolina, but as adults they moved to the North, joined the abolitionist movement, and delivered speeches in New York and Massachusetts during the late 1830s. Karlyn Kohrs Campbell observes, "Their lectures were the beginning of major efforts to break the barriers against women speaking in public" (*A Critical Study of Early Feminist Rhetoric*).

3. Barbara Bardes and Suzanne Gossett's *Declarations of Independence: Women and Political Power in Nineteenth-Century American Fiction* is one of the first and most comprehensive of the critical studies about feminist activism's relationship to American literature. They look at several ways that women's political participation influenced American literature, but they dismiss what they call "pro-woman's rights novels" as "little more than fictionalized didactic tracts" (180) and reduce them summarily to a single thesis: "All agree that the vote, and only the vote, can ensure protection for women" (180).

In her book, *Passions of the Voice: Hysteria, Narrative, and the Figure of the Speaking Woman, 1850–1915*, Clare Kahane specifically explores the nineteenth-century phenomena of women entering the public arena as speaking subjects. However, *The Bostonians* is the lone example of novels representing feminist activists in her book. Thus, her picture of the fictional incarnation of the speaking woman is incomplete because she omits novels less ambivalent about the value of reform and the positive potential of women's political intervention.

In contrast to Kahane's book, which offers a psychoanalytic reading, Caroline Levander's *Voices of the Nation: Women and Public Speech in Nineteenth-Century American Literature and Culture* looks at the social work accomplished by novels that pay attention to women's voices and how they helped construct and solidify the emerging middle-class culture of the nineteenth century. Levander ultimately argues that depictions of women speaking in public serve a conservative function by devaluing such public performance, a contention that is problematized considerably by the tradition of feminist activist fiction discussed in this book.

4. Davidson and Hatcher are the editors of *No More Separate Spheres* (2002), a collection of essays that includes many articles from the *American Literature* issue of the same name and whose goal is to begin this dismantling. Another collection of essays, *Separate Spheres No More: Gender Convergence in American Literature, 1830–1930*, edited by Monika M. Elbert, was published two years earlier, attesting to the current scholarly determination to deconstruct this pervasive binary.

5. In her influential *Dimity Convictions: The American Woman in the Nineteenth Century*, Barbara Welter defines this cultural ideal as having four characteristics: purity, piety, submissiveness, and domesticity (21).

6. In *The Grounding of Modern Feminism*, Nancy Cott notes that the word "feminism" was not widely used until 1910 and was not listed in the *Oxford English Dictionary* until 1933 (3–4).

CHAPTER ONE. "True Christian Philanthropy"; or,
a Release from the "Prison-House" of Marriage

1. Elizabeth Cady Stanton, along with Lucretia Mott, is credited with getting the woman's rights movement underway in America by organizing the Seneca Falls Convention in 1848. She met Susan B. Anthony (who began her activist career working for the temperance movement) a few years later. The two became lifelong friends and activist partners. In 1869 they founded the National Woman Suffrage Association (NWSA) and began publishing *The Revolution*, which was the official journal of the organization. William D'Arcy Wentworth Thompson (1829–1902) was a classics scholar and became chair of the Greek department at Queen's College Galway (in Ireland) in 1864. He was quite progressive in both his politics and his pedagogy. The passage quoted in *The Revolution* comes from his book, *Wayside Thoughts* (1868), and the poet laureate he refers to here is Alfred Lord Tennyson whose poem "The Day-Dream" was published in his 1842 *Poems*.

2. The simultaneous founding of two national suffrage organizations happened, in part, because of a dispute over the passage of the Fourteenth and Fifteenth Amendments.

NWSA was founded by Elizabeth Cady Stanton and Susan B. Anthony, both of whom disapproved of these amendments, because they inserted the word "male" into the Constitution with regard to suffrage. Henry Blackwell and Lucy Stone, who supported passage of the amendments, started AWSA. Beyond this dispute, there were other differences in the two organizations. AWSA is considered by most historians to be the more moderate and mainstream association, confining its interests pretty narrowly to woman suffrage and supporting state-by-state referendums for achieving this goal. The NWSA, on the other hand, concerned itself with a diffuse set of issues such as prostitution, dress reform, divorce, and sexual abuse, and it supported a federal amendment on the grounds that it was the best way to insure women's enfranchisement. See Flexner 136–48 for further discussion.

3. See Barbara Welter's book *Dimity Convictions* for an explanation of the Cult of True Womanhood in nineteenth-century America.

4. As I noted in my introduction, recent scholarship has challenged the idea that there was such a division of gendered roles, arguing that the boundary between these ostensibly separate spheres was blurred in the lives of men and women in the nineteenth century. My interest is more in the rhetorical discourse of separate spheres that proscribed narrow gender roles and influenced the attitudes of all classes in America. This rhetoric reached a fever pitch as the nineteenth century progressed, suggesting that its power was waning. See *Separate Spheres No More*, edited by Monika M. Elbert, and *No More Separate Spheres*, edited by Cathy Davidson and Jessamyn Hatcher, for further discussion.

5. Of course, many critics, including Dobson, have identified subversive potential in even these two novels, which seem the most conventional. Nevertheless, most scholars agree that the novels overtly promote to their female readers the virtues of self-sacrifice and confinement to the domestic sphere.

6. Aileen Kraditor was the first to identify these two strains of discourse and to label them arguments of justice and arguments of expediency. Kraditor clarifies the rationale underscoring justice arguments: "In asserting that natural right applied also to women, the suffragists stressed the ways in which men and women were identical. Their common humanity was at the core of the suffragist argument" (44). On the other hand, Kraditor explains, expediency arguments stressed "the ways in which [women] differed from men, and therefore had the *duty* to contribute their special skills and experience to government" (66).

7. All biographical information about Harbert comes from the Elizabeth Boynton Harbert Collection, Huntington Library, San Marino, California.

8. This speech is taken from the Elizabeth Boynton Harbert Collection, Huntington Library, San Marino, California.

9. Harbert is perhaps suggesting to her readers that the time for abolitionist reform is over ("the slaves are free"), and that it is now time to focus on questions of gender, a suggestion that brings white women's concerns to the fore.

10. Kraditor's terms "arguments of expediency" and "arguments of justice" suggest

a value judgment on her part about which ideology is more ethically sound. Justice arguments from natural rights seem preferable to those from expediency, which imply a short-term, short-sighted agenda. I use Kraditor's terms without qualification, first, because they are standard in the discipline of speech communications but also and just as importantly because I agree with her assessment.

11. The WCTU was founded in 1874 as part of what Eleanor Flexner describes as a "crusade" against alcoholism that had an overtly religious tone (174). Although the overwhelming majority of alcoholics were men, temperance was clearly a "woman's issue," because the consequences of this alcoholism, including destitution and domestic violence, affected many women and children. The WCTU, thanks in large part to Frances Willard's charismatic appeal, rapidly became a nationally popular organization with thousands of members. Willard used her platform to lobby for woman suffrage, making her a strong ally of the suffragists. However, the temperance support of woman suffrage also created a backlash among the liquor interests, who were afraid that if women were given the vote then prohibition laws would be passed more quickly.

12. These letters can be found in the Elizabeth Boynton Harbert Collection.

13. Many scholars have pointed out the exclusionary nature of the construct that pits white females against black males. See "Racism and Feminism: The Issue of Accountability," in bell hooks's *Ain't I a Woman: Black Women and Feminism*, for a particularly astute analysis.

14. The Quakers are something of an exception because they have always allowed women to speak as freely as men during meetings. It is no coincidence that many early feminist activists, like Lucretia Mott, were Quakers.

15. Once again, Stowe's influence seems pertinent. Jane Tompkins has argued that *Uncle Tom's Cabin* is "typological" and that Tom's story is Christ's retold as the story of a slave, an idea that likely would have struck contemporary readers as odd. The suggestion that Harbert's heroine is the story of the Virgin Mary retold as the story of a white feminist activist would no doubt have seemed similarly unorthodox to contemporary readers.

16. Because more egalitarian living conditions were a necessity on the frontier, many western territories and states granted women either full or partial suffrage in the late nineteenth century. See Flexner 147–56 for further discussion.

17. For further discussion of the misappropriation of slave experience by suffragists, see Karen Sánchez-Eppler's essay "Bodily Bonds: The Intersecting Rhetorics of Feminism and Abolition."

The Seneca Falls Convention, organized by Elizabeth Cady Stanton and Lucretia Mott, is generally considered to have officially launched the woman's rights movement in America. During it, Stanton read a Declaration of Sentiments, modeled on the Declaration of Independence, which was primarily a list of specific gender reforms the delegates were asked to support; the most controversial of these reforms at the time was woman suffrage.

18. Lydia Maria Child (1802–80) was a nationally known writer (her first novel, *Hobomok*, was published in 1824) and abolitionist; she also was the editor of Harriet

Jacobs's slave narrative, *Incidents in the Life of a Slave Girl* (1861). Lucretia Mott (1793–1880), a Quaker, was one of the first important female abolitionists in America and a founder of the woman's movement. Frances Anne "Fanny" Kemble (1809–93) was a famous British actress who married an American slave-owner, Pierce Butler. After seeing the conditions in which their slaves lived, Kemble divorced her husband and became active in the abolitionist movement.

19. Farrell is referring specifically to Woolf's fictional heroine Judith Shakespeare.

20. I do not mean to suggest here that white women *were* more vulnerable than other women—if anything, history shows that women of color were (and are) more susceptible to sexual abuse—only that it was a commonly held belief that they were.

21. The characters Biddy and Patrick Maloney, for example, are stereotypically named and characterized in racist ways.

22. It is also interesting to note that it is Frank, and not Guy, who rescues Laura from being kidnapped on two occasions.

23. Also during the interim between Guy's two proposals, Laura learns of Frank's true identity, thus eliminating the possibility of an alternate, unconventional love affair for Laura.

24. Rhoda's death in particular is reminiscent of another fallen woman's sacrificial death, that of Rosa's in *Hope Leslie*, though this literary precursor's end is much more dramatic. Rosa, believing that Hope has been captured by her former lover, the evil Sir Philip, and that he has plans to rape her, blows up a ship with all three of them on board, preferring to die herself rather than see her friend assaulted. It turns out that it was not Hope, but Jennet the housekeeper, who had been captured; still, this event reinforces the notion that fallen women can redeem themselves through a heroic death and also the idea that it is better to die than to be sexually defiled.

25. *Harper's New Monthly Magazine* was an internationally distributed, very popular, monthly periodical published in New York by Harper & Bros. from 1850–99.

CHAPTER TWO. Expanding the Vision of Feminist Activism

1. The National Woman Suffrage Association (NWSA) and the American Woman Suffrage Association (AWSA) merged in 1890 to form the National American Woman Suffrage Association (NAWSA). By this time, many of the philosophical differences between the two had been erased and, deploying expediency arguments, the NWSA increasingly focused on the vote; however, there was still a disagreement over the best tactic for gaining suffrage (state referendum or national amendment) that would not be settled until 1916 with Carrie Chapman Catt's "Winning Plan." See Flexner 208–17 for further discussion.

2. For further discussions of Jim Crow laws, see, for example, Floris L. B. Cash's *African American Women and Social Action: The Clubwomen and Volunteerism from Jim Crow to the New Deal, 1896–1936* (2001).

3. The argument that northern white feminists must appease the racism of their southern counterparts was often used to mask the racism of the northerners themselves. See chapter 3 and the work of Marjorie Spruill Wheeler and Rosalyn Terborg-Penn for further discussion.

4. Stanton delivered this speech to the Congressional Committee of the Judiciary on January 18, 1892, and again the next day as her resignation speech to NAWSA, when she stepped down as president. It was published a few days later in two periodicals affiliated with the association, the *Woman's Journal* and the *Woman's Tribune*, and also in pamphlet form by NAWSA headquarters.

5. For a fuller account of Stanton's racist rhetoric, see chapter 1. See also Ellen Carol DuBois, Angela Davis, and Louise Michele Newman.

6. Little is known about the identity of Harper's parents, although there is speculation that her father was white. See Frances Smith Foster's introduction to *A Brighter Coming Day: A Frances Ellen Watkins Harper Reader* for a thorough biographical sketch of Harper.

7. These earlier novels include *The Bondswoman's Narrative* by Hannah Crafts, first published in 2002 (edited by Henry Louis Gates), as well as Harriet Wilson's *Our Nig*, published in 1859, and some of Harper's own serialized works.

8. "Colorism" is a term used both within the African American community and in society at large to describe the prejudice based on relative lightness of skin tone.

9. See, for example, Deborah McDowell, Marilyn Elkins, Barbara Christian, and Elizabeth Ammons.

10. By "privileged readers" I mean both white readers and members of the African American "elite," the black middle class whom Du Bois called the "Talented Tenth" and who had social, financial, and educational opportunities not available to most African Americans.

11. Lauren Berlant also notes the pivotal role of this scene, observing that Iola's "transition between lexicons, laws, privileges, and races takes place, appropriately, as a transition from dreaming to waking" (557).

12. Iola is not central to the first few chapters, which describe an African American slave community before emancipation.

13. M. Giulia Fabi claims that in rejecting Dr. Gresham, Iola is "able to assert [her] free will and negotiate, at least, less victimizing conditions of survival through the exercise of negative freedom, that is the liberty of turning down offers, rather than that of making choices" (231). Certainly Iola's turning down Dr. Gresham's offer is crucial for her survival, but I do not see it as a merely passive exercise in "negative freedom;" in fact, I see her refusal as part of an active choice-making process.

14. Racial uplift in the nineteenth and early twentieth century was a broad-based, often contradictory movement plagued by internal and external debates and disagreements about its major tenets; I can only touch on its complexity here.

15. Some critics note that Lucille Delany is probably named after the historical Lucy A. Delany, a slave woman who sued for her freedom in 1844 and who had published her autobiography in the 1880s. See, for example, P. Gabrielle Foreman's essay.

16. The earlier incarnations of this movement, which began in the 1870s, were known as the Grange movement and then the Farmer's Alliance.

17. The *Forum* was a periodical conceived as an arena in which experts on reform issues could express their views. It was published from 1886–1930, when it merged with *Century* magazine.

18. While there is not enough material evidence to argue persuasively that Ida B. Wells was a role model for Garland's heroine as well as Harper's, it is certainly worth noting the resonance in their names.

CHAPTER THREE. Making It New

1. Harriot Stanton Blatch was Elizabeth Cady Stanton's daughter and a leader of the twentieth-century suffrage movement, especially in New York, where she founded the Equality League. The years 1896–1910 are widely known as the "doldrums" for the suffrage movement, a time during which no new states voted for woman suffrage and when the matter was not discussed on the floor of either house in Congress. Many factors contributed to this malaise, including the narrow but dispiriting defeat of woman suffrage in California in 1896 and the new system of national conventions under a unified National Woman Suffrage Association (NWSA) that took the meeting out of Washington, D.C., every other year, thus lessening the pressure on the federal government. See Flexner 241–54.

2. I use the term "suffragist" in this chapter more often than "woman's rights activist," because at this historical moment, the movement had narrowed its goal almost exclusively to enfranchising women.

3. It should also be remembered that reform was a major concern of Americans in general during the first two decades of the twentieth century, hence the name, the "Progressive Era."

4. See Andreas Huyssen's *After the Great Divide: Modernism, Mass Culture, Postmodernism* (1986).

5. Robert and Helen Lynds went to Muncie, Indiana, in 1924 to conduct what they called "a small town study." They documented many aspects of the town's culture, paying particular attention to the way industrialization had changed it. The subsequent book they published, *Middletown* (1929), became a popular success. Dorothy Canfield was one of the most popular American authors of the early twentieth century. She is also a contributor to *The Sturdy Oak*.

6. While the epistolary novel was a conventional early form, its use was unprecedented in the tradition of American literature depicting feminist activism.

7. Jacobson also quotes from this essay at length.

8. The book is *Woman Suffrage and Politics: The Inner Story of the Suffrage Movement* (1923). Carrie Chapman Catt was president of NAWSA from 1900–1904 and 1915–20. Marjorie Shuler was also an officer in NAWSA, serving as corresponding secretary during the final years of the campaigns. She, too, wrote a well-known suffrage book (besides *For Rent*) entitled *The Woman Voter's Manual*, for which Catt wrote the introduction.

9. Like Delight Dennison and Marjorie Shuler, Harriot Stanton Blatch was also a second-generation suffragist, perhaps the most influential one in America, given that her mother was Elizabeth Cady Stanton.

10. As my earlier discussions reveal, however, Delight's "face" is not wholly "new" among feminist activist heroines. One sees her precursor in Laura Stanley in Lillie Devereux Blake's *Fettered for Life*, also a college-educated, self-supporting white heroine. However, I would argue that the primary differences between Delight and this predecessor are first, the latter's jocularity and lightheartedness and second, her initial unawareness of the precariousness of her situation as a working woman. Both of these traits suggest the relative ease with which white women entered the workforce in the twentieth century as compared to their nineteenth-century counterparts.

11. Blatch founded the Equality League of Self-Supporting Women in 1907, realizing her dream of an oppositional community of women who worked for a living, both in the professions and as skilled and unskilled labor. The organization's name later changed to the Women's Political Union, and it lost its emphasis on the woman-as-worker.

12. In this way, Blake's *Fettered for Life* (1874), discussed in the first chapter, is more prophetic in its vision of oppositional community formation than other nineteenth-century books that stress women's domesticity and maternity.

13. There are countless recent books about the "New Woman" in history and literature, both in England and America. For further discussion, see for example, Ann Heilmann's *New Woman Fiction* (2000) and *The New Woman in Fiction and in Fact* (2000), edited by Angelique Richardson and Chris Willis.

14. I discuss the tropes of white woman-as-moral-arbiter and white woman-as-civilizer in this book's first chapter.

15. See Vron Ware's *Beyond the Pale: White Women, Racism and History* and Louise Michele Newman's *White Women's Rights* for further discussion of white women's appropriating the role of "protectors" of marginalized groups.

16. Matthew Frye Jacobson discusses the correlation between Anglo-Saxon ancestry and one's perceived "fitness for self-government" in *Whiteness of a Different Color: European Immigrants and the Alchemy of Race* (1998).

17. Several readers of this text have pointed out the parallels between Delight's biscuit-making contest and *Family Circle*'s Cookie Cook-off, which pitted Hillary Clinton's cookie recipe against Barbara Bush's in 1992 and against Elizabeth Dole's in 1996. Clinton won both contests.

18. In this way, *For Rent*'s depiction of maternal role models seems a specialized version of a common theme Maureen Honey identifies in New Woman fiction of this time period: "[W]hile the mother is usually absent, symbolizing the death of a past, home-centered community, a memory of her remains, as a negative role model, yes, but as also as a source of love and moral support" (Introduction 19).

19. One need only think of Samuel Richardson's *Pamela* and *Clarissa*, classic examples of the form, to see the validity of this statement.

20. *Harper's Bazar*, a popular women's magazine launched in 1867 and still published under the name *Harper's Bazaar*, is known for its fashion advice and clothing patterns.

21. Elizabeth Jordan was probably chosen not only because she was prosuffrage, but also because she had previous experience with this type of collaboration. In 1908, she and William Dean Howells orchestrated the serial publication of another composite novel, *The Whole Family*, which includes chapters by writers such as Henry James and Mary E. Wilkins Freeman.

22. The *Dial* magazine, originally published from 1840 to 1844 as a vehicle for the American transcendentalist movement, was revived by Marianne Moore in the twentieth century as one of the "little magazines" that published modernist poetry.

23. See, for example, Helen Damon-Moore's *Magazines for the Millions: Gender and Commerce in the "Ladies' Home Journal" and the "Saturday Evening Post," 1880–1910* (1994); Joan Shelley Rubin's *The Making of Middlebrow Culture* (1992); Julia Ehrhardt's *Writers of Conviction* (2004); and *Middlebrow Moderns* (2003), which has a section entitled "The Middlebrow and Magazine Culture" that includes essays by Maureen Honey and Jaime Harker.

24. Of course, *Collier's* paid three thousand dollars for *The Sturdy Oak* seven years later; nonetheless, it seems that if it were an exorbitant price in 1910, it would still be a competitive one in 1917.

25. Authorial correspondence about *The Sturdy Oak* excerpted here can be found in the Elizabeth G. Jordan Collection at the New York Public Library and is quoted with permission.

26. Elizabeth Jordan to "Miss Bjorkman" (most likely Frances Maule Bjorkman, a third-generation suffragist and writer affiliated with the *Woman Citizen*), October 23, 1917. One conflict that is mentioned specifically is William Allen White's virulent opposition to serializing *The Sturdy Oak* in any of the Hearst publications. He writes to Jordan that although he understands Jordan's desire for wide circulation, he believes "for the suffrage novel to appear in a Hearst magazine along with the smutty, sex stuff that Hearst puts in his magazines, will hurt the suffrage novel and propaganda and the suffrage cause as a righteous cause infinitely more than the suffrage cause will be helped by appearing in the Hearst papers."

27. "Trimmer" is an informal term for one who "modifies a policy, position or opinion, especially out of expediency" (*Merriam-Webster Dictionary Online*, February 3, 2003).

28. One earlier scene in *The Sturdy Oak* also points to the ethnic and class differences among the women. George fires Betty Sheridan because she is spearheading the public campaign to make him speak out about factory conditions. For Betty, this is a moral blow but not a material one. However, she (and the reader) is given a "sudden, sinister illumination upon the relations of working women to their employers," wondering what would have happened if "instead of being a prosperous, protected young woman playing the wage-earner more or less as Marie Antoinette had played the milkmaid, she had been Mamie Riley across the hall, whose work was bitter earnest, whose earnings were not pin money, but bread and meat and brother's schooling and mother's health—would George still have made the stifling of her views the price of her position?" (79–80).

29. While this story is clearly a sympathetic portrait of interclass and intercultural

bonding among women, the story's indebtedness to the Rudyard Kipling poem "The Ladies," and specifically to its final couplet, "For the Colonel's Lady and Judy O'Grady / Are sisters under their skins," problematizes this positive portrayal. The poem, written in what seems to be Irish dialect, is about the sexual conquests of the speaker, a soldier in the British army. The stereotypical depiction of this speaker as well as his contention that "But the things you will learn from the Yellow an' Brown / They'll 'elp you a lot with the White" reveal a disturbing racial and gender hierarchy that undermines any notion of genuine commonality among women of different races or of compassion between women and men.

30. *Banner Bearers* is 350 pages long, almost twice the length of *For Rent—One Pedestal* and *The Sturdy Oak.*

31. The Reverend Dr. Anna Howard Shaw (1847–1919) was a Methodist minister, a medical doctor, and one of the most accomplished orators of the suffrage movement. She served as president of NAWSA from 1904 to 1915. Carrie Chapman Catt was perhaps the best-known twentieth-century suffragist; she was president of NAWSA from 1900 to 1904 and then again from 1915 to 1920, during which time she engineered and implemented the organization's "Winning Plan," which accelerated considerably the passage of the Nineteenth Amendment.

The lines between fictional feminists and their real-life counterparts break down in many ways in this text. For example, the microfilm copy of *Banner Bearers*, available through the *History of Women* microfilm collection, was made from Carrie Chapman Catt's personal copy of the book housed at the Schlesinger Library that bears the following inscription: "To *The Boss*: With love and with hope that you will enjoy these little glimpses into the past days of You, Us, and Company. From the Author. Nov 12, 1920." Further, the second story in the collection is entitled "Sizing Up a Boss" and its theme is the multifaceted personality and tireless work of Mary Genston Hale, the president of the state NAWSA affiliate.

32. "Short story sequence" is Kennedy's preferred term for the genre, and he explains his reasons in the introduction to his edited volume *Modern American Short Story Sequences.* However, it is clear from this introduction that he is discussing the same tradition as Nagel and others (Forrest Ingram and Susan Garland Mann, for example), all of whom use the term "short story cycle."

33. In the first volume of *No Man's Land*, Sandra Gilbert and Susan Gubar discuss at length the use of military rhetoric in suffrage polemics, both British and American. Furthermore, they link this rhetoric to larger concerns about gender in modernist literature at this historical moment, which they see as driven by a "battle of the sexes."

34. Alice Paul was a suffragist who, like Harriot Stanton Blatch, had spent time in England and had embraced British suffragists' more militant tactics. Consequently, she disagreed with Carrie Chapman Catt and other mainstream NAWSA members about the best publicity strategies. These disagreements led her to form a subcommittee within the organization called the Congressional Union, which then broke completely with NAWSA and renamed itself the National Woman's Party (NWP). This organization was the one

that led the picketing outside Woodrow Wilson's White House during World War I and whose members were arrested and subsequently went on hunger strikes. Eleanor Flexner criticizes NAWSA for not speaking out against the inhumane treatment of NWP members when they were mobbed, arrested for picketing outside the White House, and force fed in prison: "No disagreement as to the merits of the picketing and hunger strikes should be allowed to obscure [. . .] the fact that, with all too few exceptions, the leaders of the National suffrage association, including Mrs. Catt, tacitly acquiesced by their silence in the injustice done" (279).

35. As I note in chapter 2, however, there were many women committed to race reform who were equally committed to woman suffrage during the Progressive Era, including Frances E. W. Harper and Ida B. Wells.

36. Lester Ward (1841–1913) is known as "the Father of American Sociology," and he wrote several foundational texts in the discipline, including *Outlines of Sociology* (1898) and *Pure Sociology* (1903). He was also very progressive in his thinking about gender, race, and class.

37. The organizations include the National Association of Colored Women's Clubs and the Alpha Suffrage Club, the first all-black suffrage organization, founded by Ida B. Wells in 1913.

CHAPTER FOUR. The Political Is Personal

1. In his introduction to the Penguin edition of the novel, Charles Anderson notes, "*The Bostonians* is unique among the thirty-six volumes of Henry James's fictions. It is one of the very few to be set in America with an all-American cast of characters, the great majority being set in Europe. It is the only one of his novels, with the single exception of *The Princess Casamassima*, that deals with a sociological subject. One is impressed by James's progressiveness in choosing a subject in the 1880s that is so much in the air today: the problem of equal rights for women" (7).

2. The review is actually signed "L.T.A."; however, critics who discuss the review, most notably Alfred Habegger, attribute the review to Ames, who was a zealous suffragist and contributor to the *Woman's Journal*. See Habegger, *Henry James and the "Woman Business,"* 228–29.

3. This trend continues to the present date. With the exception of Nan Bauer Maglin's article "Fictional Feminists in *The Bostonians* and *The Odd Women*," Sara deSaussure Davis's "Feminist Sources in *The Bostonians*," and (to a lesser degree) Habegger's book, I have found no critical analysis of the novel that pays more than perfunctory attention to its relationship to the historical woman's rights movement.

4. See Caroline Levander's chapter in *Voices of the Nation*, "Bawdy Talk: The Politics of Women's Public Speech in Henry James's *The Bostonians* and Sarah J. Hale's *The Lecturess*." For readings of *Hannah Thurston* that claim it was an inspiration for *The Bostonians*, see Barbara Bardes and Suzanne Gossett's *Declarations of Independence*, 171–76 and Andrew Taylor's *Henry James and the Father Question*, 152–54.

5. Critics who read *The Bostonians* as an affirmation of the heterosexual status quo include Lionel Trilling, Alfred Habegger, Barbara Bardes and Suzanne Gossett, and Thomas F. Bertonneau. Critics who see the novel as approving or at least sympathizing with "the agitation on [women's] behalf" include Judith Fetterley, Kathleen McColley, and Terry Castle.

6. While Ames is ostensibly writing about all of Boston, it would not be implausible to assume she was applying this injunction specifically to the woman's rights movement, given that the review is published in its official journal.

7. Joyce A. Rowe applies Nussbaum's ideas about *The Princess Casamassima* to *The Bostonians* in her essay "'Murder, what a lovely voice!': Sex, Speech, and the Public/Private Problem in *The Bostonians*."

8. The story of a heterosexual romance in which the hero is converted to gender reform by his love interest—a convention in much feminist activist fiction—*is* contained in *The Bostonians*, if only to be parodied. Miss Birdseye's fantasy in which Verena converts Basil imagines just such a relationship.

9. For discussions of Olive as a tragic heroine, see for example, Terry Castle, Judith Fetterley, and Claire Kahane.

10. The original passage that Whitehead parodies is: "Did Verena's strange aberration, on this particular day, suggest to Olive that it was no use striving, that the world was all a great trap or trick, of which women were ever the punctual dupes, so that it was the worst of the curse that rested upon them that they must most humiliate those who had most their cause at heart! Did she say to herself that their weakness was not only lamentable but hideous—hideous their predestined subjection to man's larger and grosser insistence? Did she ask herself why she should give up her life to save a sex which, after all, didn't wish to be saved, and which rejected the truth even after it had bathed them with its auroral light and they had pretended to be fed and fortified? These are mysteries into which I shall not attempt to enter, speculations with which I have no concern; it is sufficient for us to know that all human effort had never seemed to her so barren and thankless as on that fatal afternoon" (James, *Bostonians* 397).

Bibliography

Alsen, Eberhard. "Hamlin Garland's First Novel: *A Spoil of Office*." *Western American Literature* 4 (1969): 91–105.
A[mes], L[ucia] T. "The Bostonians." *Woman's Journal* 18 Mar. 1886: 82–83.
Ammons, Elizabeth. *Conflicting Stories: American Women Writers at the Turn into the Twentieth Century*. New York: Oxford University Press, 1991.
Anderson, Benedict. *Imagined Communities: Reflections on the Origins and Spread of Nationalism*. Rev. ed. London: Verso, 1993.
Anderson, Charles. Introduction. *The Bostonians*. By Henry James. London: Penguin, 1984. 7–30.
Auerbach, Nina. *Communities of Women: An Idea in Fiction*. Cambridge, Mass.: Harvard University Press, 1978.
Bakhtin, Mikhail. *Dostoevsky's Poetics*. Ed. and trans. Caryl Emerson. Minneapolis: University of Minnesota Press, 1984.
Bardes, Barbara, and Suzanne Gossett. *Declarations of Independence: Women and Political Power in Nineteenth-Century American Fiction*. New Brunswick, N.J.: Rutgers University Press, 1990.
Baym, Nina. *Woman's Fiction*. Ithaca: Cornell University Press, 1978.
Berlant, Lauren. "The Queen of America Goes to Washington City: Harriet Jacobs, Frances Harper, and Anita Hill." *American Literature* 65.3 (1993): 549–74.
Bertonneau, Thomas F. "Like Hypatia Before the Mob: Desire, Resentment, and Sacrifice in *The Bostonians*." *Nineteenth-Century Literature* 53.1 (1998): 56–90.
Blair, Sara. "Realism, Culture and the Place of the Literary: Henry James and *The Bostonians*." *The Cambridge Companion to Henry James*. Ed. Jonathan Freedman. Cambridge, U.K.: Cambridge University Press, 1998. 151–68.
Blake, Katherine Devereux, and Margaret Louise Wallace. *Champion of Women: The Life of Lillie Devereux Blake*. New York: Fleming H. Revell, 1943.
Blake, Lillie Devereux. *Fettered for Life*. 1874. New York: The Feminist Press, 1996.
Blatch, Harriot Stanton, and Alma Lutz. *Challenging Years: The Memoirs of Harriot Stanton Blatch*. New York: G. P. Putnam's Sons, 1940.
——. "Self-Supporting Women." *Woman's Journal* 17 Aug. 1907: 129.
Botshon, Lisa, and Meredith Goldsmith, eds. *Middlebrow Moderns: Popular American Women Writers of the Twenties*. Boston: Northeastern University Press, 2003.

Boudreau, Kristin. "Narrative Sympathy in *The Bostonians.*" *The Henry James Review* 14.1 (1993): 17–33.

Bower, Anne. *Epistolary Responses: The Letter in Twentieth-Century American Fiction and Criticism.* Tuscaloosa: University of Alabama Press, 1997.

Brant, C. "The Epistolary Novel." *History of European Literature.* Ed. Annick Benoit-Dusausoy and Guy Fontaine. Trans. Michael Woolf. London: Routledge, 2000. 377–80.

Brantlinger, Patrick. "What Is 'Sensational' about the 'Sensation Novel'?" *Wilkie Collins.* Ed. Lyn Pykett. New York: St. Martin's, 1998. 30–57.

Bromley, Dorothy Dunbar. "Feminist—New Style." *Harper's Magazine* Oct. 1927: 552–60.

Brown, Bill. "The Popular, the Populist, and the Populace—Locating Hamlin Garland in the Politics of Culture." *Arizona Quarterly* 50.3 (1994): 89–110.

Brownstein, Rachel. *Becoming a Heroine: Reading about Women in Novels.* 1982. Rev. ed. New York: Columbia University Press, 1994.

Buechler, Steven M. *Women's Movements in the United States: Woman Suffrage, Equal Rights, and Beyond.* New Brunswick, N.J.: Rutgers University Press, 1990.

Campbell, Elizabeth. "Re-visions, Re-flections, Re-creations: Epistolarity in Novels by Contemporary Women." *Twentieth Century Literature* 41.3 (1995): 332–49.

Campbell, Jennifer. "'The Great Something Else': Women's Search for Meaningful Work in Sarah Orne Jewett's *A Country Doctor* and Frances E. W. Harper's *Trial and Triumph.*" *Colby Quarterly* 34.2 (1998): 83–98.

Campbell, Karlyn Kohrs. *A Critical Study of Early Feminist Rhetoric.* Vol. 1 of *Man Cannot Speak for Her.* Westport: Praeger, 1989.

———. *Key Texts of the Early Feminists.* Vol. 2 of *Man Cannot Speak for Her.* Westport: Praeger, 1989.

Carby, Hazel V. *Reconstructing Womanhood: The Emergence of the Afro-American Woman Novelist.* New York: Oxford University Press, 1987.

Carp, Roger E. "Hamlin Garland and the Cult of True Womanhood." *Women, Women Writers and the West.* Eds. L. L. Lee and Merrill Lewis. Troy, N.Y.: Whitston, 1979. 83–99.

Carter, Joseph. "Hamlin Garland's Liberated Woman." *American Literary Realism* 6 (1973): 255–58.

Cash, Floris Loretta Barnett. *African American Women and Social Action: The Clubwomen and Volunteerism from Jim Crow to the New Deal, 1896–1936.* Westport, Conn.: Greenwood Press, 2001.

Castle, Terry. *The Apparitional Lesbian: Female Homosexuality and Modern Culture.* New York: Columbia University Press, 1993.

Catt, Carrie Chapman. Introduction. *Woman Citizen: A General Handbook of Civics, with Special Consideration of Women's Citizenship.* Ed. Mary Sumner Boyd. New York: Frederick A. Stokes, 1918. 8–9.

Chesnutt, Charles. "The Wife of His Youth." 1899. *Conjure Tales and Stories of the Color Line.* Ed. William L. Andrews. New York: Penguin Books, 1992. 103–14.

Christian, Barbara. *Black Women Novelists: The Development of a Tradition, 1892–1976.* Contributions in Afro-American and African Studies 52. Westport, Conn.: Greenwood Press, 1980.

Clanton, Gene. *Populism: The Humane Preference in America, 1890–1900.* Boston: Twayne, 1991.

Clark, Suzanne. *Sentimental Modernism.* Bloomington: Indiana University Press, 1991.

Conrad, Charles. "The Transformation of the 'Old Feminist' Movement." *The Quarterly Journal of Speech* 67.3 (1981): 284–97.

Cooke, Marjorie Benton. Letter to Elizabeth Jordan. July 191?. Elizabeth Garver Jordan Papers. Manuscript and Archives Division. The New York Public Library. Astor, Lenox, and Tilden Foundations.

Cooper, Anna Julia. *A Voice from the South.* 1892. Introd. Mary Helen Washington. The Schomberg Library of Nineteenth-Century Black Women Writers. Gen. Ed. Henry Louis Gates Jr. Oxford: Oxford University Press, 1988.

Cott, Nancy. *The Grounding of Modern Feminism.* New Haven, Conn.: Yale University Press, 1986.

Cummins, Maria S. *The Lamplighter.* 1854. Ed. Nina Baym. New Brunswick, N.J.: Rutgers University Press, 1988.

Dalke, Anne French. "The Sensational Fiction of Hawthorne and Melville." *Studies in American Fiction* 16.2 (1988): 195–207.

———. "'The Shameless Woman Is the Worst of Men': Sexual Aggression in Nineteenth-Century Novels." *Studies in the Novel* 18.3 (1986): 291–303.

Darwin, Charles. *The Descent of Man and Selection in Relation to Sex.* 1871. Princeton, N.J.: Princeton University Press, 1981.

Davidson, Cathy N., and Jessamyn Hatcher. Introduction. *No More Separate Spheres! A New Wave American Studies Reader.* Ed. Cathy N. Davidson and Jessamyn Hatcher. Durham, N.C.: Duke University Press, 2002. 7–26.

Davis, Angela. *Women, Race and Class.* New York: Vintage Books, 1983.

Davis, Sara deSaussure. "Feminist Sources in *The Bostonians.*" *American Literature* 50.4 (1979): 570–87.

DeKoven, Marianne. "Modernism and Gender." *The Cambridge Companion to Modernism.* Cambridge, U.K.: Cambridge University Press, 1999.

Deutsch, Sarah Jane. "From Ballots to Breadlines: 1920–1940." *No Small Courage: A History of Women in the United States.* Ed. Nancy F. Cott. New York: Oxford University Press, 2000. 413–72.

Dobson, Joanne. "The Hidden Hand: Subversion of Cultural Ideology in Three Mid-Nineteenth-Century American Women's Novels." *American Quarterly* 38.2 (1986): 223–42.

———. Introduction. *The Hidden Hand: Or, Capitola the Madcap.* By E.D.E.N. Southworth. New Brunswick, N.J.: Rutgers University Press, 1986. xi–xlii.

Dow, Bonnie. "*The Revolution*, 1868–1870: Expanding the Woman Suffrage Agenda." Solomon 71–86.

DuBois, Ellen Carol. Introduction. *The Elizabeth Cady Stanton–Susan B. Anthony Reader: Correspondence, Writings, Speeches.* Ed. Ellen Carol DuBois. Rev. ed. Boston: Northeastern University Press, 1992.

———. *Feminism and Suffrage.* Ithaca: Cornell University Press, 1978.

———. "Harriot Stanton Blatch and the Transformation of Class Relations among Woman Suffragists." *Gender, Class, Race and Reform in the Progressive Era.* Ed. Noralee Frankel and Nancy S. Dye. Lexington: University Press of Kentucky, 1991. 162–79.

Dunn, Maggie, and Ann Morris. *The Composite Novel: The Short Story Cycle in Transition.* Studies in Literary Themes and Genres 6. New York: Twayne, 1995.

Dupee, F. W. *Henry James.* Westport, Conn.: Greenwood Press, 1973.

DuPlessis, Rachel Blau. *Writing Beyond the Ending: Narrative Strategies of Twentieth-Century Women Writers.* Bloomington: Indiana University Press, 1985.

"Editor's Literary Record." *Harper's New Monthly Magazine* 49.291 (1874): 440–44.

"Education of Girls." *The Revolution* 12 Mar. 1868: 151.

Ehrhardt, Julia C. *Writers of Conviction: The Personal Politics of Zona Gale, Dorothy Canfield Fisher, Rose Wilder Lane, and Josephine Herbst.* Columbia: University of Missouri Press, 2004.

Elbert, Monika M., ed. *Separate Spheres No More: Gender Convergence in American Literature, 1830–1930.* Tuscaloosa: University of Alabama Press, 2000.

Elkins, Marilyn. "Reading beyond the Conventions: A Look at Frances E. W. Harper's *Iola Leroy, or Shadows Uplifted.*" *American Literary Realism* 22.2 (1990): 44–53.

Ernest, John. "From Mysteries to Histories: Cultural Pedagogy in Frances E. Harper's *Iola Leroy.*" *American Literature* 64.3 (1992): 497–518.

Fabi, M. Giulia. "Taming the Amazon? The Price of Survival in Turn-of-the-Century African American Women's Fiction." In *The Insular Dream: Obsession and Resistance.* Ed. Kristiaan Versluys. Amsterdam, Netherlands: VU University Press, 1995. 228–41.

Fairbank, Janet Ayer. *Rich Man, Poor Man.* New York: Houghton Mifflin, 1936.

Farrell, Grace. Afterword. *Fettered for Life.* By Lillie Devereux Blake. New York: The Feminist Press, 1996. 381–430.

Felski, Rita. *Beyond Feminist Aesthetics: Feminist Literature and Social Change.* Cambridge, Mass.: Harvard University Press, 1989.

Ferber, Edna. *Emma McChesney and Co.* 1915. Urbana: University of Illinois Press, 2002.

———. *Roast Beef, Medium.* 1913. Introd. Lawrence R. Rodgers. Urbana: University of Illinois Press, 2001.

Ferguson, Ann. "Can I Choose Who I Am? And How Would That Empower Me? Gender, Race, Identities and the Self." *Women, Knowledge and Reality.* Ed. Ann Garry and Marilyn Pearsall. 2nd ed. New York: Routledge, 1996. 108–26.

———. "Feminist Communities and Moral Revolution." *Feminism and Community.* Ed. Penny A. Weiss and Marilyn Friedman. Philadelphia: Temple University Press, 1995. 367–98.

———. "Moral Responsibility and Social Change: A New Theory of Self." *Hypatia* 12.3 (1997): 116–41.

"Fettered for Life." *The Literary World* 5.12 (1874): 87.

Fetterley, Judith. "'My Sister! My Sister!': The Rhetoric of Catharine Sedgwick's *Hope Leslie*." Davidson and Hatcher 67–92.

———. *The Resisting Reader: A Feminist Approach to American Fiction*. Bloomington: Indiana University Press, 1978.

Finnegan, Margaret. *Selling Suffrage: Consumer Culture and Votes for Women*. New York: Columbia University Press, 1999.

Flexner, Eleanor, and Ellen Fitzpatrick. *Century of Struggle: The Woman's Rights Movement in the United States.* 1975. Enlarged Ed. Cambridge, Mass.: Harvard University Press, 1996.

Flower, B. O. "Review of *A Spoil of Office*." *Arena* 6 (October 1892): xi–xvi. Rpt. in Nagel. *Critical Essays on Hamlin Garland*. 48–52.

Foreman, P. Gabrielle. "'Reading Aright': White Slavery, Black Referents, and The Strategy of Histotextuality in *Iola Leroy*." *The Yale Journal of Criticism* 10.2 (1997): 327–54.

Foster, Frances Smith. Introduction. *A Brighter Coming Day: A Frances Ellen Watkins Harper Reader*. New York: The Feminist Press, 1990. 3–40.

———. Introduction. *Iola Leroy*. By Frances Ellen Watkins Harper. The Schomberg Library of Nineteenth-Century Black Women Writers. Gen. Ed. Henry Louis Gates Jr. New York: Oxford University Press, 1988. xxvii–xxxix.

———. *Written by Herself: Literary Production by African American Women, 1746–1892*. Bloomington: Indiana University Press, 1993.

Frye, Northrop. *Secular Scripture: A Study of the Structure of Romance*. Cambridge, Mass.: Harvard University Press, 1976.

Fulton, Valerie. "Rewriting the Necessary Woman: Marriage and Professionalism in James, Jewett, and Phelps." *Henry James Review* 15.3 (1994): 242–56.

Gaines, Kevin. *Uplifting the Race: Black Leadership, Politics and Culture in the Twentieth Century*. Chapel Hill: University of North Carolina Press, 1996.

Garland, Hamlin. "The Land Question and its Relation to Art and Literature." *Arena* 9 (1893): 165–75.

———. "Productive Conditions of American Literature." *Forum* 17 (1894): 690–98.

———. *A Spoil of Office: A Story of the Modern West.* 1892. Introd. Eberhardt Alsen. New York: Johnson, 1969.

———. *A Spoil of Office: A Story of the Modern West.* New and Rev. Ed. New York: D. Appleton, 1897.

Gilbert, Sandra M., and Susan Gubar. *No Man's Land: The Place of the Woman Writer in the Twentieth Century*. Vol. 1. New Haven, Conn.: Yale University Press, 1988.

Gooder, Jean. "Henry James's *The Bostonians*: The Voices of Democracy." *Cambridge Quarterly* 30.2 (2001): 97–115.

Graham, Sara Hunter. *Woman Suffrage and the New Democracy*. New Haven, Conn.: Yale University Press, 1996.

Grant, Robert. "The Limits of Feminine Independence." *Scribner's Magazine* June 1919: 729–34.

Griffin, Farah Jasmine. "Frances Ellen Watkins Harper in the Reconstruction South." *SAGE* Student Supplement 1988: 45–47.

Habegger, Alfred. *Henry James and the "Woman Business."* Cambridge Studies in American Literature and Culture. New York: Cambridge University Press, 1989.

Hall, Sallie J. "Henry James and the Bluestockings: Satire and Morality in *The Bostonians*." *Aeolian Harps: Essays in Literature in Honor of Maurice Browning Cramer*. Ed. Donna G. Fricke and Douglas G. Fricke. Bowling Green, Ohio: Bowling Green University Press, 1976.

Hanaford, Phebe A. *Women of the Century*. Boston: B. B. Russell, 1877.

Hapke, Laura. *Tales of the Working Girl: Wage Earning Women in American Literature, 1890–1925*. New York: Twayne, 1992.

Harbert, Elizabeth Boynton. *Out of Her Sphere*. Des Moines: Mills, 1871.

Harker, Jaime. "Progressive Middlebrow: Dorothy Canfield, Women's Magazines, and Popular Feminism in the Twenties." Botshon and Goldsmith 111–34.

Harper, Frances E. W. *Iola Leroy, or Shadows Uplifted*. 1892. Introd. Frances Smith Foster. The Schomberg Library of Nineteenth-Century Black Women Writers. Gen. Ed. Henry Louis Gates Jr. Oxford: Oxford University Press, 1988.

Haskell, Oreola Williams. *Banner Bearers: Tales of the Suffrage Campaigns*. Geneva, New York: W. F. Humphrey, 1920.

Heilmann, Ann. *New Woman Fiction: Women Writing First-Wave Feminism*. New York: St. Martin's Press, 2000.

Hogeland, Lisa Maria. *Feminism and its Fictions: The Consciousness-Raising Novel and the Women's Liberation Movement*. Philadelphia: University of Pennsylvania Press, 1998.

Honey, Maureen. Introduction. *Breaking the Ties that Bind: Popular Stories of the New Woman, 1915–1930*. Ed. Maureen Honey. Norman: University Oklahoma Press, 1992. 3–36.

———. "Feminist New Woman Fiction in Periodicals of the 1920s." Botshon and Goldsmith 87–109.

hooks, bell. *Ain't I a Woman: Black Women and Feminism*. Boston: South End Press, 1981.

Howe, Irving. "Introduction to *The Bostonians*." In *Critical Essays on Henry James: The Early Novels*. Ed. James W. Gargano. Boston: Hall, 1987. 154–69.

Howlett, Caroline. "Femininity Slashed: Suffragette Militancy, Modernism and Gender." *Modernist Sexualities*. Ed. Hugh Stevens and Caroline Howlett. Manchester, U.K.: Manchester University Press, 2000. 72–91.

Huyssen, Andreas. *After The Great Divide: Modernism, Mass Culture, Postmodernism*. Bloomington: Indiana University Press, 1986.

Ingram, Forrest. *Representative Short Story Cycles of the Twentieth-Century: Studies in a Literary Genre*. The Hague, Netherlands: Mouton, 1971.

Irwin, Inez. *The Story of the Woman's Party*. New York: Harcourt, Brace, 1921.

Jacobson, Matthew Frye. *Whiteness of a Different Color: European Immigrants and the Alchemy of Race*. Cambridge, Mass.: Harvard University Press, 1998.

James, Henrietta [Celia B. Whitehead]. "Another Chapter of 'The Bostonians.'" Bloomfield, N. J.: S. Morris Hulin, 1887.

James, Henry. *The Bostonians.* 1886. Introd. Charles R. Anderson. London: Penguin, 1984.
———. *The Complete Notebooks.* Ed. Leon Edel and Lyall H. Powers. Princeton, N.J.: Princeton University Press, 1989.
Jameson, Frederic. *The Political Unconscious: Narrative as a Socially Symbolic Act.* Ithaca: Cornell University Press, 1981.
Jordan, Elizabeth. Letter to Miss Bjorkman. 23 Oct. 1917. Elizabeth Garver Jordan Papers. Manuscript and Archives Division. The New York Public Library. Astor, Lenox, and Tilden Foundations.
———, ed. *The Sturdy Oak: A Composite Novel of American Politics.* 1917. Introd. Ida H. Washington. Athens: Ohio University Press, 1998.
Kahane, Claire. *Passions of the Voice: Hysteria, Narrative, and the Figure of the Speaking Woman, 1850–1915.* Baltimore, Md.: The Johns Hopkins Press, 1995.
Kaye, Frances W. "Hamlin Garland's Feminism." *Women and Western American Literature.* Ed. Susan Rosowski. Troy, N.Y.: Whitston, 1982. 135–61.
Kelly, Mary. Introduction. *Hope Leslie; or Early Times in Massachusetts.* By Catharine Maria Sedgwick. New Brunswick, N.J.: Rutgers University Press, 1987. ix–xxxviii.
Kennedy, J. Gerald. "The American Short Story Sequence—Definitions and Implications." Introduction. *Modern American Short Story Sequences: Composite Fictions and Fictive Communities.* Ed. J. Gerald Kennedy. Cambridge, U.K.: Cambridge University Press, 1995. vii–xv.
———. "From Anderson's *Winesburg* to Carver's *Cathedral*: The Short Story Sequence and the Semblance of Community." *Modern American Short Story Sequences: Composite Fictions and Fictive Communities.* Ed. J. Gerald Kennedy. Cambridge, U.K.: Cambridge University Press, 1995. 194–216.
King, Grace. "Bayou L'Ombre: An Incident of the War." 1892. *Grace King of New Orleans: A Selection of Her Writings.* Ed. Robert Bush. Southern Literary Studies. Gen. Ed. Louis D. Rubin Jr. Baton Rouge: Louisiana State University Press, 1973.
Kraditor, Aileen. *Ideas of the Woman Suffrage Movement, 1890–1920.* New York: Columbia University Press, 1965.
Lang, Amy Schrager. "Slavery and Sentimentalism: The Strange Career of Augustine St. Clare." *Women's Studies* 12.1 (1986): 31–54.
"Latest Works of Fiction." *New York Times Book Review* 11 Nov. 1917: 42+.
Lazenby, Walter. "Idealistic Realist on the Platform: Hamlin Garland." *The Quarterly Journal of Speech* 49 (1963): 138–45.
Leach, William. *True Love and Perfect Union.* New York: Basic, 1980.
Levander, Caroline. *Voices of the Nation: Women and Public Speech in Nineteenth-Century American Literature and Culture.* Cambridge, U.K.: Cambridge University Press, 1998.
Lewis, Sinclair. *Ann Vickers.* 1933. Introd. Nan Bauer Maglin. Lincoln: University of Nebraska Press, 1994.
Linton, Eliza Lynn. "The Girl of the Period." 1868. *Prose by Victorian Women: An Anthology.* Ed. Andrea Broomfield and Sally Mitchell. New York: Garland, 1996. 355–60.
Lowell, James Russell. "Democracy." 1884. *James Russell Lowell: Representative Selections,*

with Introduction, Bibliography and Notes. Ed. Harry Hayden Clark and Norman Foerster. New York: American Book Company, 1947. 407–30.

Lundén, Rolf. *The United Stories of America: Studies in the Short Story Composite*. Costerus New Series 122. Amsterdam, Netherlands: Rodopi, 1999.

Maglin, Nan Bauer. "Fictional Feminists in *The Bostonians* and *The Odd Women*." *Images of Women in Fiction: Feminist Perspectives*. Ed. Susan Koppelman Cornillon. Bowling Green, Ohio: Bowling Green University Popular Press, 1973. 216–36.

Martin, Quentin E. "'This Spreading Radicalism': Hamlin Garland's *A Spoil of Office* and the Creation of True Populism." *Studies in American Fiction* 26.1 (1998): 29–50.

Maxwell, Joan. "Delighting in a Bite: James's Seduction of His Readers in *The Bostonians*." *Journal of Narrative Technique* 18.1 (1988): 18–33.

McColley, Kathleen. "Claiming Center Stage: Speaking Out for Homoerotic Empowerment in *The Bostonians*." *Henry James Review* 21.2 (2000): 151–69.

McCullough, Joseph B. "Hamlin Garland's Romantic Fiction." *Critical Essays on Hamlin Garland*. Ed. James Nagel. Boston: Hall, 1982. 349–62.

McDowell, Deborah. "'The Changing Same': Generational Connections and Black Women Novelists." *New Literary History* 18.2 (1987): 281–301.

McMath, Robert C. *American Populism: A Social History, 1877–1898*. New York: Noonday-Hill, 1993.

Morson, Gary Saul, and Caryl Emerson. *Mikhail Bakhtin: Creation of a Prosaics*. Stanford: Stanford University Press, 1990.

"Mrs. Jellaby." Rev. of *Bleak House*, by Charles Dickens. *Una* 1 Febr. 1853: 4.

Nagel, James. *The Contemporary American Short-Story Cycle: The Ethnic Resonance of Genre*. Baton Rouge: Louisiana State University Press, 2001.

―――, ed. *Critical Essays on Hamlin Garland*. Boston: Hall, 1982.

"New Figures in Literature and Art: Hamlin Garland." *Atlantic Monthly* Dec. 1895: 840–44.

Newlin, Keith. "Melodramatist of the Middle Border: Hamlin Garland's Early Work Reconsidered." *Studies in American Fiction* 21.2 (1993): 153–69.

Newman, Louise Michele. *White Women's Rights: The Racial Origins of Feminism in the United States*. New York: Oxford University Press, 1999.

Norris, Kathleen. Letter to Elizabeth Jordan. March 1915. Elizabeth Garver Jordan Papers. Manuscript and Archives Division. The New York Public Library. Astor, Lenox, and Tilden Foundations.

"Notes on New Fiction." *Dial* 31 Jan. 1918: 117.

Nussbaum, Martha C. *Love's Knowledge: Essays on Philosophy and Literature*. Oxford: Oxford University Press, 1990.

Parrington, Vernon Louis. "Hamlin Garland and the Middle Border." 1930. Rpt. in Nagel. *Critical Essays on Hamlin Garland*. 152–67.

Peterson, Carla L. "'Further Liftings of the Veil': Gender, Class, and Labor in Frances E. W. Harper's *Iola Leroy*." *Listening to Silences: New Essays in Feminist Criticism*. Ed. Elaine Hedges and Shelley Fisher Fishkin. New York: Oxford University Press, 1994. 97–112.

Pizer, Donald. "Hamlin Garland in the *Standard*." *American Literature* 26.3 (1954): 401–15.

———. *Hamlin Garland's Early Work and Career*. New York: Russell, 1960.

Pykett, Lyn. *The Sensation Novel: From* The Woman in White *to* The Moonstone. Writers and Their Work Series. Plymouth, U.K.: Northcote House, 1994.

Quebe, Ruth Evelyn. "*The Bostonians*: Some Historical Sources and their Implications." *Centennial Review* 25.1 (1981): 80–100.

Reynolds, David. *Beneath the American Renaissance*. Cambridge, Mass.: Harvard University Press, 1989.

Richardson, Angelique, and Chris Willis, eds. *The New Woman in Fact and Fiction: Fin-de-Siècle Feminisms*. New York: Palgrave, 2001.

Rosenthal, Debra J. "Deracialized Discourse: Temperance and Racial Ambiguity in Harper's 'The Two Offers' and *Sowing and Reaping*." *The Serpent in the Cup: Temperance in American Literature*. Ed. David S. Reynolds and Debra J. Rosenthal. Amherst: University of Massachusetts Press, 1997. 153–64.

Rowe, Joyce A. "'Murder, what a lovely voice!': Sex, Speech and the Public/Private Problem in *The Bostonians*." *Texas Studies in Literature and Language* 40.2 (1998): 158–83.

Rubin, Joan Shelley. Foreword. Botshon and Goldsmith i–xvii.

———. *The Making of Middlebrow Culture*. Chapel Hill: University of North Carolina Press, 1992.

Sale, Maggie. "Critiques from Within: Antebellum Projects of Resistance." *American Literature* 64.4 (1992): 695–718.

Sánchez-Eppler, Karen. "Bodily Bonds: The Intersecting Rhetorics of Feminism and Abolition." *The Culture of Sentiment: Race, Gender, and Sentimentality in Nineteenth-Century America*. Ed. Shirley Samuels. New York: Oxford University Press, 1992. 92–114.

Saum, Lewis O. "Hamlin Garland and Reform." *South Dakota Review* 10.4 (1972): 36–62.

Schneider, Dorothy, and Carl J. Schneider. *American Women in the Progressive Era, 1900–1920*. New York: Facts on File, 1993.

Scott, Bonnie Kime. *Refiguring Modernism: The Women of 1928*. Bloomington: Indiana University Press, 1995.

———, ed. *The Gender of Modernism: A Critical Anthology*. Bloomington: Indiana University Press, 1990.

Scott, Anthony. "Basil, Olive, and Verena: *The Bostonians* and the Problems of Politics." *Arizona Quarterly* 49.1 (1993): 49–72.

Sedgwick, Catharine Maria. *Hope Leslie; or Early Times in Massachusetts*. 1827. Ed. Mary Kelly. New Brunswick, N.J.: Rutgers University Press, 1987.

Showalter, Elaine. "The Other Bostonians: Gender and Literary Study." *The Yale Journal of Criticism* 1.2 (1988): 179–87.

Shuler, Marjorie. *For Rent—One Pedestal*. New York: National Woman Suffrage Publishing, 1917.

Shulman, Robert. *Social Criticisms and Nineteenth-Century American Fictions*. Columbia: University of Missouri Press, 1987.

Solomon, Martha, ed. *A Voice of Their Own: The Woman Suffrage Press, 1840–1910*. Tuscaloosa: University of Alabama Press, 1991.

Stanton, Elizabeth Cady. "Address to the National Woman Suffrage Convention." 1869. Rpt. in *The Concise History of Woman Suffrage: Selections from the Classic Work of Stanton, Anthony, Gage and Harper*. Ed. Mari Jo Buhle and Paul Buhle. Urbana: University of Illinois Press, 1978. 249–56.

———. "Marriages and Mistresses." *The Revolution* 15 Oct. 1868: 233–34.

———. Preface. *Pray You Sir, Whose Daughter?* By Helen H. Gardener. Boston: Arena, 1892.

———. "To Susan B. Anthony." 1 Mar. 1853. *The Elizabeth Cady Stanton–Susan B. Anthony Reader: Correspondence, Writings, Speeches*. Ed. Ellen Carol DuBois. Rev. ed. Boston: Northeastern University Press, 1992. 55–56.

Stowe, Harriet Beecher. *Uncle Tom's Cabin; or, Life Among the Lowly*. 1852. Introd. Alfred Kazin. New York: Bantam, 1981.

Tate, Claudia. *Domestic Allegories Of Political Desire: The Black Heroine's Text at the Turn of the Century*. New York: Oxford University Press, 1992.

Taylor, Andrew. *Henry James and the Father Question*. Cambridge, U.K.: Cambridge University Press, 2002.

Terborg-Penn, Rosalyn. *African American Women in the Struggle for the Vote, 1850–1920*. Bloomington: Indiana University Press, 1998.

Tompkins, Jane. *Sensational Designs: The Cultural Work of American Fiction, 1790–1860*. New York: Oxford University Press, 1985.

Tonn, Mari Boor. "The *Una*, 1853–1855: The Premiere of the Woman's Rights Press." Solomon 48–70.

Tracey, Karen. *Plots and Proposals: American Women's Fiction, 1850–90*. Urbana: University of Illinois Press, 2000.

Trilling, Lionel. *The Opposing Self*. New York: Viking, 1955.

"The Truth of Fiction, and Its Charms." *Una*. 1 Febr. 1853: 5.

Van Leer, David. "A World of Female Friendship: *The Bostonians*." *Henry James and Homo-Erotic Desire*. Ed. John R. Bradley. New York: St. Martin's, 1999. 93–109.

Wagner, MaryJo. *Farms, Families and Reform: Women in the Farmer's Alliance and Populist Party*. Diss. University of Oregon, 1986. Ann Arbor: UMI, 1989.

Walker, Francis. "Restriction of Immigration." *Atlantic Monthly* June 1896: 822–30.

Ware, Vron. *Beyond the Pale: White Women, Racism and History*. London: Verso, 1992.

Warner, Susan. *The Wide, Wide World*. 1850. After. Jane Tompkins. New York: The Feminist Press, 1986.

Wells-Barnett, Ida B. *Crusade for Justice: The Autobiography of Ida B. Wells*. Ed. Alfreda M. Duster. Chicago: University of Chicago Press, 1970.

Welter, Barbara. *Dimity Convictions: The American Woman in the Nineteenth Century*. Athens: University of Ohio Press, 1976.

Wheeler, Marjorie Spruill. *New Women of the New South: The Leaders of the Woman Suffrage Movement in the Southern States*. New York: Oxford University Press, 1993.

White, William Allen. Letter to Elizabeth Jordan. 6 Mar. 1917. Elizabeth Garver Jordan Papers. Manuscript and Archives Division. The New York Public Library. Astor, Lenox, and Tilden Foundations.

———. Letter to Elizabeth Jordan. Undated. Elizabeth Garver Jordan Papers. Manuscript and Archives Division. The New York Public Library. Astor, Lenox, and Tilden Foundations.

Wilkins (Freeman), Mary E. "Love and the Witches." *Century* June 1891, 286.

Willard, Frances. "Temperance and Home Protection." *Outspoken Women: Speeches by American Women Reformers, 1635–1935*. Ed. Judith Anderson. Dubuque, Iowa: Kendall Hunt, 1984. 221–24.

———. "A White Life for Two." Campbell, Vol. 2. 317–38.

"Women in Art." *The Revolution* 19 Oct. 1868: 236.

Yezierska, Anzia. *Hungry Hearts*. 1920. Introd. Vivian Gornick. New York: Signet, 1996.

Young, Elizabeth. "Warring Fictions: *Iola Leroy* and the Color of Gender." *American Literature* 64.2 (1992): 273–97.

Index

abolitionism, 1, 6, 7, 18, 67, 70, 157, 163, 199n2; relation to feminism, 19–20, 22, 40, 42, 202n17, 202–3n18; in *Uncle Tom's Cabin*, 24–25, 40, 41
AERA. *See* American Equal Rights Association
Alsen, Eberhard, 88, 99, 101
American Equal Rights Association (AERA), 20, 67
American Woman Suffrage Association (AWSA), 20, 67; founding of, 18, 201n2, 203n1; and *Women's Journal*, 8, 169
Ames, Lucia: pseudonym of, 209n2; review of *The Bostonians*, 169, 170–71, 173, 179, 187, 210n6
Ammons, Elizabeth, 81
Anderson, Benedict, 19
Ann Vickers (Lewis), 190–93
"Another Chapter of 'The Bostonians'" (Whitehead), 185–88
Anthony, Susan B., 9, 17, 65, 100; and NWSA, 20, 43, 44, 200n1, 201n2
arguments of expediency (Kraditor), 53, 62, 82, 201–2n10; definition of, 21, 27–28, 201n6; and Harbert, 23, 31, 35, 37; in woman's rights movement, 66, 97, 203n1
arguments of justice (Kraditor), 62, 92, 201–2n10; and Blake, 48, 59–60; definition of, 21, 201n6; and Garland, 97; and NWSA, 42
Auerbach, Nina, 172, 178
Austin, Mary, 124

AWSA. *See* American Woman Suffrage Association

Bakhtin, Mikhail, 108
Banner Bearers (Haskell), 15, 108, 121, 143–64, 165, 166; African American characters in, 156–57; "collective protagonist" of, 144–45, 147–48; eugenics promoted in, 145–46, 162–63; heroines, depiction of, 144, 145, 146, 147–48, 149–50, 160, 162–63; heterosexual romance plot in, 144, 157–61, 164; immigrants as characters in, 153–54, 155, 158–59; male characters in, 154–57, 158–59, 164; oppositional community formation in, 144, 145, 148–49, 150, 151, 152, 153, 154, 155–56; race and politics, relationship between, 155–56, 158, 164, 166; racial hierarchy, depiction of, 151–52, 162; and short story cycle form, 144, 149, 165; and "Soap and Water," 152; spectacle as a political tactic in, 163–64
Banner Bearers (Haskell), stories in: "Four Generations," 163; "The Great Shortcut," 163–64; "The Heart of the Chief," 151–52, 159; "The Invader," 145–46, 158; "Methods," 162; "A Musical Martyr," 149–50, 159; "The Nail," 158; "Rea, the Orator," 147; "Silent Forces," 158; "Sissies," 154–55; "Sizing Up Boss," 146–47, 159, 208n31; "Stallfed," 153–54; "Switchboard Suffrage," 149; "Tenements and Teacups," 148–49, 151,

Banner Bearers (*continued*)
153, 189; "A Touch of Romance," 160–61; "When Hester Hikes," 158; "Winds and Weathervanes," 155, 158; "The Yellow Button," 156–57
Bardes, Barbara, 98, 199n3, 209n4, 210n5
"Bayou L'Ombre: An Incident of War" (King), 70
Blackwell, Henry, 201n2
Blair, Sara, 184
Blake, Lillie Devereux, 14, 18, 21, 42, 43, 82, 102; and abolitionist rhetoric, 20, 41; biography of, 63; as member of NWSA, 44. See also *Fettered for Life*
Blatch, Harriot Stanton, 103–4, 105, 166, 208n34; and Elizabeth Cady Stanton, 205n1, 206n9; and *For Rent—One Pedestal*, 114, 115; and "Sisters Under Their Skin," 135
Bleak House (Dickens), 5
"Born Thrall, or Woman's Life and Experience, The" (Cary), 6
Bostonians, The (James), 1, 15, 168–88, 199–200n3; "Another Chapter of 'The Bostonians,'" 185–88, 209n10; critical reception of, 169–71, 209n2–4, 210n5; existential communitarianism in, 171, 173, 175–76, 181, 184, 185; heterosexual romance plot in, 179–83, 187, 210n8; homoeroticism in, 178–79; James's plan for, 168; oppositional community formation in, 171, 173, 175–76, 177–78, 179, 180–85, 187; and *The Princess Casamassima*, 182, 209n7; revolutionary love in, 171, 175, 182–83, 184, 185, 187
Botshon, Lisa, 106, 107, 165
Boudreau, Kristin, 174
Bower, Anne, 113, 119
Brantlinger, Patrick, 44–45

Campbell, Elizabeth, 117, 121–22
Campbell, Jennifer, 84

Campbell, Karlyn Kohrs, 7, 199n2
Canfield, Dorothy, 106, 124, 205n5
Carby, Hazel, 69
Carp, Roger, 98–99
Cary, Alice, 6
Castle, Terry, 179, 210n5, 210n9
Catt, Carrie Chapman, 112, 144, 151, 203n1, 205n8, 208n31, 208–9n34
Century, The, 93, 205n17
Chestnutt, Charles, 78–79
Child, Lydia Marie, 43, 202–3n18
Clark, Suzanne, 105, 107, 113
Collier's Magazine, 124, 207n24
Communism, 190, 191–92, 194–95, 197
composite novel, 15, 108, 125, 127, 165, 207n21
Conscription Act of 1863, 141
Cooke, Marjorie Benton, 125
Cooper, Anna Julia, 64, 66, 101, 163; and *Iola Leroy*, 81, 85; and *A Spoil of Office*, 92, 97
Cott, Nancy, 200n6
Cummins, Maria Susanna, 20, 21. See also *Lamplighter, The*

Dalke, Anne French, 45, 46
Davidson, Cathy, 2, 3, 200n4, 201n4
Davis, Paulina Wright, 4, 5
"Day-Dream, The" (Tennyson), 200n1
Declaration of Sentiments, 162–63, 202n17
DeKoven, Marianne, 105
Delany, Lucille, 204n15
"Democracy" (Lowell), 110
deSaussure, Sara Davis, 169
Deutsch, Sarah Jane, 190–91
Dial, The, 124, 207n22
Dobson, Joanne, 21, 47, 56, 201n5
domestic fiction. See sentimental novel
double-proposal plot (Tracey), 38–39, 58–59
Douglass, Frederick, 65, 67

DuBois, Ellen Carol, 6, 103–4, 114, 133, 166, 204n5
DuPlessis, Rachel Blau, 9

"Education of Girls," 17
Elkins, Marilyn, 77, 204n9
Emma McChesney & Co. (Ferber), 135
epistolary novel, 15, 108, 112–13, 114, 116–19, 121–22, 165, 205n6
Equality League, 114, 135, 205n1, 206n11
eugenics, 7, 145–46, 162–63
existential communitarianism (Ferguson), 10, 70, 171, 175–76, 184
existential moment (Ferguson): in *The Bostonians*, 132, 173, 175, 181, 185; definition of, 10, 72; in *Iola Leroy*, 71–72; in *A Spoil of Office*, 87, 90

Fabi, M. Giulia, 84, 204n13
Fairbank, Janet Ayer, 190, 191, 194, 195, 196, 197
Farmer's Alliance. See Populism
Farrell, Grace, 47, 60, 203n19
Felski Rita, 12, 13–14
feminist activist fiction: connection between literary history and formal properties of, 12–13; critical neglect of, 1; formal innovations of, in twentieth century, 105, 107–8; heterosexual romance plot in, 9, 18, 109, 113; influence on reform movements of, 2, 4–6, 161, 189; oppositional community formation in, 11, 13, 14, 21, 32–33, 69, 101–2, 107–8, 149, 165; revolutionary love in, 11–12; separate spheres and, 3; as "symbolic act," 12–13, 196; tradition of, 1, 168–69, 189, 196–97, 199–200n3. *See also specific titles*
feminist activist heroine: created by male and female authors, 3; definition of, 7–9; origin of, 1; post-ratification change to, 193. *See also specific titles*

Ferber, Edna, 106, 110–11, 116, 135–36, 137, 166. See also *Emma McChesney & Co.*; *Roast Beef, Medium*; "Sisters Under Their Skins"
Ferguson, Ann, 32, 70, 89, 94; "class traitor," 97; existential moment, 71–72, 132, 173, 175; imagined communities, 19; oppositional communities, 10–11, 32, 125, 126, 171, 196; revolutionary love, 11–12, 78, 175. *See also* existential communitarianism; existential moment; oppositional community; revolutionary love; self-horizon
Fettered for Life (Blake), 14, 15, 20, 45–63, 67, 102; corruption in, 48–51; cross-dressing in, 55–56, 58, 60–62, 82, 203n22–23; heterosexual romance plot in, 56–61; and *Hidden Hand*, 47–48, 54–56, 63; and *Hope Leslie*, 47–48, 54–55, 60, 63; oppositional community formation in, 21, 42–43, 50–55, 60, 62–63; race/whiteness in, 44, 49–50, 51, 60, 62, 63, 203n21; and *The Revolution*, 44, 61; as sensation novel, 44–46, 48–49, 61; true womanhood in, 46, 48, 203n24, 206n10; violence against women in, 48–49, 50–51, 52, 54–55
Fetterley, Judith, 5, 60, 210n5, 210n9. *See also* "resisting reader"
Fifteenth Amendment, 20, 43, 200n2, 203n1
Finnegan, Margaret, 114, 115–16
first-wave feminism. *See* suffrage movement; woman's rights movement
Flexner, Eleanor, 201n2, 202n11, 202n16, 203n1, 205n1, 208n34
Flower, B. O., 86, 91, 99
For Rent—One Pedestal (Shuler), 15, 108, 112–23, 164, 208n30; and *Banner Bearers*, 144, 145; corruption in, 117–18; epistolary style, 112–13, 114, 116–19, 121–22, 165, 205n6; heterosexual romance

For Rent—One Pedestal (continued)
  plot in, 122–23, 137; New Woman,
  depiction of, 114–16, 117, 120–21, 206n9–
  10, 206n17–18; oppositional community
  formation in, 119–21; political action,
  117–18, 122–23; racism/xenophobia
  in, 115, 118, 119–20, 122; spectacle as
  political tactic in, 117; and *The Sturdy
  Oak*, 131
Foreman, P. Gabrielle, 84, 204n15
Forum, 87, 205n17
Foster, Frances Smith, 67, 204n6
Fourteenth Amendment, 20, 43, 200n2
Freeman, Mary Wilkins, 93, 207n21
frontier suffrage, 40, 202n16
Frye, Northrop, 161

Gaines, Kevin, 76, 101
Gardener, Helen, 6
Garland, Hamlin, 3, 14, 63, 67, 109, 193,
  195; aesthetic and political values of,
  86–88, 97; and "Love and the Witches,"
  93; and Populist movement, 86, 97; on
  revision of *A Spoil of Office*, 99–100, 101.
  See also *Spoil of Office, A*
Gilbert, Sandra, 208n33
"Girl of the Period, A" (Linton), 34
Goldsmith, Meredith, 106, 107, 165
Gooder, Jean, 169–70, 181
Gossett, Suzanne, 98, 199n3, 209n4, 210n5
Grange. See Populism
Griffin, Farah Jasmine, 76
Grimké, Angelina, 1, 199n2
Grimké, Sarah, 1, 199n2
Gubar, Susan, 208n33

Habegger, Alfred, 179, 181, 209n2, 209n3,
  210n5
Hale, Sarah Josepha, 1, 169, 196, 199n2
Hall, Sallie, 173
Hannah Thurston (Taylor), 169, 183, 209n4
Hapke, Laura, 133

Harbert, Elizabeth Boynton, 14, 63, 102,
  112, 201n7–9, 201n12; biographical
  information about, 22–23; political
  ideals of, 18, 19, 20, 22–25, 41;
  relationship to Frances Willard, 28. See
  also *Out of Her Sphere*
Harker, Jaime, 107, 112, 124, 207n23
Harper, Frances E. W., 67, 204n6; political
  and literary activities of, 8, 67–68, 78,
  204n7, 209n35; and Reconstruction
  South, 76. See also *Iola Leroy*
Harper, Ida Husted, 158
Harper's Bazar, 123, 206n20
Harper's New Monthly Magazine, 62,
  203n25
Haskell, Oreola Williams, 143–44, 166. See
  also *Banner Bearers*
Hatcher, Jessamyn, 2, 3, 200n4, 201n4
heterosexual romance plot: in nineteenth-
  century literature, 8, 9; and revolutionary love, 11–12; in twentieth-century
  suffrage fiction, 109, 113, 165. See also
  double-proposal plot; *and specific
  titles*
Hidden Hand (Southworth), 21, 47, 54,
  55–56, 63
Hogeland, Lisa, 12, 13–14
homosexuality, 190, 191–92, 197. See also
  Fettered for Life; *Bostonians, The*
Honey, Maureen, 124, 207n23; definition
  of New Woman fiction, 106–7, 116, 121,
  165, 206n18
Hope Leslie (Sedgwick), 47, 48, 54, 55, 60,
  63, 203n24
Howe, Irving, 179
Howells, William Dean, 65, 88, 99, 207n21
Howlett, Caroline, 160
Hungry Hearts (Yezierska), 136
Huyssen, Andreas, 105, 205n4

Incidents in the Life of a Slave Girl
  (Jacobs), 202–3n18

Iola Leroy (Harper), 14, 63, 66–84, 95, 102, 109; and Christianity, 68, 72, 80, 81–82, 84, 86; heterosexual romance plot in, 73–74, 83–85; and moral responsibility, 70–72, 73; nationalism in, 85–86; oppositional community formation in, 69–70, 73, 75–78, 81, 83, 85–86; race/whiteness in, 68–70, 72, 73–74, 75, 76–77, 81, 82, 83; and racial uplift movement, 75–76, 79, 84–85; and reconciliation literature, 70–71, 78–79; temperance movement in, 79–80; "tragic mulatta" in, 69; true womanhood in, 69, 80; woman's rights movement in, 73, 79, 80, 81–82

Irwin, Inez, 167

Jacobson, Matthew Frye, 7, 43, 109, 141, 146, 205n7, 206n16. *See also* whiteness

James, Henry, 15, 207n21, 209n1; feminist activists' opinions of, 169–71; plan for *The Bostonians*, 168; on reception of novel, 184. *See also Bostonians, The*

Jim Crow laws, 65, 95, 167, 203n2

Jordan, Elizabeth, 15, 108; as editor of *The Sturdy Oak*, 123–25 *passim*, 207n21, 207n25–26. *See also Sturdy Oak, The*

Kahane, Clare, 183, 199–200n3, 210n9
Kaye, Frances, 97
Kearney, Belle, 167
Kelly, Mary, 47
Kemble, Fanny (Frances Anne), 43, 203n18
Kennedy, J. Gerald, 144–45, 147, 149, 208n32
King, Grace, 66, 70–71
Kraditor, Aileen, 27, 42, 201n5, 201–2n10. *See also* arguments of expediency; arguments of justice

"Ladies, The" (Kipling), 208n29
Lamplighter, The (Cummins), 20–21, 23, 47, 63
"Land Question, and Its Relation to Art and Literature, The" (Garland), 86
Lang, Amy Schrager, 25–27 *passim*
Leach, William, 18
Lease, Mary Elizabeth, 97, 101
Lecturess, The (Hale), 1, 169, 196
lesbianism. *See* homosexuality
Levander, Caroline, 61, 90, 200n3, 209n4
Lewis, Sinclair, 190, 191, 192, 193
"Limits of Feminine Independence, The," 190
Linton, Eliza Lynn, 34
"Love and the Witches" (Freeman), 93
Lowell, James Russell, 110, 111
Lynds, Helen, 205n5
Lynds, Robert, 205n5

Maglin, Nan Bauer, 191, 209n3
marriage plot. *See* heterosexual romance plot
Martin, Quentin, 88, 95, 100, 101
McColley, Kathleen, 179, 210n5
McDowell, Deborah, 69, 204n9
middlebrow literature, 106–7, 110–11, 124, 165, 207n23; mentioned, 9, 15, 102, 133, 141, 158
Middletown, 106, 205n5
Millay, Edna St. Vincent, 106, 113, 116
modernism (literary), 104–8, 113, 116, 166
Mott, Lucretia, 4, 25, 43, 200n1, 202n14, 202n17, 203n18
Mumford, Ethel Watts, 126
"My Own People" (Yezierska), 136–37

Nagel, James, 144, 208n32
National American Woman Suffrage Association (NAWSA), 65, 162, 167, 203n1; Anna Howard Shaw, president

National American Woman Suffrage Association (*continued*)
of, 156; becomes League of Women Voters, 167; break with National Woman's Party (NWP), 150, 208–9n34; Carrie Chapman Catt, president of, 112, 144, 151, 205n8, 208n31; Elizabeth Cady Stanton, president of, 66, 204n4

National Association of Colored Women, 65, 167, 209n37

National Council of Negro Women, 67

National Woman Suffrage Association (NWSA), 8, 20, 44; history of, 18, 200n1, 201n2, 203n1

National Woman's Party (NWP), 150, 162, 167, 193, 208–9n34

NAWSA. *See* National American Woman Suffrage Association

New Woman: characteristics of, 113, 114, 116; depiction of, 114–15, 117, 120–21, 145; fiction about, 106, 116, 121, 165, 206n13

New York State Woman Suffrage Party (NYSWSP), 123, 124

Newlin, Keith, 88

Newman, Louise Michele: on perceived role of white women, 22, 26, 40, 73, 157, 206n15; on racism in politics, 46, 50; on racism in woman's rights movement, 7, 20, 21, 43, 109, 111, 204n5

Nineteenth Amendment, 6, 15, 108, 143, 163, 189, 208n31

Norris, Kathleen, 106, 124, 125

Nussbaum, Martha, 182, 210n7

NWP. *See* National Woman's Party

NWSA. *See* National Woman Suffrage Association

NYSWSP. *See* New York State Woman Suffrage Party

oppositional community (Ferguson): definition of, 10–12; and existential communitarianism, 10, 70, 171, 175–76; feminist activist fiction as model of, 13, 14, 15, 43, 101–2, 107–8, 112, 165–66, 189, 196–97; and revolutionary love, 11–12, 56, 78, 93, 119, 163, 171, 196. *See also specific titles*

Osgood, J. R., 168

Out of Her Sphere (Harbert), 14, 15, 47, 63, 82, 102; corruption in, 50; depiction of heroine in, 24, 25, 27, 28, 30–33, 35–36; female education in, 30, 36; heterosexual romance plot in, 25, 26, 37, 38–39, 41, 59; oppositional community formation in, 32–34, 39–41, 42; race/whiteness in, 20, 28–29, 36, 39–40, 42, 63, 201n9; religious duty in, 27–28, 30–32, 37, 41, 42; sentimental genre, as revision of, 24; and true womanhood/manhood, 24, 25–28, 30–31, 35–37, 41–42; and *Uncle Tom's Cabin*, 24–25, 28, 39–40, 63, 202n15

Parrington, Vernon, 97

Paul, Alice, 150, 167, 193, 208n34. *See also* National Woman's Party

People's Party. *See* Populism

Peterson, Carla, 76–77, 83

Plessy v. Ferguson, 65

Populism: Garland's involvement with, 86; racism in, 101; in *Rich Man, Poor Man*, 193; in *A Spoil of Office*, 14, 88, 89, 91, 94–96, 97, 98

Pound, Ezra, 104–5

Pray You Sir, Whose Daughter? (Gardener), 6

Princess Casamassima (James), 182, 209n1, 210n7

Progressive Era, 8, 104, 106, 111–12, 137, 155, 205n3, 209n35

Progressive Party. *See* Populism

public speaking by women: in *Banner Bearers*, 145–47, 153, 160–61; beginnings of, in America, 1, 199n2, 199–200n3; in

The Bostonians, 172–73, 183–84, 185; in *Iola Leroy*, 81–82; Levander's discussion of, 90; in *Out of Her Sphere*, 33, 37, 39; in *Rich Man, Poor Man*, 195–96; in *A Spoil of Office*, 89, 90, 92, 96–97
Pykett, Lyn, 45

race: "absent present" of, 3, 21–22, 44, 156; history of, in America, 7, 20, 43, 65–66; and reconciliation literature, 9, 66, 70–71, 78–79. *See also* abolitionism; racial uplift; suffrage movement (American): racism/xenophobia in; whiteness
racial uplift, 14, 65, 75–76, 79, 84–85, 101, 204n14
realism, 9, 65–66, 102
reconciliation literature, 9, 66, 70–71, 78–79
"resisting reader," 5, 171, 197
Revolution, The, 6, 17, 44, 61, 163, 200n1
revolutionary love (Ferguson): definition of, 11, 175; and heterosexual romance, 12, 59–60, 84–85, 93, 98; and oppositional community formation, 11–12, 56, 78, 93, 119, 163, 171, 182–83; and women's friendships, 11–12, 119, 149, 153, 160, 184, 185, 187. *See also specific titles*
Reynolds, David, 62
Rich Man, Poor Man (Fairbank), 190–91, 193–97
Roast Beef, Medium (Ferber), 110–11
Rosenthal, Debra, 79
Rubin, Joan Shelley, 106, 165, 207n23

scientific racism, 110, 146, 151
Scott, Anthony, 177, 178, 179
Scott, Bonnie Kime, 105, 116
self-horizon (Ferguson), 71, 90, 92, 94
Seneca Falls Convention, 4, 18, 42, 200n1, 202n17

sensation novel, 21, 44–46, 48–49, 61; mentioned, 8, 14, 54, 63, 102, 107. *See also Fettered for Life*
sentimental novel, 20–21, 24–26, 44, 46; mentioned, 8, 14, 41, 102, 107. *See also Lamplighter, The*; *Out of Her Sphere*; *Uncle Tom's Cabin*; *Wide, Wide World, The*
separate spheres: critical reliance on paradigm of, 3, 200n4; feminism and, 4, 23, 27–28, 36, 41, 42, 84; rhetoric of, 3–4, 14, 131, 199n2; and sentimental literature, 3, 20–21, 25–26, 41
Shaw, Anna Howard, 144, 156, 208n31
short story cycle, 15, 108, 165, 208n32
Showalter, Elaine, 184
Shuler, Marjorie, 15, 108, 112–13, 205n8, 206n9. *See also For Rent—One Pedestal*
Shuler, Nettie Rogers, 112, 205n8
"Sisters Under Their Skin" (Ferber), 135–36, 207–8n29
"Soap and Water" (Yezierska), 152–53
Spoil of Office, A (Garland), 14–15, 63, 66, 86, 87, 102, 109; heroine in, 89–92, 96, 98, 99–101; heterosexual romance plot in, 91–93, 95, 98–99, 100; and Ida B. Wells, 205n18; nationalism in, 87; oppositional community formation in, 88, 89, 91–97; plot changes in revised edition of, 99–101; and Populism, 86, 88, 89, 91, 94–96, 97, 98; race in, 93–94, 95; woman's rights movement in, 88, 91–92, 94, 96–98, 100
"Spring Romance, A" (Garland), 93
Stanton, Elizabeth Cady, 8, 9, 25, 43, 67; and Harriot Stanton Blatch, 205n1, 206n9; and NAWSA, 66, 201n2; racist rhetoric of, 49–50, 204n4; as *The Revolution* editor, 6, 17, 44, 61, 163; and Seneca Falls Convention, 4, 18, 42, 200n1, 202n17
Stewart, Maria W. Miller, 1, 199n2

Stone, Lucy, 201n2
Stowe, Harriet Beecher, 24–26, 28, 29, 39, 41, 202n15. See also *Uncle Tom's Cabin*
Sturdy Oak, The (Jordan, ed.), 15, 108, 121, 123–43, 164, 165, 205n5, 207n24–26, 208n30; and *Banner Bearers*, 144, 145, 154, 155, 156; class in, 128–29, 130–31, 133, 134–35, 139–40, 141; composite novel, 125, 127, 165; corruption in, 129–31, 138–39, 141–43; heroines in, 128–29, 131–35; heterosexual romance plot in, 137–38, 139, 140; "Lady Bountiful," 133–37; and "My Own People," 136–37; oppositional community formation in, 135, 138–40; oppositional community of authors of, 124–26; as publicity stunt, 123–24; race/ethnicity in, 126, 127, 129–32, 134–35, 139, 141–43, 154, 156; and "reverse Cinderella," 133–35; and separate spheres rhetoric, 131; and "Sisters Under Their Skin," 135–36, 137; spectacle as political tactic in, 128, 129, 130, 140–42
suffrage movement (American), 14, 15; conflict over militant strategies in, 208–9n34; conservative developments in, 163–64; "the doldrums" in, 103, 205n1; and eugenics, 145–46, 162–63; Harriot Stanton Blatch's influence on, 103–4, 114, 206n11; military rhetoric in, 208n33; mother/daughter relationships in, 112; the New York campaigns of 1915 and 1917, importance of, 108, 113, 123, 144, 155, 164; post-ratification demise of, 189–90, 191, 192; racism/xenophobia in, 15, 111–12, 119–20, 127, 140–43, 155–57, 165–66; spectacle as political tactic in, 15, 103–4, 117, 128, 129, 130, 140–42, 163–64; use of term, 205n2. *See also* woman's rights movement
suffrage movement (British), 103–4, 160, 208n33–34

Tammany Hall, 155, 164
Taylor, Bayard, 169. See also *Hannah Thurston*
temperance movement, 6, 14, 41, 65, 67; in Frances E. W. Harper's writings, 79–80; and Frances Willard, 27, 202n11
Terborg-Penn, Rosalyn, 111–12, 156, 204n3
Thompson, D'Arcy W., 17–18, 38, 200n1
Thompson, Dorothy, 190–91
Tompkins, Jane, 28, 106, 202n15
Tonn, Mari Boor, 5
Tracey, Karen, 9, 38, 59
Trilling, Lionel, 210n5
true woman: and "Cult of True Womanhood," 5, 26, 46, 54, 62, 98, 200n5; and feminist activism, 19, 21, 32–36, 41, 48; in *Iola Leroy*, 69, 80; in *Out of Her Sphere*, 24, 26–28, 30–31, 37, 42; and "true men," 35–36

Una, 4–6, 15, 171, 197
Uncle Tom's Cabin (Stowe), 6, 21, 63; and *Out of Her Sphere*, 19, 24–25, 28–29, 39–40, 41, 202n15

Van Leer, David, 181
Vanity Fair (Thackeray), 34–35
"variegated whiteness" (Jacobson), 7, 109–12, 134, 146

Wagner, MaryJo, 97
Walker, Francis, 143
Ward, Lester, 158, 209n36
Ware, Vron, 22, 206n15
Warner, Susan, 20, 21. See also *Wide, Wide World, The*
Washington, Ida H., 125
Waste Land, The (Eliot), 166
Wayside Thoughts (D'Arcy Thompson), 200n1
WCTU. *See* Women's Christian Temperance Union

Webster, Henry Kitchell, 126
Wells, Ida B., 65, 66, 84, 205n18, 209n35, 209n37
Welter, Barbara, 26, 200n5, 201n3. *See also* true woman
Wheeler, Marjorie Spruill, 156, 203–4n3
White, William Allen, 124–25, 207n26
Whitehead, Celia (Henrietta James), 185–88, 210n10
whiteness: and citizenship, 7, 43, 109–12, 117, 122, 140, 206n16; and scientific racialism, 110, 146, 151; and "variegated whiteness" (Jacobson), 7, 109–12, 134, 146. *See also* race; suffrage movement (American): racism/xenophobia in; *and specific titles*
Whole Family, The (Jordan), 207n21
Wide, Wide World, The (Warner), 20–21, 47, 63
"Wife of His Youth, The" (Chesnutt), 78–79, 205n1
Willard, Frances, 26, 31, 133; WCTU, association with, 8, 27–28, 97, 202n11
Wilson, Harry Leon, 127
woman suffrage movement. *See* suffrage movement; woman's rights movement

Woman's Journal, 8, 169, 204n4, 209n2
woman's rights movement (American): and abolitionism, 19–20, 22, 40, 42, 202n17, 202–3n18; beginning of, 4; and the Fourteenth and Fifteenth Amendments, 7, 20, 43; and ideas about white womanhood, 22, 43, 49–50, 115, 134–35, 147; importance of literature to, 4–6, 14, 62–63; post–Civil War changes in, 6–7, 18, 168–69, 203n1; Quakers as leaders in, 202n14; racial exclusivity of, 63–65, 203–4n3; relationship to other reform movements, 8, 14–15, 64–67, 79–81, 92, 96, 97–98, 101, 202n11; and the Seneca Falls Convention, 4, 18, 42, 200n1, 202n17; use of singular noun "woman" in, 199n1. *See also* suffrage movement
Woman's Voter's Manual, The (Nettie Rogers Shuler), 205n8
Women's Christian Temperance Union (WCTU), 8, 27, 65, 67, 97, 202n11
Women's Political Union. *See* Equality League

Yezierska, Anzia, 106, 136, 152–54, 166

www.ingramcontent.com/pod-product-compliance
Lightning Source LLC
Chambersburg PA
CBHW011753220426
43672CB00017B/2947